DINGO

THE STORY OF OUR MOB

Sally Dingo was born in Latrobe, Tasmania in 1953. After completing a Bachelor of Arts degree in politics and history at the University of Tasmania, she left the apple isle to see if life really was different on the 'mainland'. After a variety of jobs, including waitressing at the Last Laugh Theatre Restaurant in Melbourne, youth worker and proofreader's assistant at the *Age*, she stumbled into the world of television, working firstly in promotions, then in sales, before transferring to TCN 9 in Sydney and on to radio at 2Day FM, proving that mediocre sales results are not necessarily life threatening. However an urge to write saw her back at study, obtaining a Diploma of Journalism from Sydney's Macleay College, after which she worked for an insurance company, translating policies into plain English and doing freelance work. All of which was put on hold with the arrival of children. A few nannies later, this is her first book. Sally lives in Queensland with husband Ernie Dingo and their two children.

DINGO

THE STORY OF OUR MOB

SALLY DINGO

RANDOM HOUSE AUSTRALIA

Published by
Random House Australia Pty Ltd
Level 3, 100 Pacific Highway, North Sydney, NSW 2060
http://www.randomhouse.com.au

Sydney New York Toronto
London Auckland Johannesburg
and agencies throughout the world

First published 1997
First paperback edition published 1998
This paperback edition published 2001
Copyright © Sally Dingo

National Library of Australia
Cataloguing-in-Publication Data

Dingo, Sally
  Dingo: the story of our mob

  ISBN 978 1 74051 102 5
  ISBN 1 74051 102 6

  1. Dingo, Sally. 2. Dingo, Ernie. 3. Dingo family. 4.
  Aborigines, Australian—Social life and customs. 5.
  Motion picture actors and actresses—Australia—Biography. I. Title.
  791.43028092

Cover design by Gayna Murphy, Greendot Design
Internal design by Yolande Gray
Typeset by Asset Typesetting Pty Ltd
Printed and bound by Griffin Press

Dedication

To Ernie, Wilara and Jurra who teach me

Acknowledgements

A book like this emerges only through people's generosity and I am grateful to many. My heartfelt thanks to my family, to Bessie (who I call Mum), to Auntie Pearlie, Uncle Owen, Michael Ryan and my brothers and sisters. To Clarrie Whitehurst—who Pearlie said talked more than she had ever known him to before. To my 'not quite family', the Moorheads and Peets, who looked after me, fed me, taxied me, talked on the phone at odd hours of the night answering questions and giving to me as generously as they had given to Pearlie and Bessie over the years; to Mrs Elizabeth Peet, now in her nineties, with her beautiful Scottish accent; to Obbie, Eddie, Bill and Horrie; and especially to Helen Moorhead, for her enthusiastic and unstinting help and support. To Helen and her parents, Margaret and Harry Moorhead, I am indebted.

Many people willingly shared their stories and expertise, to them my sincere thanks: to Norm and Val Armstrong, Liz (Officer) Robson, Les Clayton, John P. (Happy) Gill, Peter Poole, Neroli Douglas, Dora Dann, Joy and Dick Johnson, Jim Trevaskis, Lee Peters, Steven Comeagain, Len Broad, John McPherson, Robert Jenson, Jock Sharpe, Les Kempton, Bob and Delys Chitty, Francis Kahn and members of the Western Australian Police Force. My thanks also to Dawn Wallam, Rose Mitchell and Sue Beverley for assistance with official records. To Richard Walley, Bob Ellis and Jane Cameron. To Vaughan Barndon of Yallalong Station for his generosity towards Bessie and for the hospitality extended to us. So too Ted and Meg Officer of Woolgorong Station. To Dr Neville Green for advising me so generously.

To Joan Sauers for her friendship and support throughout the writing of the book and to Deb Callaghan and Rose Creswell for understanding immediately the story I wanted to write.

And my sincere thanks to my editor, Roger Milliss, who sought to preserve my voice retrieving me when I lost my way. I am overwhelmingly grateful for his thoroughness and commitment to my story.

Foreword

Just a quick yarn up front to tell you about what you may be in for reading on.

You see my people are called Yamatji, that's the official spelling anyway, but we pronounce it Yum-a-gee. Must be the way we talk—and boy, do we love to talk or yarn about everything. We'd yarn that much that no-one had time to write it down, no-one that is until Sally started to.

My two Yugu's (mothers) my Mum, Bessie, and her sister, my Aunt Pearlie, yarned and yarned to Sally. And all their friends yarned some more and pretty soon she had yarns coming out of her ears.

She went about her task—and let me tell you it wasn't easy because Yamatji people yarn in circles and one question with four or five different approaches *may* result in the answer you require, that is if you ask a couple more times over. Now if all that made sense to you, you could only be a blackfella, or married to one—or should be married to one!

A couple of bush excursions later, endless phone calls, faxes, photos, visits, revisits and 75 x 1 hour recorded tapes, some containing strong Yamatji accents, Wadjarrie (pronounced Wud-juddi) language and songs that had to be transcribed, all were the raw material for the book that follows.

They revealed their lives to Sally, sprinkled with sadness and hurt, laughter and celebration, strength and unity and above all love—and no malice.

When Sally married me, little did she know what was to happen to her. My family had lived these extraordinary lives, and it was only fair, I reckon, that she had to do some work to catch up and put it all into perspective for herself. You mob reading this will get the armchair ride.

When you read through the eyes of Sally Dingo, I know you will enjoy the story of our mob. Now this might sound silly, but personally, I am learning about *my* family, from my *wife*.

Cheers,

Ernie Dingo

Contents

THE DINGO FAMILY

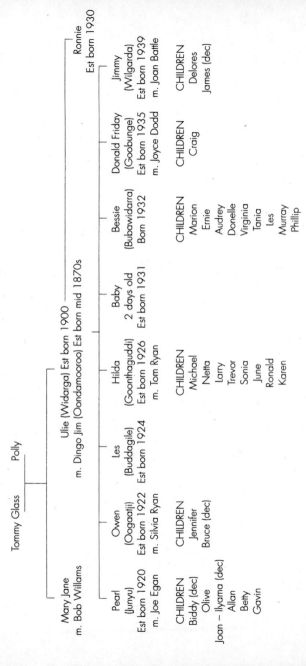

Tommy Glass —— Polly

Ulie (Widargal Est born 1900
m. Dingo Jim (Oondamooroo) Est born mid 1870s

Ronnie
Est born 1930

Mary Jane
m. Bob Willams

Pearl
(Junyu)
Est born 1920
m. Joe Egan

CHILDREN
Biddy (dec)
Olive
Joan – Ilyama (dec)
Allan
Betty
Gavin

Owen
(Oogaaiji)
Est born 1922
m. Silvia Ryan

CHILDREN
Jennifer
Bruce (dec)

Les
(Buddagile)
Est born 1924

Hilda
(Goonthaguddi)
Est born 1926
m. Tom Ryan

CHILDREN
Michael
Netta
Larry
Trevor
Sonia
June
Ronald
Karen

Baby
2 days old
Est born 1931

Bessie
(Bubawidarra)
Born 1932

CHILDREN
Marion
Ernie
Audrey
Donelle
Virginia
Tania
Les
Murray
Phillip

Donald Friday
(Goobunge)
Est born 1935
m. Joyce Dodd

CHILDREN
Craig

Jimmy
(Wilgarda)
Est born 1939
m. Joan Battle

CHILDREN
Delores
James (dec)

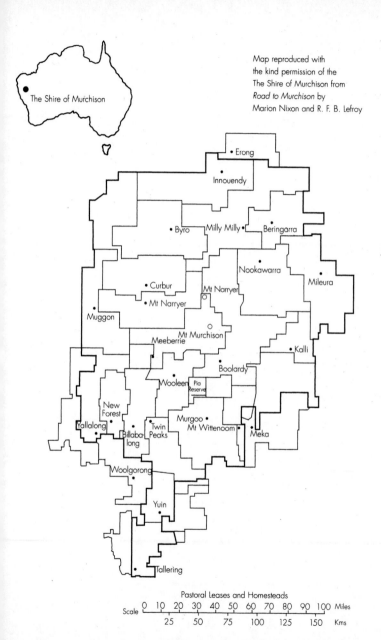

The Shire of Murchison

Map reproduced with
the kind permission of the
The Shire of Murchison from
Road to Murchison by
Marion Nixon and R. F. B. Lefroy

Erong

Innouendy

Byro • Milly Milly • Beringarra

Nookawarra

Mileura

Curbur

Mt Narryer

Mt Narryer

Muggon

Mt Murchison

Meeberrie

Kalli

Boolardy

Wooleen

Pia Reserve

New Forest

Murgoo

Yallalong

Twin Peaks

Mt Wittenoom

Meka

Billaba-long

Woolgorong

Yuin

Tallering

Pastoral Leases and Homesteads

Scale   0   10   20   30   40   50   60   70   80   90   100 Miles

25   50   75   100   125   150 Kms

Chapter One

He took the call. Trouble. The parcel was gone. Dingo Jim's parcel. Oondamooroo's parcel. Something was dangerously amiss. The family whispered down the line. Too much power to fool with. Too much power in the wrong hands. Ernie put down the phone and stared right through me. It was happening again. More strangeness. More evidence of a world totally outside my own. Only it wasn't. This was now my world too. I had married into it. And I was still learning how to accompany him.

'They don't know who's got it,' he said, coming out of it. 'Or *how* they got it.'

But someone had got it for sure. The spirit dingo puppies had gone strangely quiet, their familiar squeaky yelps no longer heard. Dingo Jim's messages were not getting through and Junyu, Ernie's Auntie Pearlie, was alarmed. No family member was safe. The parcel had to be retrieved, put back, just as her father had left it before he departed this earth. The cave should never have been disturbed. This was bad, bad business.

But retrieval would never be easy. Death hovered, waiting for a chance. No ordinary man, including Dingo Jim's own family, should touch the seemingly innocuous package. Even an initiated man would not be spared. Nobody less than a Clever Man Dingo Jim's equal would know how to harness its forces.

I listened and drew breath. I had seen many things since I married Ernie in 1989, and scenarios such as this, alien, weird even, with a fantasy component worthy of any Hollywood film, were now very real. Life had changed. And the only thing I now knew with certainty was that I could no longer be certain of anything.

'Who would do this?' I asked.

'Many people,' Ernie said, matter-of-factly. 'A Clever Man always has enemies, people who are jealous of him. They want Grandfather's powers for themselves. Now they can get any one of us. In any way they want.'

He shrugged it off and went outside to play footy in the backyard. There was nothing he could do but wait. He and his family all knew how to wait. The parcel or its other awful consequences would reveal themselves soon enough. Time to deal with it then. Everything in its own time, everything at the right time. He would wait for the word.

Waiting was not as easy for me. I stayed inside and worried instead. We both did as our backgrounds had trained us, anxiety seeming a larger part of mine. I wanted this to be over as soon as possible. I wanted to pretend it wasn't happening. And most of all I wanted to believe it couldn't possibly be real.

This was no longer so easy to achieve. My years with the Dingos had left me in no doubt that life for Dingo Jim's progeny, and partners, was complicated. And hazardous. No matter where you were. The phone, damn phone. Message after message. Even into suburban Sydney. There was no escaping his shadow which loomed so large. Or his name, both within his family and beyond. I heard tell of people who envied, feared and coveted his powers still, even though it was a good fifty years since he had left this world, and even though his wife, Ulie, had done as she should and gone into the night to send his spirit where Yamatji spirits go. I heard tell of havoc those cave desecrators wreaked, of scheming and plotting, of feuding carried forth, of Aboriginal law misused. I heard of the lawbreakers spreading fear so their lust for power could continue unimpeded. I felt the fear they spread. And I heard a lot. Frightening and unsettling if faced alone. Manageable if part of a family with ties which could still bind and protect. My Yamatji family fought to make sure it stayed so, but it was hard. 'Too much of it,' said Pearlie. 'And very strong.' Sometimes it looked like they wouldn't make it, my family. But always they tried. And they had friends. And there was always Dingo Jim. After all his Yamatji name meant shield. He would be there when it mattered, wouldn't he?

'Mrs Bingo?' the doctor enquired when I entered.

'No, Dingo,' I corrected. I was used to this, although here was a new slant.

'Surely you should have kept your maiden name,' he said,

looking at me over his glasses, without any notion there could be any other opinion.

'My husband is very proud of it'.

He held my gaze and raised his eyebrows. I wished for another doctor.

It had only been since Dingo Jim's death in 1948 that the Dingo family line began. White officialdom calls for standard practice, and surnames were standard—in the white world, that is. On his death certificate, Dingo Jim, a Wadjarri Yamatji of full descent, and a former dingo trapper, suddenly metamorphosed into Jim Dingo, his tribal name Oondamooroo ignored long ago by the whitefellas. In line with new Native Welfare department instructions that everyone should have a family name, a surname had been duly created and presented. So too his so-called Christian name, his full name in the Native Affairs file suddenly showing up a few official letters later as James Dingo. The new surname was then progressively assigned to his tribal wife Ulie, and their children, as they came under official administrative attention over the following years. Up until that time Native Affairs had filed his daughter, Ernie's mother, under 'Subject: Native—Bessie. Of Yallalong Station.' Her surname came later as well. Bigger sister Junyu, Pearlie her widpella name, never knew herself as a Dingo. On her wedding day, a ceremony imposed on her by well-meaning but sanctimonious whitefellas insistent her children be given respectability, she began the morning as 'Pearlie, native, daughter of Dingo Jim and Ulie. Full blood.' She ended her day with a surname for the first time, her husband's, and a second name, Brigid, which she relates the widpella also said she had to have. From one name to three, and a husband, because it must be so. 'We just a wild one! Bush man!' Junyu says, laughing at the judgement she knows was being made.

The name Dingo Jim also had been one of those generous whitefella gifts. Before his dingo-hunting, that is dogging, days, Dingo Jim, then still Oondamooroo, had been a tracker for the police. The family has lost part of his life story over the years, but the presumption seems reasonable that it was from here he first became known as Jim, when trackers were often called jimmy-jimmies. Many subsequently became Jimmy or Jim. Jim the tracker, one of the many throughout Australia, neatly became Dingo Jim when dogging with a whitefella already dubbed Dingo Ross. In the name game, Dingo Jim didn't do too badly. First names handed out liberally by the whitefellas around this time, in place of cultur-ally significant tribal names, included the derisive Sambo, Cinder-ella, and Sandy Claus, and surnames such as Moneyjingler, Piebald, Walkup, Shillingsworth and Painkiller. All flippantly assigned as if it were of no consequence. Their descendants still carry some of those names today. Recently a major city newspaper carried an anecdote meant to amuse when it reported an inmate Freddy Flatfoot had escaped, on foot, from a lockup in the far north. Poor Freddy Flatfoot. Still the butt of whiteman's jokes, just as his grandfather would have been when originally tossed the name. Other blackfellas were luckier, if lucky is the appropriate word when your identity is summarily denied. They were given whiteman's own names, or the names of places such as the sheep or cattle stations they worked on. It seems their tribal names were either too taxing, too foreign to contemplate, or quite frankly, just too darned native. Dingo Jim, like blackfellas all over Australia, had no say in the matter.

Now, on first hearing the Dingo name, and always oblivious to the fact it was their brethren who assigned it, whitefellas often recoil with evident distaste. Or disbelief, when it is me they are introduced to. It is as if it is too harsh, obscene even, as if the name carried the threat of violence and the stigma of the native dog itself. Fox, Hawke or Peacock are names so much easier on the ear. And acceptable after centuries of use. Dingo instead speaks of an animal which refuses to toe the line, a cunning and clever animal, a particularly native animal. Dingo speaks of an Australia before the whiteman. The name Dingo, then, can sound subversive, and for those who do not wish to hear such reminders, too loudly Aboriginal. My husband was proud to call himself Dingo after his grandfather, the name passing to him through mother Bessie who never married whitefella way. Me, the white girl, I took it as well.

I had no idea my life was going to veer in the direction it did. The girls at the office liked what they saw. I did too. But come on. Ernie Dingo, voted number three in a glossy magazine's fifty most eligible bachelors, complete with cute quotes, was surely to be avoided. I chuckled and left the throng poring over the photos. People who allow themselves to be paraded this way must be too convinced of their own attractiveness. Testosterone and sleazy charm on the loose. I had him pegged. I had met the type. 'What do you think of my home?' he asked almost as soon as I stepped inside the small inner city flat. A publicity job had taken me there, to drive him to a television interview.

His question astonished and embarrassed me. I searched through my store of requisite glib comments from every duty visit I had ever made. 'Very nice,' I offered, almost in a panic. The room was remarkable mostly for its brownness. Modest would be the kindest euphemism. I felt middle-class and out of place, and tried not to look anywhere in particular. He wouldn't retreat from the question. 'My home,' he repeated. Finally in exasperation he came to my assistance and pointed—at a painting. Spinifex desert country. Scrappy country. Strange, dramatic country. 'My country!' he said. And I was completely thrown. We had been speaking two different languages, two different value systems. I knew instantly which one I preferred. I decided I could ignore the show-biz way he was dressed.

He knocked at my door a few days later. His Mum Bessie was in town for the first time, and he wanted her to meet me. 'How many womans you got?' she asked in the cab on the way to my place, admonishing him sweetly as only Bessie can. He had introduced her to half of Sydney. Ernie wasn't short of female companions. He was someone who wrapped you in his arms almost on meeting. He loved living. He loved people. He hugged men and he hugged women. People in turn wanted to be near him, particularly women. Ernie was an attractive man with a rare spontaneity and exuberance which caught you up and carried you with it. He also qualified as exotic, his Aboriginal looks, colouring and ability to spin a funny yarn not often seen on the Sydney happening scene. Or the amusing party tricks he could perform on cue. His irreverent playing of a vacuum cleaner as a didgeridoo was always greeted with amazement. He was a sparkling centre-piece, and social mileage was to be had from his presence. He was in demand. There was kudos in knowing him, in whatever sense you chose.

Again he came to my door, although this time I didn't hear him arrive. My flatmate let him in. I was in the bathroom, shower cap pulled over my hair as I scrubbed my face clear of make-up. It wasn't a look I presented in public too often, especially not Sydney, a town concerned with trappings and appearances. After a faint knock, he poked his head round the door and came in. He had been at a function, and was spruced up Dingo-style, emu oil through his long curls, emu leather jacket on his back. He looked breathtakingly handsome. I felt horribly plain, fully exposed in all my blotchiness and my faded bathrobe. I wondered why he was there. I wasn't part of his circle.

'I'm so lonely,' he said, low and sad. 'You're the only one who doesn't want anything from me.'

We married. Ernie, like his grandfather Dingo Jim, is a Wadjarri Yamatji, from the centre of Western Australia. I am non-Aboriginal, a Tasmanian. We came from different places, from totally different experiences into a world which regarded me as of them, and him as the other. 'Yes, we have a mixed marriage,' he would say. 'My wife is Tasmanian, and I … am from the mainland.' It was a joke which played on the shock inter-racial marriages still delivered. On hearing the punchline, many laughed with outright relief. Dealing with our home-grown race issue was uncomfortable in a country where most had never met an Aboriginal and preferred it that way. Ernie did the work for them. He mentioned the unmentionable. In a weird twist, he helped them deal with his Aboriginality. He eased their way.

In his world, things were so very different. 'You a Yamatji now,' Sister Betty, Ernie's cousin, had announced. 'You belong to us.' Junyu, Auntie Pearlie, said it herself a day later, adding 'She our *gudja* (child)'. Junyu was the overseer of the family. These were important words. My place had been spoken, decreed. And I was astonished. I had been included. Surely my differences, my mistakes, must be apparent to all who had eyes and ears. At best I had hoped to be politely tolerated. In my world families do not always accept their members' partners, and I expected to remain on the fringes, the wrong wife, the white wife way over in Sydney. But I was a babe in the woods. I had no real knowledge of the daily lives Aboriginal people lived or indeed who they really were. I was now of the Dingos. Family. And talk could begin.

Chapter Two

We stepped onto the tarmac at Darwin airport. Darwin is a place for heat, and I was certainly feeling it. I was going to meet many of my new in-laws, now mostly living here. Ernie and I had married a few months earlier in Sydney, in a small registry office ceremony, both a little shaken and uneasy that we were taking such a step, even though we were both in our thirties. Neither of us was from families which pushed or insisted on marriage. In my family, my schoolteacher mother had emphasised self-reliance and the need to make your own way, after my father had died in his forties leaving her with three of her four children still at home to care for. In Ernie's family, whitefella marriage was seen as exactly that, what whitefellas liked to do, or what whitefellas said should be done to give children a name. Ernie's mum Bessie had never married whitefella way. 'What's that word … facto?' she answered in explanation when I asked her why not. Another whitefella term, unfamiliar in both language and meaning. As a result we married with no members of his family present, and only my sister from mine. Few friends were invited, and even then some did not show. Of those that did several were confused. Ernie had not understood the official term 'witness', and had invited more than were needed to fill that role. To him, all our guests were witnessing our wedding. And so they waited for their moment to step forward next to us, the bridal couple, only to find two people there before them. The many nuances and meanings in whitefella ways still confused Ernie. Friends gave us six months till bust.

I was nervous. I had only met his mother for those few minutes back in Sydney, no-one else. And there were many to meet. Ernie was the second of nine children, all mostly parents themselves now. A crowd of young black faces pressed against the airport window, straining, climbing over each other, desperate to get the first glimpse of Uncle Ernie and new Auntie. The glass was left with steamy lip and nose marks, and a few hundred finger-prints. They were eager. They clambered. 'Uncle Ernie, Uncle Ernie,' they sang frantically, competing for his attention.

I smiled a lot, and tried to remember names. But it was hard to concentrate. Children were tugging at me, arms were out-stretched, and there were lots of beautiful faces beaming up. So much activity, so much goodwill. Children had never been this way with me before. Bessie, my new mother-in-law, ushered me to where we could all be seated. Ernie and some of the kids rolled over and over, wrestling the length of the airport and back. White family groups stared, but I couldn't tell whether it was from disapproval or envy. Ernie and the kids were having a ball.

Bessie sat next to me and saw to my every whim, even though I didn't have many. I was trying to fit as much as they were trying to accommodate. Later Ernie explained the positioning had been deliberate. Her place was beside me, her role to look after me. I was her new daughter.

Both my arms clutched children, another niece perched on my knee. One spoke of Uncle David. My sisters-in-law glanced at me sheepishly and laughed. 'Uncle David?' I asked. They all knew who. And knew how strange it would seem in white eyes. The uncle the children referred to with absolute inclusion and possession was David Boon the cricketer, a distant cousin of mine—third in fact. I had never met him, but this did not matter. He was now part of their family, and because of his age had been given the title Uncle. They loved their new connection. Ernie loved the incorrectness of it all according to the way the white world interpreted family, and grinned when he thought of David Boon blissfully going about his life, unaware a mob of black kids was running around claiming him. Test matches were now watched with immense pride and concentration in many a Darwin household. You should always know what your family is up to.

Our visit to Darwin was extremely brief, a stopover on the way to Broome, where Ernie had some work waiting. Bessie stayed with me as we all moved to catch the connecting flight. She did not leave my side. A cousin of mine from home in Tasmania suddenly fronted, a close cousin I hadn't seen since I was a child and whom I could no longer say I really knew. Bessie stood with me, waiting. To my eternal shame, I did not introduce her. I did not say I'd like you to meet my mother-in-law. I chatted with him as if I were alone, and tried to edge round as soon as I could. My cousin had been in Darwin for many years, and I knew the unapologetic and ugly racism which ran rampant in some sections of the Territory. I also remembered his father's politics and attitudes, and was unsure whether he had taken them up. I feared his response. I feared the problem. I failed badly—unforgivably. In the decency stakes, Bessie soared above. She didn't mention the rebuff, the difference in the way I had been treated and the way she had been. Bessie, the sweetest person I have ever encountered, never would.

I spent endless hours travelling with Ernie. He was just beginning to make a name for himself in the entertainment industry as an Aboriginal actor to watch out for. But his name always seemed bigger than his fee. Our travel then was often by bus. And it was here I learnt much about myself, and who Ernie really was.

We had a good table at the roadhouse edging the Nullarbor Plain, my new husband and I. We could see everyone. We were on our way to a suburban school fundraising effort in Perth, and the charity budget stretched to a choice of air travel for one or a bus fare for two. There we were—bus. It wasn't so bad. It reminded me of our recent honeymoon to Alice Springs where our self-funded bus and train ticket delivered us to the memorable post-nuptial setting of a single mattress on cousin-sister Betty's spare bedroom floor. I saw two men at a nearby table gazing at the food stand. Longingly, I thought.

'Go and ask if they want something to eat,' I said, nominating myself party hostess.

Ernie hesitated, the floral plastic tablecloth suddenly of extreme interest. He kept checking in their direction, but making no attempt to do as I bid. He sat. I knew it was not my place to approach, and worried aloud to Ernie that they would be hungry and thirsty on their journey. He stayed seated. The man missing a tooth finally nodded and smiled. After pleasantries and at my insistence, they both joined our table. I wanted to give them the shop, my overly drilled small town politeness on full throttle.

'Would you like breakfast?' I asked. Courteous nods, smiles and averted eyes. Shy, I noted. Not used to white people, I patronisingly thought.

'Do you want tea or coffee?'

'Yes.' Barely audible.

I was confused, but undaunted. I ordered tea. Determined to put them at their ease, I listed the roadhouse meal choices. They simply and quietly said yes or nodded at whatever offer I made. So much agreement. So few firm decisions. Ernie was little help. He ignored my attempts. Eventually so did they.

The three men established each other's country and family connections. I established how confused a girl can get, how spectacularly blind I could be, and how much I had to learn. My efforts, perfectly acceptable back home in the Anglo-Celtic world I had grown up in, were out of place here. Greeting was not a simple procedure, and yes can often mean no. There are rules you need to abide by, and signs you need to attend to. I didn't. I hadn't. I had no idea. And each of my offers had merely increased the men's discomfort. To openly refuse any offer or request is considered rude and insulting, and therefore highly shameful. The word 'no' could never, would never, be uttered in such circumstances. So to avoid offending me, and embarrassment for themselves, the two Yalata men, Nungas from South Australia, who had merely wanted to connect and talk with a fellow desertman, said no the only way they could—by imprecision, by lack of enthusiasm, by deflection. In the end, given my persistence, they had but one choice: to pretend I wasn't there.

Ernie had demonstrated this trait many times. And many times I had delivered a sermon on how unfair and impolite it was to agree to something you had no intention of doing. I had no idea it was culturally determined. In my eyes it had merely been a personal failing on his behalf and, with a bit of commitment to straight-talk, could be overcome. Yes means yes. But no. Not here. And not always.

The missing front tooth distracted me momentarily from my hostessing duties. Luckily my effusiveness didn't extend to an offer of dental treatment as well. And there was a danger of this. Wonder-woman was on a roll, determined to give them something, anything. I had seen a number of Aboriginal people with what I took to be the same problem, had noted the similarities, and yet failed to figure anything other than the need for regular brushing. It was something I was a stickler for. But an initiated man from this part of the country has no need of such advice. The gap in his teeth was a badge of honour, the tooth knocked out with a wedge and a block of wood during one of the initiation ceremonies. Women the same. It announced status and certain abilities to those who knew. And even with his telltale missing tooth, there was still no indication of who he really was. Traditional Aboriginal people do not publicly display their overall position and power. Ernie, however, was fully aware of all the possibilities. The man could easily have been the head man, the boss man for his people. Out of respect, Ernie was on his best behaviour.

They continued talking, quietly, now setting out the reasons for their journey, the conversation following a time-honoured pattern prescribed in Aboriginal law—declaring yourself, in a particular sequence, unrecognisable to those who do not know. The Nungas were returning home full of joy having just completed a park rangers' course in Central Australia. Up-to-date information enhanced traditional knowledge. They were going home, to rejoin their families and to continue caring for their country.

By now I had the good sense to realise I hadn't a clue and shutting up seemed the best move. The initiated man left first. He politely thanked us and went outside, his visit complete and duty done. His countryman stayed, bolted to his seat, staring at the floor. The heavy silence put me in a spin, again I was completely baffled. I desperately wanted to tell him to go if that was what he wanted. I could see nothing preventing him.

'You better go out and keep an eye on the old fella,' Ernie suggested at last, almost to the room in general, rather than to the person beside him.

He granted permission in the loose, indirect manner Aboriginal people with traditional links couch all directives. His phrasing and inflection allowed the young man to choose whatever it was he wanted to do. Such looseness grants each person a degree of interpretative freedom, an escape clause. It is a personal freedom totally at odds with Western culture which always demands straight and definitive responses, even against your will. Here no-one is forced to take an action, outside those set down in Aboriginal law and custom, which they do not wish to take. It often leads, in interactions with non-Aboriginal people, to accusations of unreliability, vagueness and even of lying. In my marriage I have learnt to rephrase my questions, or approach from a different angle. And I am becoming skilled at recognising when I have received a negative reply in among all the seemingly affirmative words. As problematic as this style of communication is for interaction with non-Aboriginal society, in Aboriginal culture itself it allows great personal autonomy within a complex and highly structured social network. It is a perfect fit.

Ernie's suggestion was taken up immediately. As soon as he spoke, the young man was up and gone, obedient to the end to the undeclared but strictly observed seniority order which had been at play. Etiquette must be followed, no matter how long it took. Ernie knew these rules too. I knew by now to let it happen around me, my self-appointed role as the driving force unnecessary, unwanted, and loaded with paternalism and prejudice.

Even saying hello in this encounter had been swathed in all sorts of considerations, unbeknown to me. The non-Aboriginal way of greeting whomever you feel like, expecting a friendly response as your right, even from strangers, is way off the mark for blackfellas mindful of their cultural duties and responsibilities. Ernie and his brothers from the desert had been unable to speak openly until the approximate purpose of each other's journey had been divined. It was unusual for desert people to travel alone like that, without family. The reasons could therefore be serious, either important family business itself or being on the way to a sorry ceremony, a funeral. If this were indeed the case, a sense of ceremony must be observed, with interruptions and inappropriate joviality unwelcome and rude.

Our cultural stand-off was sorted out only when the lawman, the one whose eyes scanned the room but whose head didn't move, finally gave the nod and talk had been able to begin.

We travelled on to Geraldton, north of Perth, to attend an Aboriginal basketball carnival, a new concept for me. I could not understand why Ernie was insisting on getting there no matter what. My cultural all-knowingness had still not been sufficiently dented. I knew what to expect, I thought—a few motley teams in a small regional competition. I was mistaken and amazed—Aboriginal people en masse, about 3000 of them, from all over the State, entire families, grandmother and pop included, travelling for days to attend, often with just enough money to get there. Someone from within the still strong kinship system will provide what is needed to return. Someone always does, even if a few grumbles go with it. Many teams compete from A grade, through to the under-12s, men and women, boys and girls, all well decked out, and all looking flash on the court. It's important to look your best when you are a showcase for your mob, even if it has taken every cent your entire family has. Aunties, nieces and cousins, uncles, nephews and more cousins, team-mates together. These were proud people.

I marvelled from the stands. All this vibrance, purpose, and organisation didn't fit with the sub-culture stereotype brought to me by the daily news. The spectators, the teams—so many, so skilful. I felt as if I had entered a new world. But at the same time I felt ill at ease. I had never seen so many Aboriginal people in the one place before, and experienced what must be for them a familiar feeling when out in the overwhelmingly white world of mainstream Australia. I became acutely aware of my colour, of how different I was. I felt like an interloper, an obvious one, but this seemed my interpretation alone. No-one treated me that way. Instead, my family relationships were paraded and identified. I was not white. I was a Dingo, and introduced to all who should know me.

It was soon obvious, even to my untrained eye, what an important function the carnivals serve in Western Australia. A modern meeting place. Noongar, Wongi, Yamatji people, even the Kimberley and Pilbara mob—they're all there. Much important family work goes on. Connections are maintained, kinship ties reinforced. And in a country which presents a white Anglo-Celtic vision of itself in magazines, on television and in the employment market, here is a safe place to feel complete in who you are. With your mob. Watching the young demonstrate their athleticism and their expertise.

Even the not so young. Ernie was playing in an old boys' team, re-formed after many years. Now in their thirties, they still managed to scrape into A-grade competition. The 'old dawgs', as they called themselves, were out for the kill, refusing to concede the dominance they had held in their twenties. To them reputations were on the line. This was serious business, as it was to all the teams. But no-one would have known until they took to the court. Not from such nonchalance.

Ernie's team-mate and closest friend, Richard Walley, had collected us from Perth, and we travelled up together. It was night-time, black, and I could just make out the shapes of the coastal trees, bent to the ground in response to the unrelenting sea wind.

'Have we got somewhere to stay?' I asked as we neared the town itself. It was late, and I hoped someone had thought of this already. I'd given up trying to run things my way and had left the arrangements to the locals, Richard and Ernie. But I wasn't completely at ease. My view of how the world should work still lingered. I presumed phone calls had been made, and beds were waiting.

'Yep,' replied Richard. A definite yep.

'So where are we staying?'

'Up here.' A definite up here.

But clearly no more information was on offer. And clearly nothing was clear.

Richard and Ernie. Frustrating as all hell if you're set on a direct, linear question-and-answer way of speaking. Neither of them would respond fully if the information or response you sought could not be. It was the roadhouse experience again—the avoidance of actually saying no, of actually refusing anybody anything, coupled with a desire to please, a belief system and response pattern learned and practised since birth resulting in behaviour which doesn't slot neatly into the Western way of communicating. It is a trait which, throughout Australia, creates problems for Aboriginal people in the law courts, at school and in general social interaction. Aboriginal people themselves generally know what is being said, know when to leave it alone, or know how to re-word a question so that no shame will be involved in any answer, for either party. Non-Aboriginal people discover this after many confusing encounters. In this case, Richard said whatever would placate me, whatever was close enough to the truth without him having to openly deflate my expectations. I had enough experience by now to recognise the signs. Pushing would achieve little. I did what Ernie was doing. I waited.

There were many cars parked at odd angles when we pulled up. Must all be expecting someone, I presumed. A team-mate perhaps, still on the road. This looked a perfect place for teams to meet and make final arrangements for the competition which began early in the morning. I hoped they wouldn't be long. I was tired, and country motels closed early. And if instead we were staying with a relative, I figured it would be even longer before we actually got to bed. Surely we would have to be polite and at least have a cup of tea and chat for a while. I was anxious to move. Richard seemed in no hurry. He traded humorous insults and greetings. He knew everybody.

It was the first riverbed I had ever slept in. A bit gritty, but soft enough. However, the towel he handed us could have been wider. Longer would have helped as well. Ernie and I fought for its warmth all night. I found a motel in the morning. Richard came too.

In time I came to see our conversation could not have been

any other way, our foremost intentions so completely at odds. Richard's concern had been to just get to the carnival, fix the details later, mine the creature comforts. I had always envied Richard's ease within the world and began to glimpse how burdened I was with anxiety-inducing inessentials. I suspected I had a lot of paring back to do.

After the first day's competition, it was entertainment time. A social evening had been arranged at a large hall, disco lighting thrown in. Gavin, Auntie Pearlie's son and Ernie's cousin-brother, fronted his band, Dirtwater. He played music to suit all tastes— four styles. Country. Western. Rock. And its partner, roll. The place was jumping, and crowded. But I had little idea of what was going on outside my field of vision. As the new Auntie, I was chaperoned and safeguarded. My recently acquired nephews, all men, fine-looking men, seated me on a chair. Some placed themselves on the floor, a respectable distance around me, while others stood, appearing to take up positions. They arranged themselves so they could see all angles, facing out. No stranger or trouble was allowed near, no drunks to approach. Whatever I wanted was before me in an instant. Each time they spoke, these men, they addressed me respectfully as Auntie. No hint of insincerity or play-acting. Every now and then the line-up would change. Nephew would change shifts with nephew.

Gavin, my brother-in-law, watched from the stage, giving directions to which they instantly responded.

'That's your Auntie Sally there. Go and introduce yourself. Look after her,' he'd say to one young man, and the whole duty roster would spring into action.

I'd never experienced anything like it in my life. One chair, with me on it, surrounded and pampered by handsome young men. I was delighted but bewildered, yet once again nothing was

explained. I was left to work out what was happening as it unfold-
ed. Full explanations come out over time, information released as
you learn how to ask the questions. Knowledge is built, bit by bit.
This was my first real taste of what it meant to be part of this
family.

With family and interwoven kinship relationships still
adhered to, I have cousins, nieces and sisters, as well as nephews,
uncles and brothers, who all know my position in the family and
my relationship to that position. They know I am prone to make
mistakes, cultural mistakes, social mistakes, any mistake at all
really. And even though I have caused a few giggles, constantly I
am guided, protected, often without me seeing the moves. It was
a new and wonderful feeling for me. I loved being with my own
mob.

Chapter Three

Several years later:

Basketball was the furthest thing from our minds on this trip to Geraldton. It was a family visit, intended to reconnect, and to yarn. It was also a time for Ernie to attend to any family business which must be seen to with relations or kin. For me it gave time to spend with my family who never ceased to astonish me with their endurance, their resoluteness in the face of the hardships they faced, or with the humour that would emerge at every opportunity. I learnt to love and laugh with my Yamatji family. It also gave me time to do some recording for the Dingo story they had agreed I would write.

Geraldton, Western Australia, is not exactly family stamping ground for the Dingos but is close enough for Junyu, Ernie's Auntie Pearlie. It is central. Not far from her beloved Gascoyne and Murchison rivers and the cattle and sheep stations where she lived and worked all her life. Nearby are the grannies and great-grannies, grandchildren so-called because they become herself in the cycle Yamatjis follow. So too her faithful old friends. And mother Ulie and father Dingo Jim, as well as her husband and daughter, are buried at Mullewa, only an hour's car trip away. Geraldton will do—as it has to do for many Yamatjis, now that bush and station life has ended.

Auntie Pearlie was looking forward to our visit, eager to tell a few yarns. The whole family was glad we were coming. Yet when we pulled into Auntie's driveway, on time, no-one came out to meet us. The house sat in stillness. Trees. Grass. Her two well-tended, but stunted rose bushes. Nothing moved. We opened the wire door and went inside. There they were, in Pearlie's bedroom, waiting. Pearlie was sitting on the side of the bed, with her daughter, Ernie's cousin, Sister Ollie, on a chair, both women motionless.

Ernie dropped his bags and went straight to Auntie Pearlie. They clung to each other, arms circling, heads buried, and sobbed in utter, utter sadness. Sister Ollie stayed at the foot of the bed with a handkerchief across her face, crying alone underneath the cotton shield waiting for Ernie's turn with her. They cried together for those who had died since last they met. This time there had been several deaths, one of them Auntie Pearlie's husband, Sister Ollie's father, Joe.

I watched from the doorway, eyes wet, and struggled with the force of such a scene. And I knew more grief would come, probably soon. Death comes too regularly to Aboriginal families. 'We all upside down,' Bessie told me on the phone after another dearly loved cousin-brother, not much older than Ernie, had died, leaving Ernie one of only two remaining male Dingos of his generation. Grief mixed with confusion. Why the young ones, 'the good ones' as Pearlie says? And how to stop it?

To be Aboriginal in Australia is to know sorrow to the core, I have come to believe. There is so much trouble and sadness, so many deaths. Struggle upon struggle. Most families have someone in gaol, most deal with alcohol and its problems and the results among their kin. Most experience family members dying early. Since I married Ernie, there have been so many calls reporting another death. In my own family, few. Aboriginal people have to be strong in a way I will probably never know, or never have the need to be.

I waited my turn. This is a strictly choreographed routine, carried out in a definite order. I was ready. Behind Ernie. I was then to take my place beside my two mothers-in-law, Auntie Pearlie and Bessie, who was expected to arrive at any moment. It is a practical system which includes all in the family and prevents petty claims of favoured status. The crying respects and honours those who have passed away. It also openly deals with what has happened. There is no stoic pretence life is still the same. Remembering is allowed, death acknowledged, and grief permitted in its fullness. The family moves on when it is time.

Ernie cried with every family member as they turned up to see us, day after day, men and women alike. When each cry finished, and tears were wiped away, the present returned. Conversation buzzed and the noisy energy noticeable in most Aboriginal households filled out the room. It was an energy I loved. It wasn't too long before a game of cards began.

Auntie Pearlie's laminate and chrome kitchen table took only a cloth to be transformed from utilitarian shelf on legs to dream-maker, a card table, where a few dollars could be won or lost. Sometimes those few dollars made all the difference.

Auntie's table was well travelled—around the yard. An important social tool, it seemed in perpetual motion, moved endlessly from the verandah to the small front yard to the concrete driveway. It even came inside. However, it was a bit of a squeeze in the tiny one-bedroom rented unit.

It was a sight I enjoyed immensely. I would go away for an afternoon and return to find a mob of people around the table in a different place—one side of the tree for morning light, another for afternoon. Seasons within seasons were duly noted, and of course the wind. The cry went up. Better move the table. Ah, better move the table. But it spent each night on the verandah, never left out. The table was almost an honorary family member. It was also one of the few possessions Pearlie had.

Auntie Pearlie made her way out to the table under the tree in the middle of the front lawn. Shade had been the deciding factor for today's initial placement. Her skin was playing up. We sat yarning, great-grannies around our feet, huge enamel pannikins of tea in front of us. At one stage Pearlie burst into full voice for her grandson-in-law who was on a short visit from America and about to go back. The traditional Wadjarri song soared round the garden, rich and big. It sympathised with the sorrow he felt at having to leave. She had sung this for him before, when she thought she would never see him again, and had personalised it. The song was Randy's now. He was deeply moved, and embarrassed as well. What is the right way to respond when somebody sings their heart for you? The sound came from the depths of her being, full and guttural, the Wadjarri language busy and beautiful. We were transfixed. She sang him a place here in Australia. He would never really be away.

Pearlie finished, joked that no-one was to replay my tape and cry over it when she was gone, and moved on to the business at hand. Taming those bloomin' ants. They were everywhere. Meat ants, about two centimetres long. She leant down, in this open air, and gave them another jolly good squirt with an economy-sized insect spray. But they were bustling. This seemed to be their meeting ground and market place, and they weren't going anywhere, regardless of Pearlie's determination. Eventually we worked out who was boss—they were!—and moved the table again, this time to the driveway about a metre from the front gate. The cloth was produced. It was time. Let the cards begin.

Money hit the table. About three dollars each. It was off-pension week. A couple of children lounged on their mothers' knees or draped arms lazily around the nearest adults' shoulders. They'd done a lot of waiting in their short lives, these kids. But it was no problem, not when you were with family. And besides, around the card table you got to listen to all the gossip and stories. You learnt all about your own mob. You learnt all about being Yamatji together. This was an important social gathering.

I could see the game would last a while. Coins were pushed between players to keep everyone in. Today was about enjoying the moment. And maybe, just maybe, it was also about an extra few bucks at the end of the day. Next week would be serious. Next week, pension week, was when income redistribution really took place. Someone would go home about $300 richer—and their big bills, electricity, phone, maybe even repair that washing machine, would all be paid first thing in the morning. The following pension day, a fortnight later, would be someone else's turn to win and pay their bills. An ingenious system enabling them to cope with their poverty, but fraught with inherent dangers I calculated from the security of my comfortable existence. Gambling habits could develop, losses could be sustained several weeks in a row and then there was the problem of just feeding your family between pensions, if your game had been too far down. But having seen first-hand how little money each family had, knowing how few Aboriginal people are able to find jobs, and knowing how both Pearlie and Bessie owned next to nothing after decades of earning next to nothing on nearby sheep stations, it was easy to see the lure of a potential boon.

'Buy food,' Bessie said without missing a beat in the hand she was playing, when I asked why did people play with their precious few dollars. I had rarely ever had to look at life from the perspective of literally scraping by. And even when I did, I always had a few fall-backs. I had a decent education. I knew people who had jobs and houses, and money. And my own family, who certainly were never wealthy, would always be able to help me out. Lending me a hundred dollars would not mean empty food cupboards or eviction for them. Bessie's family and friends did not have such a stable safety net. No-one owned a house. If any had jobs, they were mostly seasonal or very poorly paid, and it was not always possible to share those few dollars among so many. And sharing was no longer so fairly or freely given. They tried to help one another, but poverty always brings its own baggage. Sometimes it looked as if it had become each man for himself or be brought down. Powerlessness, and what it creates, is never pretty. And then there was the constant search for dollars to cover the costs of family or kin funerals, and the costs of travelling to them. People were spread far and wide now traditional land and life was all but gone, and they had been forced to disperse. Funerals would mean many bills fell behind. On one of my visits to Geraldton, one of Ernie's cousins, a non-drinker, had been without power for two months. Yet she always put in her bit when a funeral collection was taken for another family friend or relative. I was aghast at how regularly they came, and how regularly people had to travel. There was no choice in this. Respect must always be paid. Ties with your people are still very strong, and obligations must be delivered upon.

Those who had managed to resist the feelgood solution alcohol is to the dispirited and the dispossessed tried hard to be seen as decent and upstanding in the eyes of white society. One woman who visited Junyu regularly from the country always wore the same second-hand dress. Clean, but always the same one. If she stayed for two days, the dress came out again. This was her only dress neat enough for wear in town. It meant she could hold her head up when shopping for her stores. I admired her self-respect, and her ability to raise her family with some dignity. But each time she appeared I was slapped in the face with how privileged my position was. My admiration for her would have meant little. She probably would have appreciated instead, to be in a situation where it wasn't needed.

Cars cruised past, the driver and occupants staring in at our surreal scene. The news was out Ernie was in town, and as he was the local boy who had made good on television, people were out for a look. We were all shapes, sizes, and colours around the table stuck smack bang in the middle of the white drive-way. Pearlie and Bessie were full-descent Yamatji, both big women, black-black, with snow-white hair. Randy was African-American. Others were varying shades of brown, the many children every possible tanned hue. And then there was me, blending with the concrete. We all stared back. I knew the ins and outs of the neighbourhood in no time. I even learnt to lift my chin, point with my lips, and say 'Who that?' at any car, pushbike or pedestrian coming our direction. And mean it.

On the other side of the road a neatly dressed Yamatji man shuffled past, his trouser creases razor sharp. Our scene was of no concern, and probably a familiar sight. He was intent on getting home.

'How yer goin'?' Sister Betty called.

He turned, grinned at being acknowledged and, as fast as his stiff legs would move, crossed the road and came over to us.

'I turned the big six oh!' he proclaimed. 'Been celebrating with my nephew.'

Round the table he went, sloppy kisses given to the side of everyone's cheeks. He was full of good cheer, green eyes twinkling. His face had been disfigured through cancer, and his chin and lower jaw had all but disappeared. But the indomitable spirit which had seen him through still shone brightly and it was easy to see evidence of the good-looking man he had been.

'Can I join in?' he asked, edging in without waiting for a reply. 'Only got seventy cents though.' He eagerly took a seat on a battered milk crate. 'What's the pot?'

'A dollar!' was the uncompromising reply. After all, we had been women together before his arrival, Randy and Ernie just lounging and watching.

I could see no court was being given and pushed him a coin. He played and won the hand. More cheer.

'This is Randy,' Betty said between deals, adding proudly. 'He's from America.'

'I'm Ray Kelly, and I'm from Mooney Mia,' the newcomer punched out with just as much importance. He laughed with delight at his own joke, fully aware Mooney Mia, the Yamatji name for tiny Northampton, stood nowhere in the eyes of the world. We all laughed with him, enjoying his audacity—and his pride. He knew who he was even if the world would never recognise him. And he would say so, wherever and to whomever he chose.

'Go 'way now,' laughed Pearlie. 'You're winning all our money.'

'I'm stayin',' he reckoned.

But he left soon after, fifteen dollars richer, and happy. The women weren't, or didn't seem to be. Ernie later suggested they had influenced the result. A birthday present. I'm still undecided. But I liked the idea.

'How come all Yamatjis play cards?' I asked Bessie, hoping she would ignore the generalisation I was making. I knew I was wrong in one respect. It was now essentially a women's pastime. 'Where did it come from?' I don't know why I asked. The answer was fairly obvious.

'From the whitefellas,' she replied, eyes still on her cards, concentration undisturbed.

'Did your Mum and Dad play?'

'No,' she said, and then added, as if remembering another recent whitefella gift to her mob, 'They never even drink.'

Life had changed a lot for Yamatjis, in such a short space of time. It wasn't so long ago that Dingo Jim, her father, had first appeared at the sheep station with his new tribal bride. It wasn't so long ago that he sang and danced *nyumbi loo binya* just for fun, and at corroborees. And it most certainly wasn't so long ago that Bessie was born. By the river. At an outcamp. Under the makeshift bough shed.

Dora and Pearlie had been close since early childhood, Dora's grandfather and Pearlie's father being firm friends. They shared a history. I wanted to meet Dora, hear her stories of Dingo Jim, and had arranged it. Or so I thought.

We had breakfast at Auntie Pearlie's 'camp', her rented flat, washing it down with those enormous pannikins of tea, and gently began the morning. Pearlie was no longer able to move about as easily as in her youth. Now in her seventies, big, and suffering from a lifetime of hard work and the complications aging can bring, she would mostly stay on the side of her bed, facing out through the door into the small kitchen-living space and hold court from there. I joined her often, immediately feeling warmer and somehow at home as I sat on the bed next to her. I noticed myself moving closer by the day. It put me, inexplicably, in a different state. In no time, I would simply sit and lean, and we would talk and giggle, yarning about our lives, saying things we would never be permitted under Yamatji law to say in front of men. We were two girls together. And Pearlie was the naughtier one of the two. I loved it. And her.

I was in the kitchen when the young man came to the door. He was Yamatji, but not a direct relative. He spoke to everyone and then asked if Pearlie was ready, peeking in to where he knew she would be. After a long pause, a torrent of words rushed out. She wasn't going anywhere this morning, or today or the next. She was too sick, and nobody understood or helped her. And everybody wanted to use her up. 'And why I gotta teach them Yamatji? Why didn't they learn?' And so it went on. Pearlie was forthright. She had had enough. He copped an earful.

She was one of the few remaining people who could speak Wadjarri fluently, and I knew many Aboriginal people were increasingly irritated with their race and themselves being studied over and over, poked and prodded they said, almost as if they were insentient objects. I presumed Pearlie had reached that point too.

He listened, appeared to take no offence, and politely took his leave. We all tiptoed around, not wanting to add fuel to the fire. I sat on the verandah, presuming our visit to Dora was no longer happening, and wondered what I could do to ease the tension. Suddenly the wire door opened with great gusto, and Pearlie surged forth, puffing heavily, but pushing her walking frame as fast and as furiously as she could manage. 'I'm going to see my old mate,' she cried. She would have sprinted if she had been able. Instead, she pulled herself into the car, grinning mischievously. 'Come on, daughter!' she shouted to me, looking round to make sure he was really gone. We all raced to get in before she changed her mind. But Pearlie was doing what she had wanted all along. Her performance, worthy of an Oscar, had been a variation on how to avoid saying no. I can only presume, since he was a fellow Yamatji, that he read the signs correctly. He had plenty to go on. After all, she had used just about every other word in her vocabulary.

Her vehemence would have confused and upset many a white person used to polite apologies and a simple 'I'm sorry, I won't be able to go with you this morning. Something else has come up.' The Yamatji way meant she could not refuse him in such a direct manner. And if he had persisted, or even just hung about for longer, waiting, she would have had no choice but to acquiesce. Her play-acting was the only means she could see to avoid the obligation she considered herself to be under.

Dora was almost prim—neatly dressed, hair perfectly in place and her house filled with family photographs, plants, flowers and things Christian. Along with the odd doily or two. We sat around her table trying to make sure our china mugs didn't stain the lace cloth. I listened at first while she and Pearlie chuckled, talked, and chuckled some more. They enjoyed being together. Dora, for all the trappings of an anglicised white woman, is Yamatji—knows it, proclaims it, and is proud of it. Like Pearlie she also speaks Wadjarri well. She pulled out two photo albums of plants from her country, and proceeded to go through them one by one, with its Yamatji name and use. She, Pearlie and Bessie were in heaven, each plant a good friend. They reminisced about plants they had known, where to find them, when to find them, and how to eat them, house plants and decorative foliage considered to be of no interest for the moment. Dora hesitated over a photo of a tree.

'O my brother,' Pearlie said wistfully. 'Well,' she continued softly, 'you can say it.'

She had given permission for her dead brother's name, her brother Jimmy's Yamatji name, to be spoken.

'That's a wilgarda tree,' said Dora sensitively, and went on to explain it was like a split pea.

To grant permission like that, to allow his name *Wilgarda* to be said aloud after all this time was an offering for me, an offering I did not recognise straightaway, so anxious was I after the morning's events. Pearlie's outburst, contrived though it was, meant I was still treading lightly and examining my motives with each word. I worried that she had, in the true Yamatji way of never addressing an issue head-on, actually given me her opinion about my questioning and taping. By now I had years of experience at receiving information, requests and directives in what amounted to a sideways and sometimes circular manner. Sentences looped about, often seeming to contradict the one before, sometimes appearing to go nowhere, and confusion often reigned while I looked for what was really being said. It was more of the politeness offered to a fellow human being. The old Yamatji ways had trained them never to presume to tell anyone what to do or think. If their hints were taken, so be it. Otherwise it was not for them to comment or complain. For me, this time it was a hard one. The guilt I felt about the whitefella writing the Aboriginal story came to the surface, and I imagined disapproval and criticism.

I asked questions gingerly. They responded eagerly. They had been waiting. For my lead. They wanted to relive those times, to revisit their memories, to show me their photos. I was family, and this was for family, not taken away and pulled apart. All the strands of the family were to be brought together, and remaining Yamatji ways—that is, those within my understanding— preserved. I was more than welcome to know and record.

Chapter Four

Dingo Jim created a minor sensation at the bush camp at Byro Station, when he rode in with a friend. He had come as he had many times before, from Wail, an outstation on a neighbouring property, where he worked as a stockman. As usual he had ridden for over two days, pushing his horse eighty hot sweaty kilometres a day through mulga country, spinifex country and finally red sandhills, *wandarrie* country, on this long hard ride. But Dingo Jim, a skilled bush Yamatji, a tribal man tamed down as the Yamatjis say, had not been taxed at all. He knew this land, and what it required in a way not many whitefellas did. Even experienced white bushmen would never undertake such a trip without a few precautions, one in particular. Water, large quantities, had to be carried, or you'd perish. But not by Dingo Jim. A standard waterbag would do. He knew, as did all his countrymen, the location of rock hole after rock hole on the way, cradling the water whitefellas could not find. Dingo Jim always did as he had been trained since a boy, took sparingly, made sure the hole was left clean and clear, and carefully replaced the cover which effectively prevented the scorching heat turning the water to a sizzle in minutes. He and his friend arrived safely and with ease.

The Yamatjis watched in silence as the two arrived on horseback, the same way Dingo Jim always arrived. But always alone, until now. He and Dora's grandfather were in the habit of bringing bush tucker to each other—wild potatoes, small bush onions, bush bananas, and the delicious dried kangaroo meat. They watched as he and his slightly built companion dismounted. Who was he, this youth? They were puzzled. Even though there was nothing remarkable about his short cropped hair and men's working clothes, something didn't add up. Dora's mother, then a young girl, whispered 'That's a *nyarlu*. Can't you see?' But her mother in turn couldn't see. 'No, it's a man,' she corrected. The old people thought so too. But no-one was sure. And therefore, no-one knew how to approach. The Yamatjis stood back, stared, and spoke urgently between themselves. Man or woman? It was important to work it out. There were proper procedures which must be followed, and they needed to establish exactly who it was and from that, their relationship to that person. Then everything would be settled. Those who should greet would do so. Those with whom crying was necessary would wait in the order they should. And any who weren't allowed near would stay away. But they had to be sure. The dynamics of the group would change considerably if this person was a woman, and even more so if she were Dingo Jim's wife. And she was. He was here to introduce Ulie, his new bride, blackfella way, also from Wail outstation. Ulie Glass, Widarga, originally from Mooney Mia, Northampton, and about sixteen years old, was now conjoined to Dingo Jim, about twenty-five years her senior.

Dingo Jim, in his early forties, was capable, confident, and tough, Ulie shy as teenagers can be. The age difference suggested an arranged marriage, a traditional promising and giving. But this appears not to have been so. The difference was not different enough. Young girls were promised mostly to much older men, boys to older women as well. Dingo Jim was too young. Ulie had not been given. Instead, she had been fought over, fists flying, as agile Dingo Jim, determined and infatuated, had used every ounce of strength against his younger competitor.

Such disregard of the age-old tradition of carefully considered marriages designed to make sure the blood lines were correct, effectively preventing family marrying within family, and ensuring each person was partnered with someone who would teach the new spouse what they should know, sexually, socially, and domestically, before moving to someone younger, would rarely go unchecked. A punishment of some kind would be meted out. Dingo Jim, a fully initiated lawman, complete with three raised scars across his chest and three down each shoulder onto his arms, and his new wife Ulie had transgressed tribal law, and married wrong way, with wrong skin groups coupled, the transgression passing without incident, so it was believed. But not for long. Their marriage was destined to be difficult. It is possible, and likely, that interference may have come from unseen sources through unseen methods, in the ways all Yamatjis knew, and still do. And there could have been more overt disciplinary action as well. However, the family was never told beyond the stories of the sizeable scar Dingo Jim carried when the spear went through his buttocks close to his hips. Ulie sometimes mentioned that scar, the result of pushing the long spear all the way through and out the other side, a necessary if painful attempt to avoid ripping large chunks of flesh which would otherwise have caught in the barbed spear-head. When it was mentioned it was with a vagueness which suggested forbidden territory.

Dingo Jim—Jim to his new wife—and Ulie returned from their trip visiting friends and kin at Byro back to Wail, part of the vast Yallalong holding. Wail, one of two outstations to Yallalong, the station proper, was in the middle of the huge leasehold on which ran cattle to the north, sheep to the south, shared between the three main 'camps', Muggon, Wail and Yallalong itself. To an outsider, a new chum, it was harsh country with red sandy dirt changing to rocky patches, then open plains, and as quickly back to red sandhills, all covered or dotted with clumps of long dry grass and untidy bushes. The few trees were scraggly and stumpy and not quite green enough, everything above the red soil appearing sunbleached. At the Wail camp itself, however, a creek nearby looked enticing, cool and refreshing. An oasis. Instead it was deadly—salty water, useless except for picture postcards. Serene and stunning in that all-Australian outback way, especially at dawn as light bathed the sky above the water, and the horizon filled with a beautiful muted orange and yellow, but of no value. Dried salt covered the rocks next to the creek, and any thirsty man drinking would have ached with disappointment—and become very sick.

In this country, only sun-up and sundown gave any appearance of softness. And that light was so extraordinarily beautiful it made you forget how harsh the rays really were once they burst over the horizon. And burst they did. One moment you were comfortable, the next searching desperately, mostly without success, for shade. This was a hard place to live and work. The heat was unbearable for those unused to scorching temperatures. And in winter, the storms were often torrential, sleetlike, if the gods graced the land with rain. This was not paradise to many whitefellas. But it was to Dingo Jim and his fellow Yamatjis. They knew and loved this place, every tree, every red sandhill in their *wandarrie* country, every crevice in the breakaway country, even every birdcall, animal track, every sound. They knew it all.

They knew where to dig, and not too far down either, right beside the salty stuff, to find pristine water. And they knew the soak, the spring nearby which seeped to the surface. At sundown each night, kangaroos, emus, galahs and all varieties of birds and wildlife came to drink from this rare and precious spot. Warily of course, and with good reason. The soak was watched from a vantage point, well hidden, but close enough to make sure the spear found its mark, the tucker cheerfully retrieved, gutted, and taken back to the camp to be cooked in the coals. Soon rifles would be widely available, making kangarooing even easier, even though it was against the law for Aborigines to be in possession of a gun. The Yamatjis, living in an isolated area where this was often ignored, became crack shots in no time. They were masters of the bush, had been before the whiteman, and were still, if and when the whiteman would allow them to speak—and then listen.

Outstation Wail was well set up. It had a stone house for the overseer and his family and a garden which grew good vegetables, the greenness striking among the bleached native vegetation and redness of the soil. There was a blacksmith's shed where all the horses were shod, a chaff shed, and saddle rooms. And a well had been dug, with pipes connected to the windmill above, pumping the artesian water from the rocky layers far below. Wail was a good place, with the boss of Yallalong, John Mitchell, a decent man and well liked.

Dingo Jim and Ulie were content there, camped near the other Yamatji families, all in their station-supplied tents attached to their makeshift bough sheds in the scrub, close enough but away from the buildings. Their laughter, chatter and teasing banter rang through the air, especially when the men returned from a day in the saddle, and more so when they came in from a long muster. This was a happy time.

It hadn't always been so. Wail was not far from where many tribal blackfellas had been captured and taken to prison, walking, chained together at the neck, mile after blistering mile into Geraldton and then on to Fremantle gaol or Rottnest Island down south. At nearby Mt Narryer Station, an outcamp still goes by the name Jailer, across the creek from the old prison where the captives were brought on the first part of their long trek, the policeman on horseback beside them. A tree, now a stump, still stands outside, to which the men were chained. It was a time when there were some hard, cruel whitemen, I was told by a white stockman, who had ridden the Canning Stock route in his early teens, seeing and hearing much.

Mostly the Yamatjis' crime had been to spear sheep on their own traditional grounds, and often many of the prisoners had the misfortune merely to be there when it happened, or even somewhere in the immediate district. But at least they had escaped the oft-employed method of territorial and social control. They had not been massacred, as many before them. Sheep stealing was a serious offence in white eyes. So was being a witness. But blackfellas wanted tucker, and not surprisingly these other fellas to move back off their land.

At Wail, when it was merely a hut housing a lonely shepherd,

Ulie's great-uncle watched the hapless fellow as he sat inside, isolated and probably scared stiff, meat and bread set before him. Thud. The tucker was whisked away by a swift pull on the string attached to the spear. Any sheep carcass hung to drain would also vanish in no time. But it was an uneven match. The might of the new imported law was behind the shepherd, and Ulie's great-uncle was captured, so the family history goes, ending on Rottnest Island, with other poor unfortunate blackfellas, imprisoned on a place feared by many Aboriginal people from the Perth area, Noongars, believing it the place the spirits of all their dead went. Ulie's great-uncle escaped, and was captured more than once, so the family story continues, swimming the twenty-five kilometres from the island, always making his way back up bush again. There are no records in the white history books of anyone ever escaping Rottnest this way, but the story persists and is passed on.

Ulie and Dingo Jim were back in the place they loved. This was Ulie's country proper. She belonged here, as did her parents Polly and Tommy. This was home. Country. Ulie would belong here forever. Dingo Jim, then, from Meekatharra way, would stay as well. After his early years as police tracker out from Fremantle gaol, and a short stint on the Cobb and Co mail run from Albany to Perth, his family claims, Dingo Jim's home was now wherever he made it. His own country, his birthplace, would never change, the pull and hold it had over him fixed forever in his heart, but the places he lay his swag would. Dingo Jim's days with the white police had seen to that. Frequently police trackers had been forced into the role, taken out of their homeland to track many kilometres and tribal groups away. And often they learned to perform their duties too well, helping with the killing, the rounding-up, the taking of children. Death waited if they disobeyed, and death sometimes waited as punishment if they returned. In the history books, the lives of police trackers are often blurry, as were Dingo Jim's days. He talked very little of his time as a whitefella pawn. But he didn't ever try to go all the way back home.

Dingo Jim and Ulie went back to work, Dingo Jim a stockman, a musterer, a man of the saddle and of the odd fence and windmill run. Ulie was a musterers' cook. She had grown up with station life, living here with her parents when the boss wanted work done, moving about trying to avoid station leases as best they could when the 'holidays' came along. Her early days off-station were spent joining other Yamatjis on the Murchison River route, with her mother Polly and father Tommy Glass. They would follow the river as far north as Wooleen and Meeberrie stations and down as far as Kalbarri, the mouth of the Murchison, walking, hunting and fishing. But each year they could only leave for their time to be true Yamatjis again after her father had completed his special duty.

'Well, Tommy,' the boss would say. 'I want some water.' On the extensive pastoral leases, rain fell unpredictably, on some areas plenty, others not a drop. Many a year drought would come calling, the next a destructive deluge. The boss wanted consistency, and some way of control, if only he could arrange it. There were places he wanted water so the feed could grow. There were places he wanted the river to run. He wanted God and went to Tommy, who obliged.

People would gather as Tommy stepped out to stand alone, opening his hand, talking to the Clever Men, Ulie presumed.

'Now you fellas all look,' Tommy directed. Many had come to watch for another year. The flat white object which appeared in his hand suddenly turned green, lifted off and slid out of sight. Rain would come a few days later.

Dingo Jim worked the station between Wail and Muggon, the

area edging the desolate, waterless country Muggon is known for. Cattle grazed over it, sheep confined at this time to the better land towards the southern end of the Yallalong lease. About ten families worked from Wail, Ulie close to them all, but one in particular— the Egans. She had grown up with her good friend Tottie always beside her, and the two were inseparable. Ulie, just married, came back from Byro and waited. She waited and waited, but Tottie had a baby before her. Ulie was jealous, but needn't have been. Tottie shared baby Cecil, and Ulie took him for a while.

After close on six barren years, Ulie finally fell pregnant, and her long-awaited and much-loved daughter, Junyu—First Flower in her Wadjarri language—was born, Pearlie her whitefella name given because Ulie believed she should. Ulie's longing was over, but Cecil would always be part of her family, his position never usurped. Tottie followed Pearlie's example soon after, and Cecil's baby brother Clarrie was born. Everyone pitched in together to share the raising of the *mayu* (children).

One time when Dingo Jim arrived back at the camp after several weeks out mustering, he was not impressed to find Clarrie still moving through the dirt on all fours.

'I'm sick of seeing you crawling, when a boy like you should be walking,' he said in Wadjarri, and picked him up and took him away out of sight into the bushes.

In no time he returned holding Clarrie's hand, the little boy now walking well alongside him, upright and strong. From baby to toddler in an instant. Dingo Jim had worked some of his *marbarrn*, his magic, again.

Chapter Five

In the early days of their marriage Dingo Jim and his family had to leave Wail when the mustering and fencing finished for the year, and he would take his family to join the other Yamatjis at nearby rivers and at the pools along the Murchison, while they waited for the time when they could return to their traditional homelands on the leaseholds, when the station owners said they could. It was on one of these holidays young Pearlie befriended Dora.

The young girls first met on Wooramel River, in almost a different time. It was the mid-to-late1920s, a time when there still lived Yamatjis who had evaded the breaking-in process, the taming whitefellas forced upon them in the early days, often through foul means. In the Murchison Gascoyne region, Yamatjis had been allowed to survive in greater numbers than in the south because they were needed as labour, mostly for no money, on the pastoral leases. These people were useful, but only when they were actually on the sheep and cattle stations.

Dora remembers being caught in a police operation at the behest of a squatter who worried about his sheep. Her family had been following the Gascoyne River, in the wintertime living in the caves near the water holes between jobs on the sheep station to which they had now been 'assigned'. Life for her family appeared manageable. They were surviving. But Dora's young and innocent eyes were unaware of the pressures facing her old people. Their survival was not so easy. Most of the land had now been taken up by whitefellas, sheep and cattle had taken over the waterholes, and native food and game were rapidly disappearing because of the damage wreaked by hooves and grazing. Some pastoralists allowed them to use the pools they had used for thousands of years, but many hunted them away. Even so, left alone, Dora and her family were still managing to find enough food, sometimes even the exotic. At the right time of year, watermelons, rock-melons and pumpkins grew in profusion along the river, from seeds thrown away by shearers at the nearby stations. But to obtain meat, the bulk of their diet, especially if the men were away mustering or on any station work, they relied on the help of their kangaroo dogs. Similar to greyhounds, these dogs ran down and cornered kangaroos, making a kill easier, usually carried out with a club on the head with a *gurndi*, a men's fighting stick. With the areas of land Yamatjis could now move in severely limited, kangaroo dogs often meant the difference between survival and starvation. Fruit and vegetables growing in ad hoc fashion along a river known to flood were not a reliable source. And with kangaroo skins one of the few means of obtaining any money, the dogs were vital to the family's welfare.

Dora saw Doherty the policeman as he rode up on horseback, accompanied by two men sent from the squatter's station. Her father was away from their camp, her mother washing clothes in a tub. Dora saw the policeman raise his rifle and shoot their precious dogs, one by one.

The dogs ran frantically about, yelping with pain as the bullets hit, vainly searching for some rock or bush to shield them. Her mother, enraged and horrified, threw the tub of water at the horse, but there was little she or the rest of the family could do. They were powerless, and Doherty and the squatter's men knew it. The dogs died and Dora's family were left with no means to replace them and no means of getting meat. Goannas weren't that plentiful, or fleshy enough for a large family, and there looked to be only one way out of their predicament. But it would most certainly mean gaol, as it had for wave after wave of Aboriginal men in Western Australia. Two to three years was the rule, six months if you were lucky. Sheep stealing was never treated lightly.

'My old people said to them,' Dora remembers, 'right, if we don't get any meat, you come to your fence, collect your hides, collect your skins off the fence. Whether they put them in gaol or not.' The squatter who had wanted to protect his sheep was in all probability about to lose a few. The Yamatjis in turn, regardless of how hungry and desperate they were or how callous the white-man's attempts at control had been, would be charged with offending against whitefellas' property if they attempted to balance the score. They were expected to sit back and take it like good jacky jackys.

Two weeks later, Dora and her mob received their first

rations—delivered and accepted. But rather than an act of kindness or redress for a wrong it was a cold economic decision. Dora's mob had been fed to save the sheep—and rendered dependent. Like kangaroos, they had been cornered. It would take just a few more years for the dependence imposed by the whitefella to be complete.

When left alone, Dora's family lived happily in the bush, between station jobs. The bush tucker was good from ground and trees, and native animals were still about. Sometimes they drove wild goats on the stock route, which anybody could use for moving animals, and sold them at the other end. On the way they drank the goats' milk, but only ever ate the meat if times were bad. The more they had to sell the more money they made, and the longer they could survive without servitude to the whiteman.

Dora and her family were a well-organised bunch. Dora's uncle-father Charlie Dongara, the man who claimed her as his own to prevent her being taken away by the police for the crime of being what the authorities termed half-caste, had seen to that. Charlie was a stern and capable worker, taught by a white couple who had looked after him after his parents were shot and killed. Immaculately groomed in a way which belied the fact he lived in a makeshift tent, wearing the fashionable big moustache of the time, articulate and versed in the ways of the whiteman, time in the bush with him was not a time to laze about. Each person had their responsibilities. Each person had to do their bit. And Dora had been trained well. As a child about eight years old, she carted water and wood, built shades, filled the waterbags and then made the damper. It was her daily job to have it all ready and waiting for the old people and for those returning from kangarooing. 'A full grown little woman,' Pearlie used to mutter, when only a child herself, she used to stand and watch Dora in amazement.

But regardless of how organised and efficient the life they had created from their limited circumstances, Dora's family, like Pearlie's, were soon brought fully into station life. At first it was possible to live well coming and going from the stations, doing odd jobs in exchange for food and the whiteman luxury, tobacco. As long as they kept away from the towns and squatters' leaseholds, they were okay. The only trouble was there wasn't much land left after that on which to live. Full-time station life was the only life available with any connection to the land that was their home. Fait accompli. G'day, boss. And luckily they had learned to love their life 'with the horse'.

Ulie had given birth to six children by the time baby Bessie's first cry rang out at the musterers' camp at Dairy Creek in the Gascoyne River region. Dingo Jim had come to visit his good friend Charlie, Dora's uncle-father, and once he found work, Ulie had followed behind, in the horse and buggy lent by the station: John Mitchell, the Yallalong boss, was a kind man. Baby Junyu, Pearlie, had grown, and in no time was an older sister. She was now about ten years old. It was 1932, and the whitefellas at the station homestead would celebrate Christmas in four days' time. But Christmas had no meaning for Ulie and Dingo Jim. Nor did whitefella years. They had different reference points to jog their memories, varied but accurate. They knew when the emu in the sky sat down on his nest, it was time to look for eggs. They knew when the plover gave notice of impending rain. And Ulie knew Bessie's birth time in seasonal terms, whether before or after the big dry, the big winds, how far the river was up, what plants were flowering and so on. Also what major event was happening at the time. An era was always conjured, a scene sketched in many layers, the connections emphasised. Every event happened in relation to the whole, no person or object standing alone. Ulie knew her own birth had been during the Boer War in the year following the big Murchison River, and that she had married during the Kaiser's war. Her Department of Aboriginal Affairs file took the flood she referred to to be 1899, and therefore her birth 1900. And that she was probably sixteen when she married, blackfella way.

When Bessie was born it was hot on Dairy Creek Station. And dry. So hot and dry it could blister leather. It was mustering time, and the family made camp on the flat ground by the side of the river, a spot used several times a year on this station when the work demanded.

It was cattle country—sparse and scraggly, rugged and rocky, with white limestone streaking the red soil like bacon rashers and an intense beauty which shamed cultivated Anglo prissiness. This was again tough country for a whitefella, but not for a Yamatji born and bred for this land. Life was still good here. They were on the right station. In the river which they could rely on running a good six months of the year grew plenty of water lilies with especially tasty roots. *Guwiyarl* (goannas) were aplenty, *gulyu* (yams) and a variety of bush tucker were around to supplement the station rations of meat, meat and more meat. Flour, sugar and tea were given by most stations at this time as payment when the muster finished, as you were leaving, and if you were really lucky, a pair of boots and a pair of trousers were thrown in as well. Dingo Jim was fortunate. Back at Wail he sometimes left off his station duties and, with the blessing of Mr Mitchell, took to dingo trapping, dogging, the boss sending the ears and tail for him on the mail truck, a small money reward sent back from the shire Vermin Board. This way Dingo Jim saw a little money.

Here at Dairy Creek, while Dingo Jim was away mustering, Ulie gave birth in a bough shed, with midwife Amy there to help. There was nothing new in this for either woman. All Ulie's children had been born in the bush, and Amy's. And just about every Yamatji *nyarlu* (woman) knew how to be a midwife. Of course some were better than others and so were frequently requested.

The bough shed was the same design as every other time they had set up camp, a simple construction of a few sturdy forked branches supporting a roof made of saplings and leafy branches bound together. It was ideally suited for the climate, giving shade from the scorching sun and creating a breezeway to entice any wafts of air.

No-one remembers whether Ulie had to build or mend her own shelter before she gave birth, but it is likely she did. Ulie was the family bough shed specialist, usually doing all the chopping, digging and general construction. She knew the job well. Each new camp meant another shed to go up or repairs to the one still standing from before. Dingo Jim helped put them up if he was around, but the men were often away. The women had always held their own anyway. This was a lifestyle which demanded and created strong men and women. And that was precisely what Jim and Ulie were—hardy, resilient and extremely capable.

Baby Bessie's first few days tested whether this resilience had passed on down the line. Ulie's breasts were dry and Bessie was hungry. There were no other babies in camp, and so no alternate breasts to suckle. And the hot water she had been given for a couple of days did not satisfy or nourish. Ulie worried. She had already lost one baby the year before, a son, born too fat, she said, in temperatures too high. Around Dairy Creek Station, the temperature could exceed 50 degrees Celsius. She sent her eldest children Pearlie and Owen into the bush. Wild goats roamed and flourished in sheep and cattle lands—indeed, anywhere at all on the Australian mainland. They were tough and fertile, and had made their escape long ago from the early white colonists who had introduced them. They roamed in large numbers, a pest to the pastoralists and to the land, even more so today. But not to Bessie. She is indebted forever to goat's milk and a teaspoon, no-one owning a baby's bottle, no-one, in all probability, having seen one.

Out in the bush, in searing temperatures, milk does not keep. And the solution, milking a goat every time baby is hungry, is troublesome, especially when you already have a sizeable family to rear and feed. Bush tucker still needs to be found and the children attended to. Several days passed and Ulie was still unsuccessful at making her milk flow.

Pearlie and Owen were sent back into the bush, the goat set free. Their mission was so important that Amy and others from the camp joined them. They searched everywhere, through all the bushes and in every prickly tree, all scratches ignored. They found what they had been instructed to look for, down by the creek. The *ngingari*, zebra-finches, were given no choice but to relinquish their nests. Bessie's wellbeing depending on it. To Ulie's relief, Pearlie, Owen and the others returned to the camp triumphant.

She burned the nests as she knew to, the smoke billowing up around her breasts held over the fire. The smouldering twigs were well coated in bird excrement, and the smoke was thick. She scooped the fumes towards her, catching, rubbing them into her skin with both hands, washing herself in the opaqueness. Milk came, in one breast only, but enough. Bessie drank heartily, growing healthier by the day.

Ulie and Jimmy had given their new baby a Yamatji name as they had all their children. They called her Bubawidarra, meaning

Long Water, after the river which flowed past the camp where she was born. She was also named Bessie, the Anglo name Ulie was still convinced she had to give.

When Bessie was about six months old, Ulie and the other women from the camp were digging one day for yams along the side of the river. She carried Bessie strapped to her in a *gurlgu*, a sling, the cloth wrapped round her, the baby close to her body. With this, she could go kangarooing unimpeded, and when digging for tucker only had to untie it, and place baby and *gurlgu* on the ground nearby, ready for quick retrieval. This time Ulie had carefully left Bessie a safe distance from the river bank, near the other young one, Dora's baby sister, and just close enough to feel the cool breeze coming off the water. She pushed the sand into a small hollow deep enough to prevent Bessie from practising her newly developed rolling-over trick. It was a snug fit and Ulie joined the other women, reminding Pearlie to watch over baby.

But the water was clear and beautiful, its coolness enticing to skin sticky from the heat. Pearl and Dora could not resist. They played and splashed and frolicked—'In the nakety,' Dora says with a degree of embarrassment now. Then, as young girls both about ten years old, they knew none, water and bare skin perfect companions.

Ulie and Dingo Jim's second son Leslie came by. Though only about six years old, there were already hints of the independent man of initiative he was to become. He saw his little sister on the bank and worried because black goannas were about. Big ones. He lifted her and placed her in what he took to be a safe spot, closer to the water.

But he did not know the precautions Ulie had taken for the baby and so he did not make a new snug hollow for her. When he had gone, Bessie, revelling in her freedom, rolled over into the water.

This was her river, her name connecting her forever. And it wanted her. She went in headfirst, legs sticking out, considering whether to surrender to the spirits within. Dora had had enough waterplay today and was sauntering along the bank on her way to check her mother's baby and then join the women where the yams were.

'Auntie! Auntie!' she screamed, ripping Bessie from the water by the feet. 'Your baby's half-drowned! Your baby's half-drowned!' Ulie was given a good scare, Bessie a good emptying out. And Pearlie, poor Pearlie, was given a good hiding.

Chapter Six

Ulie and Dingo Jim stopped moving about soon after Bessie was born at Dairy Creek. They moved back to Wail on Yallalong, back to Ulie's mother Polly, alone now that husband Tommy had passed away some years earlier, buried with a brush fence marking his grave. They stayed put, the holidaying days all finished now, and the station wanting their labour full-time.

They went back to where they belonged. And back to John Mitchell.

John Mitchell was one of the rare ones. While no saint, he was still a good man, compassionate and caring, and the Yamatji families who worked for him were intensely loyal, treated as human beings of worth. A handful of stations in the Murchison, all within the one area, all had bosses and managers who treated the Aboriginal people with a degree of decency, even if no pay was forthcoming. Paternalistic they may have been, but it was the best treatment on offer. And in allowing the Yamatjis some dignity, there were many implications for the following generations, in the attitudes which were passed on, and for the achievements of their children. In the future it would have great significance for one of Ulie's and Dingo Jim's grandsons in particular.

John Mitchell had proved himself time and again to all his workers and their families. He made sure all the children were looked after, fed well and clothed appropriately for the seasons, including the bitterly cold winter nights. 'Doesn't matter if the mothers had no mans,' a grown-up Clarrie told me, having retired from stockwork many years ago. At Christmas time, Mr Mitchell raided his large station store and sent loads of presents to all at the outstation—fruit, boots, clothes, drinks, everything they could want, according to Clarrie.

Clarrie had spent some time working away from Wail when he was very young, doing odd jobs near the Yallalong homestead where he was still learning the ropes. On Sundays Mr Mitchell used to lounge around on the verandah overlooking the big lawn out the back, reading the paper. 'Go up there and bring all the boys from the quarters,' he would say to the housemaid. 'Let them all play round here, while I'm having a rest.' Lollies, fruit and a meal were given to them, all tumbling and playing happily on the lawn as he watched over them. 'I think you've had enough now,' he would say at sundown. 'It's time to go back home. Goodnight.'

John Mitchell was a big man and no-one stood over him, even those policemen, as reluctant as many of them were, on their state-ordered child-snatching missions. He sent them packing. On one of their visits, he refused to receive them until he was good and ready.

'See that river over there,' he said, pointing in the opposite direction from the place they had requested. 'Go back over there and camp. Then you can come back and see me in the morning.' Their wait brought little joy.

'I've been looking after these people for a long time, and I'll be looking after them till I die,' he said. And to his word, no children were taken from his property in his lifetime.

But life sometimes plays terrible tricks, and while he made sure all the Yamatji children were protected, the nanny employed to look after his dearly loved youngest daughter was not quite as vigilant. At the outside bathroom, she turned the steaming hot water from the copper on into the bath and walked out, leaving the water running. The two-year-old watched the swallows which had snuck in, squealing with excitement as they flitted and darted about above her, then she slipped backwards into the boiling water. She was buried on Yallalong, her grave still standing, still telling her story, still expressing her mother's and father's love. The nanny had to find a way out of Yallalong as quickly as she could. John Mitchell went mad with grief, and someone, anyone, had to take her away before he shot her.

Ulie and Dingo Jim made camp once more, back near Tottie's family and not far from Granny Polly's mia-mia. Cecil and Clarrie Whitehurst were glad their grandfather and grandmother, as they called them, were back. They had missed them and wanted their whole family, blood ties or not, to be together again. Cecil and Clarrie enjoyed not only the kids, but warm Ulie and happy old Dingo Jim as well. Dingo Jim enjoyed a joke and was good company for adults and children alike. And he could also tease if the mood took him. When any of the children cried, yodelling they called it, or singing hallelujah, Dingo Jim could always yodel louder and, head tilted back, sure sing to the glory of the stars.

Cecil and Clarrie had served their unofficial appenticeships as station hands, and though still only boys, had graduated to mustering. They lived for it. Leslie, Ulie's and Dingo Jim's second son, was green with envy, but still a bit too young. He dreamed of his day, one day. They had started as lamb markers, a job over a couple of days filled with excitement and adrenalin, plus a little blood and tar. A couple of blokes, grown men, sat the lamb on the stockyard fence, tail dangling, one holding the wriggling bundle of wool, the other cutting the tail with a knife. Another couple of blokes were on hand to earmark. Then there were the boys, ready with a stick and paint tin full of black tar to brush on the new wound the lambs had acquired in such an undignified manner. The lambs, lacking any appreciation whatsoever, would promptly kick it up and all over them.

Out mustering there was more chance of control. But not with the weather. It did what it liked. On a muster the two brothers did what everybody else did, getting up at three o'clock in the morning and returning to their camp sometimes as late as ten o'clock at night. In the wintertime the rain would hurl itself down, thick and miserable in the blackness. The boys battled their way through. Their good friends, the horses, would always save the day. In the dark, Clarrie and Cecil, and the other musterers, if they were unfamiliar with the country, only had to sit along, their horses delivering them safely back to the tent they called home.

John Mitchell had turned his attention to Muggon outstation, the parched and sandy country immediately north of Yallalong and Wail. A large shearing shed had been built, serviced by a kitchen, dining room and shearers' quarters clustered together to form an outcamp known as Muggon Shed. Dingo Jim and family went wherever the boss wanted and moved here, setting up their tent and bough shed close to the camp itself. The stony rise overlooking the buildings had determined the Shed's positioning, several kilometres from the place chosen for the homestead. It was the only small hill in the surrounding flat country, and its height enabled water to be pumped to four tanks twelve kilometres away. There was no other way. Any other water around was salt.

Sheep numbers were increasing rapidly, a number of wells were dug and bored on Muggon itself, windmills erected and troughs put in place. A fencing program meant proper paddocks, even if the area covered was more than 30,000 hectares. The effort paid off.

In front of Muggon Shed 300 bales of wool were stacked, ready and waiting for delivery to the buyers, but a single wagon transport along rocky sandy tracks was notoriously slow. And no sooner had a load been delivered to Mullewa on the way down south and back up to the station again, several days' travel, than the pile stacked sky high again. It seemed to never shift.

When the homestead was finally built twelve kilometres away, Dingo Jim and family once again did John Mitchell's bidding and moved camp. Men were needed at the new head-quarters and there was a lot of work to do. They camped 200 metres away from the mud brick house, built in the middle of no-where it seemed, on rockhard red dirt with no trees around. Their camp among the scraggly trees along the dried-up creekbed seemed the better bet.

Dingo Jim and the other Yamatjis had been sent to look after the Muggon country up north. It was a long way away by horse. It was big, remote, and if anything happened out there, help was many days' ride. So too if anything happened back in the camp.

Baby Bessie had drunk her fill from Ulie's one functional

breast, and had grown into a cheerful, healthy child. She was now one of the pack and wanted to be just like her older brothers and sisters. Like all small children, she was also eager to help. At sundown, Ulie and her children made their way back to their camp content with their day, and hungry. Bessie ran ahead. She was proud her little legs could match both her mother's and big sisters' strides and she reached the camp first. Brother Owen—Oogaatji his Yamatji name—had done as his mother requested and prepared a meal. The fire in the open was glowing, the coals red hot, the campfire oven placed firmly in the middle as it should.

'Got the feed on?' Ulie called to Pearlie in Wadjarri, asking her to check.

'Yeah,' Bessie said, pleased she could now answer like the big kids, and pleased her meal would soon be served. 'Oogaatji put it on!' Pearlie had been cut right out.

In her excitement, Bessie forgot the warnings both her mother and father had given her ever since her life had been spared at the river. She forgot the first law of the bush—ensuring your survival. She reached over the red hot coals and lifted the lid, with her small bare hand. Her skin burnt through and she screamed in pain. Over she fell, into the fire itself.

Dingo Jim was out bush, sheep mustering, had been for many weeks. At this time, in the 1930s, the stockmen stayed out often for long periods, coming in only for a short stay during a slack time. They would be on the move again when another problem needed seeing to, or another mob of sheep had to be moved to another part of the station. Dingo Jim was looking forward to having his own tucker, as well as a good night's sleep after a long day's work. He made his way back to his camp, took the saddle off his horse and left it to feed. Something didn't feel right. He lay on his swag outside the tent he shared with his young Yamatji co-worker, and looked at the sky getting darker.

'Can't rest,' he said without warning. 'Something home.'

His fellow worker looked blankly at him, astonished.

'I gotta go,' Dingo Jim continued. 'Something's happened to my *mayu*.'

He threw the saddle on his horse and rode. Through the *wandarrie* country, the red sandhills and the scrub he galloped, all through the night until early the following morning.

Ulie was standing watching the road and screaming his name. She knew he would come. She was sending her message as strongly as she could. Finally the faint sound of horseshoes hitting the rocks could be heard. 'Ayyy! I'm comin'. I'm comin',' Dingo Jim cried to her on the wind. At last he reached her and pulled up his horse. Exhausted from his all-night journey, he fell to the ground. Ulie knelt with him, the words pouring out. Dingo Jim realised he was too late to help his daughter and sat there in the middle of the track weeping for her.

It took a week to get her all the way firstly to the station homestead at Yallalong and then on by car into the nearest hospital at Mullewa, 130 kilometres away on rough unformed roads. Bessie healed, the scarring mainly confined to her forearms and hands, and with only the little finger of her right hand damaged, permanently bent back. But at least she was alive. From now on she was watched constantly. Dingo Jim had been married before in his blurry past, and his eldest son had fallen out of a tree and died. He now watched his children from this marriage like a hawk. While good fun, he was also strict, and could switch moods quickly if his children were not behaving sensibly and responsibly. But he could only oversee them in between the months spent mustering, droving, or fencing. The watchful eye he would have preferred to be was denied him by the disruptive nature of the station life he loved. Most men spent long periods away from their wives and children. And many marriages and families suffered the consequences. Ulie's and Dingo Jim's already had, before Bessie was born.

Alf was a station hand at Muggon when Ulie and Dingo Jim had one of their disagreements. Jim's life in the saddle meant too long away. Intimacy was hard to maintain and their partnership showed a few cracks every now and then. They separated briefly, again. Alf, a white man, offered company and affection.

It took Ulie and Dingo Jim many years to overcome the tension and jealousy the affair and the resulting baby caused. Alf once had to rescue Ulie after an argument with Jim turned nasty, and he took her and the children in his buggy way out into the bush where they set up camp. But Dingo Jim was a tracker, a good one who used to astonish whitefellas when, from the churned sand, he could tell how many sheep went where, and even distinguish goat tracks from sheep, although they had the same shaped feet. Tracking his wife then was a cinch. He followed on behind and suddenly appeared. Words were exchanged, feelings aired, promises made, and Ulie and Jim reunited. But Dingo Jim's jealousy didn't go away. They bickered too frequently about Ronnie with Ulie standing her ground. Ronnie was her son, and brother to her other children. She loved him. And so did his brothers and sisters. So did Dingo Jim, when he could overcome his sense of being aggrieved. Ronnie's position was precarious enough, without any unnecessary complications adding to it. Born about two years before Bessie, Ronnie was what the state termed a half-caste. Just by being born, he was a ready target, a black soul to whiten in the bureaucratically driven attempt at racial cleansing. He would need someone to watch over him, and luckily

John Mitchell was there to do just that. As long as he was alive, Ronnie was safe.

The Yallalong-Wail-Muggon property was too big for one man to manage in the days when the wind-up telephone was the most sophisticated communication device available. A manager was installed in the Muggon homestead, together with his wife. Arthur and Elsie Leeds had taken up residence. Pearlie went to work in the house. Owen worked as a yardman, Ulie helping outside as well.

Arthur Leeds was a different man from John Mitchell, his boss. Mr Mitchell had an affinity with his Yamatji workers. Arthur Leeds, it seems, did not. Yet Mr Leeds was popular and well liked among the white folk. He was regarded as a character, probably because of his daily inclination to repair to his office early each day to phone the overseers and ask how the sheep were doing, and take his first swig from the bottle of whisky he downed daily. Nothing unusual, or much of a problem, in this on the stations. Big drinkers were everywhere. And they were all white.

Instead the problem was with the difference between owner and manager, a problem in every industry at any time. Out here on the stations it was crucial. For the Yamatjis, that is. The type of manager employed determined the work climate, conditions and treatment of the workers. The changes could already be felt on Muggon, but at least Mr Mitchell's presence lurked somewhere in the background. There are stories of Mr Leeds hurriedly scaling a windmill when he heard of an impending visit from the big man from Yallalong, and rubbing his chest and shirt hard against the grease.

Accepting the new order was difficult for Dingo Jim and many others, who found it all a bit too much to cop. Problems arose easily. They already knew their job. Though short, Jim was a strong man, in character and physical strength, well aware of his abilities in both the Yamatji and white worlds. He took pride in his station work and pride in who he was, a lawman with a mind of his own. Such a quality meant predictable struggles with Mr Leeds, a man also with a mind of his own.

After one row, when Dingo Jim considered his work methods to be right and Mr Leeds the equivalent of office boy, he collected his swag, his two eldest children, and walked straight past the boss's nose. Dingo Jim pulled himself up to his full height, calculated at all of five feet seven inches (171 centimetres), took one last look at the place and walked on. His two eldest children relished the defiance and followed close behind, chins in the air, Owen carrying the waterbag, Pearlie swinging a billycan.

But the last look could never really be the last. Polly, Ulie's mother, was still there, now with her new husband Old Harry. They both belonged there, and that meant Ulie, even if she followed on behind, would always go back. And Mr Mitchell was still the big boss. So Dingo Jim, after a few days cooling off with friends at an outcamp on neighbouring Mt Narryer Station, returned and went straight back to station work.

When Pearlie began training with Mrs Leeds in her new duties at Muggon house—those strange new duties from another lifestyle—she was still a child. She was so young she had to stand on a box to wash up. Looking back now she has no idea what age that was. Her birth date can be calculated by guesswork alone, and she never learnt to read or write. Unlike her brothers who badgered whitefellas and then practised what they were told, she did not push to be taught, and is slightly embarrassed today if she has to reveal her inability. She still signs her name, slowly and carefully, with a shaky cross. Back then, her role in life was decided for her, as it was for many a Yamatji girl. She would make a good housemaid, a servant, if she could be buffed and polished, moulded into shape.

But Pearlie could never be servile, and showed herself every inch Dingo Jim's daughter. She had spirit. Pearlie as housemaid was therefore a problem, until she could be, in the words normally applied by the old Yamatji people to the attempted controlling of tribal Aboriginal people, 'tamed down'. As a child bent on having a childhood, the taming down took some time.

'Hurry up! Hurry up!' growled Mrs Leeds, the station manager's wife. Pearlie, determined to do things in her own time, had again taken nearly all day just to clean the one area. But regardless of how many times she was told, the bathroom always proved too fascinating for a girl who lived in a tent. Everything required testing, and games were just waiting to be invented. The bathroom held mystery which it was her duty to unravel. And best of all, it was away from the Missus' eyes. And her commands.

For a young girl, Pearlie's duties were not light, although there was some attempt to ease them. But whitefellas' deter-mination to whip everything into one shape, no matter how different it all was, meant it was unlikely the difficulty of a task, for a child, would be recognised. It had to be done, regardless of how steadfastly nature refused to toe the line. In sandy country, where high winds and willy willys were frequent, one of Pearlie's chores first thing each morning was to sweep the big verandah which encircled the house. When she finished that job, she had to move to the yard and sweep that, sweeping sand off sand and picking up any piece of rubbish lying around. If she missed a single matchstick, Pearlie was in trouble.

But the Murchison has a mind of its own, and yards and verandahs, especially at Muggon, were often covered in sand soon after sweeping, matchsticks or not. Pearlie thought it a strange exercise. Stranger still was the direction to go out and get wood without looking for bush food on the way. Mrs Leeds, obviously exasperated with her tardy charge, was forever asking what she could possibly be doing out there. Pearlie knew the real answer. Bush food was always enticing. But more so the idea of simply getting away from the job. Out in the country, Pearlie was happy to have the chance to be a child once more.

Mrs Leeds was fighting a losing battle, for a while at least. Pearlie was still convinced the world was hers to arrange as she pleased. She was too young to recognise her overall powerlessness now she 'belonged' to a station, and was innocently cocksure her parents would always be able to make everything right. She tried to do as Mrs Leeds asked this time, but the sand mound in the yard was too big and too heavy, and it genuinely took some time to finish.

'You better hurry up,' Mrs Leeds said. 'Pick it all up, or no dinner for you.'

Pearlie had been provoked. She finished her chore, went into the kitchen, took the plate that was handed to her, walked outside and emptied the lot into the rubbish bin, knife and fork included. She had had her say.

'I'm goin' back to tell my Mum on you,' Pearlie said over her shoulder, sounding just like every child that's ever been, as she marched back to the camp, her resolve never to return set in stone. That is, until Mrs Leeds asked for her a short time later.

In the meantime, Pearlie spent her brief time away from the whitefellas helping to look after her younger brothers and sisters. There were now six children in all, and Bessie was about three years old. Often Pearlie would head further into the bush, kangarooing with the other kids—Hilda, Ronnie or Owen if he was back from his yardman duties, Les working down the road at

Muggon Shed—but mostly by herself, with just a kangaroo dog who would run the favoured tucker down. Then, hoisting it on her shoulders, she would take it home to Granny Polly, who cut it up and cooked it in the open coals. Pearlie was always proud to bring a kangaroo back, especially a nice fat one. Only those were good enough for her Granny, she thought.

Ulie also would go kangarooing by herself—but in style, riding high on a camel's back. Wild camels roamed throughout much of outback Australia, having escaped from failed exploring expeditions and from Afghans and prospectors. Some of these men failed and died in the new harsh land but the camels certainly didn't. Instead they bred. Many remote Australians have been grateful to them over the years. Camels were hitched to wool wagons and even in buggies, or used in places a horse was not practical or affordable. And they were strong. A number roamed the Muggon outcamp and had been caught, branded and broken in. But Ulie's camel and kangaroo pairing came to an end after one bucked and bucked again when it smelt the blood of a newly slain carcass stuffed into the saddlebag. Ulie was forced to trek home on foot, cautiously leading the delicate creature.

Despite not always delivering what was expected of them, Ulie and Dingo Jim's two camels, Linda and Keeta, came to regard themselves as part of the camp, almost like pets. And little wonder. Dingo Jim mostly talked baby-talk to them. Mollycoddled, they demanded to be treated as one of the mob, much to the kids' horror. 'The ugly big things,' as Pearlie calls them now, insisted on being touched, patted and preferably stroked, and they went to great lengths to get what they wanted. They would chase the children, who frantically sought shelter in the middle of some scratchy bush, but the camels would drop to the ground and inch their way forward, poking their heads in underneath and straining upwards as far as their necks would stretch. The kids screamed as the camels' heads loomed closer, huge and monster-like as face met face. But it made no difference to the camels. Thorns, prickles, all meant nothing when a soft touch and a bit of affection were at stake. However, Linda's and Keeta's desire to smooch and lean was useful at times, when Dingo Jim and Ulie were travelling and camping overnight. The camels would not stray. They were too busy keeping warm, nestling right alongside the fire—that is, after they had raked through the coals searching for left-over damper.

Back at the camp, Pearlie was not allowed to languish long under the illusion her childhood could be spent free of those bossy whitefellas. Ulie and Dingo Jim wouldn't let any of their children be idle for long. Pearlie was soon back learning how to do housework, scrub floors, polish the silver and perform assorted other tasks. Bathroom play lost its lustre after a while. At least every now and then she and her sister Hilda, with Mr and Mrs Leeds' nephew, John, were able to go riding, skirts hitched up, hair flying, and sitting bareback. Pearlie would pick up a small bleached bone from the ground and hold it out as if it was bread to entice the horses. Stealing, she called it, borrowing not allowed. With just a rag strung around the horses' necks, they galloped flat out, sliding down the sandhill not too far from the homestead, just far enough away to be out of sight. These were fun times even when she had to walk home after coming a cropper, following the horse which had gone for its life straight back to the house.

Her younger brother Les had been sent down to work at Muggon Shed. From his earliest days—and there hadn't been too many of those yet, at only about seven years old—he had always been independent and self-reliant. At Muggon homestead he had even slept in the chaff shed rather than near everybody else at the camp. Down at Muggon Shed, which Pearlie sometimes visited by car with Mrs Leeds and Ulie, he camped where he felt like camping. Pearlie never knew where that was, whether up the bush, in the wool shed or under a car. Loving life, Les was king of his domain, wherever he made it. He was also desperate to grow up to be a king of the saddle, to be a stockman, just like his Dad and all the other men he watched in covetous admiration. Like every one of them, he longed to ride tall.

He learnt whatever was available, horsemanship and stockwork, and even what wasn't, whitefella reading and writing, early, pushing people to teach him, asking questions, one after the other, soaking up the answers. A happy cheerful boy with a wide smile and a knack of befriending anybody, he would seat himself next to a friendly white station hand at the long table in the workers' dining room and keep asking what's this, what's that. Tomato sauce bottles and jam tin labels he put to good use, examining them and learning to identify the letters. He would go away and practise and practise.

One of his jobs at the Shed was to get the few milking cows in each evening, not always an easy task. After all, they roamed through the scrub over a large area and he was only a little fella, on foot. But not according to him. Using a long stick with twine for reins, Les set out every afternoon on his horse. He would call his movements, galloping first, then going alongside, rounding up, and finally draughting and penning—but with make-believe cattle, the real cows nowhere in sight. Like big sister Pearlie, playing seemed to regularly bring trouble.

'Now, Leslie,' the whitefella overseeing him would say, 'you've got to go and get the cows now. And if you don't come back with them, bring a switchy stick home.'

Those sticks were piled up high, over in the corner. After each one Les would go and have a little cry. And then be back out again in the morning. The cows had to be brought in sometime and he had to go back until he succeeded, just like real mustering. And getting in all those stragglers—that was what he most wanted to do.

Down at Wail, Cecil and Clarrie had become fine horsemen and were now part of all the big musters. They enjoyed it most when the ten men from each of the three station camps got together to work the big areas, all in a mob.

The large paddock between Muggon and Wail required the type of muster film makers love. Plenty of dust, sweat and dogs, along with much noise, colour and movement. The men from Muggon, Dingo Jim and Old Harry included, joined the men from Wail, and together they would muster one side, camp, move the supply cart, muster a further side for a few days, and keep on until they'd rounded up all the sheep. When it was over, Dingo Jim, Old Harry and the others would ride back to Muggon, Clarrie and Cecil going with their lot back to Wail. They were indeed times to remember.

But in 1937, there was bad news at Yallalong. And the consequences were far reaching. John Clayton Mitchell died of pneumonia at Mullewa hospital. The Yamatjis on his station had lost their dear friend. Arthur and Elsie Leeds were moved from Muggon to Yallalong, now managers of the whole station. Much was to change.

Chapter Seven

hings were certainly going to be different, for everybody. Pearlie, who had learned to cope with working for Mrs Leeds at Muggon, as long as she returned to her parents and their camp each night, was about to have her world whisked from under her feet. Mrs Leeds asked for her to be sent across. With a deep sadness, she left Ulie and Dingo Jim and went to live in the big house at Yallalong, a lifetime away. To Ulie, Mrs Leeds' request was akin to a command. This was a Yamatji girl's lot. She had seen no other way. So she did as she understood life demanded, and sent Pearlie as directed—by the widpella.

Pearlie cried for many nights, even though Rita, another

Yamatji *nyarlu*, was also there. Separation from her family and camplife was hard. Pearlie, a teenager now, shared a bare room with Rita, and the two were servants together. Ulie and Dingo Jim continued working on Muggon, and Pearlie only saw them once a year at Christmas. The station was vast, and work could not be left unfinished. A quick two-day trip to visit your daughter was out of the question and was not seen as necessary anyway. Creating happy Yamatji families was certainly no longer a priority here. Pearlie's childhood was effectively over. Now she was a true domestic, a servant, unpaid except for a few clothes and keep. Adulthood had been thrust upon her.

At Yallalong, she became quieter, tamed down to some degree, and ironically had to rely on the sense of familiarity Mrs Leeds could provide. Pearlie was shy away from her own mob. She tried not to venture outside for some time, and when she did, another Yamatji woman accused her of wanting her man. Pearlie, shocked at the accusation, was even more shocked when Mrs Mitchell, who had stayed on for a while, suddenly appeared, and told the other woman in Wadjarri to watch her language. After a time Pearlie became bolder and would head out with Mrs Leeds, as the sun was going down. They walked and ran to the road, waiting for the boss's horse to come into view as he returned from work. When they could see him, she and Mrs Leeds would go running in the cool evening air to greet him. It gave her a welcome sense of freedom.

Pearlie over time learnt to accept the involuntary changes in her life, and she set out to cope as best she could. She now got out of the house as often as possible, putting the camel in the cart and going out to collect wood. She would go walking by herself just to get away. While doing her work in the house, she would often think of Dora, wondering what she was doing. She thought about the way they used to 'talk silly', and what fun it all was.

'What your man's name gunna be?' youthful Dora had always asked.

'I like Joe the best name,' answered Pearlie, without hesitation.

'Me too!' said Dora. Girls together, dreaming.

The mail truck arrived, always an exciting time on a station. It meant new stores for the house, mail for the whitefellas, who could just about all read and write, and maybe a visitor or two passing through. Pearlie peeped round the corner, but pulled back. She wasn't sure at first. They didn't get that many visitors at the station, and sometimes there was only the boss, his missus and the overseer there. She snuck another quick look. 'I'm *sure* that's her!' she thought. A short attractive Yamatji woman stood waiting while the truck was unloaded. A young man walked back and forth. Dora had arrived from Byro Station, over 150 kilometres away, en route to another station—Dora and her new husband, blackfella way, her new husband, Joe.

It wasn't too long before Pearlie's intended was finally presented as well, the selection and arrangement made many years back at Wail, with Pearlie having no say whatsoever. Fellow Yamatjis down at the camp used to tease her, pointing him out, saying loudly 'That's your *mardong* (boyfriend) down there.' Pearlie had been so embarrassed by it all. 'No! No!' she used to say. The whole idea of leaving her parents was frightening, and a promised man more so. And arranged marriages did not always go ahead, regardless of the punishments threatened. Pearlie felt great shame at the obligation the spoken words were conveying.

It was just before Christmas, and there was a break in the station work. Dingo Jim had been down in Mullewa, a small town which was the cornerpost, lifeblood of the Murchison stations. He had taken a bundle of dingo ears and kangaroo skins down and came back as soon as his business was done. There were family matters he had to attend to while he waited at Yallalong, before travelling through to Muggon Station. The mail truck, with which he was getting a lift, was being loaded. Everything had to be carted over—drums of fuel, fresh vegetables, big bags of flour, sugar and all the stores for the house, as well as assorted equipment such as windmill parts. And of course, the mail.

Dingo Jim waited in the big station garage. It housed quite a few cars, some of them flash, and several trucks which the men were often working on. Pearlie had never been in the garage. Mrs Leeds had forbidden her. Dingo Jim asked to see his daughter and Pearlie came from the house, peeping round the corner. She was pleased to see her father, but aware she had been summoned to territory classified out of bounds. It was the only time she went there, and what Dingo Jim had to say made it memorable.

'Well, *Gudja* [child],' he said in Wadjarri. 'I think you better get married. Live with him now.'

'No,' said Pearlie. 'No!'

'Yes,' Dingo Jim insisted. 'It's been too long now, and you've been working at Yallalong for long enough.'

On holiday that same Christmas, Pearlie was married off. Two brothers were seated side by side as they had been directed, and Pearlie's days as a single girl were all but over. She was placed firstly on the younger man's knee, then moved across to his brother, who from that moment was considered her husband. The younger man would take her husband's place if he should die. Pearlie now had a husband whether she liked it or not, and one in reserve. The match had been arranged well. Pearlie's *mardong*, Tottie's brother, was named Joe.

Two women had now realised their childhood fantasies and married two Joes. But life for Yamatjis would never be Mills and Boon. Both women had tough times ahead. And Dora had nearly missed her Joe anyway. She had originally been promised to his brother Ned who, risking the wrath of the elders, had ignored the old ways and gone off and married someone else far enough away to feel safe, probably an erroneous assumption. She was passed then, as decreed by the old Yamatji law, to his brother Joe.

The old people who had made the selection (Pearlie's and Dora's fathers, themselves not permitted to promise their own daughters) had gone against tradition to some degree and selected young husbands for the young women. Young girls were frequently promised to older men, so the men could teach them, sexually and domestically, but not in this case. They were given young ones. Young or old, the decision had to be accepted. And if you said no, look out—and just wait for the punishment to arrive.

The old people continued to rule relationships according to Yamatji law as best they could, given how disrupted their lives now were. They were still strict. Permission to talk to the opposite sex was only given if you were told that person was to be your girlfriend or boyfriend. If some brave soul requested a particular partner, and was refused, only the foolhardy failed to listen. This was still a time, the late 1930s, when if the old people were nearby, Yamatji men were not permitted to walk past their sister's face—or their mother's, or auntie's. A path had to be found all the way round. Women to men the same. Pearlie could not have married any other way.

The old people had a lot to consider when promising their kin. But most important, they thought, was merely to put the promise in place. Aboriginal people throughout Western Australia, not just Yamatjis, knew their true position. They knew how they could be herded near towns. They knew which stations had good bosses and which ones flogged the workers. They knew which foremen, bosses and managers were bunji-men, men who dabbled in what the whitefellas called black velvet, and they knew of all the unacknowledged Aboriginal children with white fathers on which stations. They knew of the children being taken away. And they knew above all, who held all the power. Pearlie and Dora were 'promised' to protect them. The old people didn't want 'the policeman' to take them. They were convinced the girls would be spared if, when 'Welfare' arrived to collect them, the same way too many children had been collected, they were able to say they were not free to be taken. They had a man on the station, waiting, working for them.

It was a sad attempt, and undoubtedly would never have worked had it been tested. The authorities were determined. '... It may appear to be a cruel thing to tear an Aborigine child from its mother, but it is necessary in some cases to be cruel to be kind,' said one West Australian politician around the turn of the twentieth century. The official policy stated in a 1937 report outlining the views of Mr A.O. Neville, the then Commissioner of Aborigines in Western Australia, was to keep the pure blacks segregated, and absorb the 'half-castes' into the white population. Pearlie would be left alone. She was full descent, meant to die out, with all 'pure blacks'. Dora, the daughter of a white man, a Scotsman, was the one really in danger, but she was fortunate, her uncle dissuading the policeman and claiming her. She was not approached again. She is still filled with gratitude and immense love for her uncle-father saviour.

With John Mitchell gone, any light-skinned Yamatjis on Yallalong were now in danger. Clarrie felt the effects almost immediately. Soon after Mr Mitchell died, Clarrie's and Cecil's mother, Ulie's friend Tottie, and her four other sons were all taken away, now that their protector was gone. All fair-skinned—as were Clarrie and Cecil, the sons of a white father as well—they were sent to Mogumber, the notorious Moore River Native Settlement down south. But Clarrie and Cecil were not taken. Instead they had been left all alone, forced to rely more than ever on each other and their relationship with Dingo Jim, Ulie and all the children.

It is possible their mother's removal was requested, once John Mitchell was dead. Cecil's and Clarrie's father had left years before, moved away from station work, back into Mullewa, and married a white woman, Clarrie never having met him. Tottie was alone and although doing what work she could for the station, was not productive in the way the men or women without children were. Almost men themselves now, Cecil's and Clarrie's labour was needed, while the station in effect supported Tottie and her younger children, a responsibility Mr Mitchell had willingly undertaken. And the trade-off, the cheap labour supplied by her sons, now went unnoted. Clarrie, still moved by John Mitchell's death, tells me exactly where he is buried. And he has good reason to be sad. Although Tottie managed to find her way back several years later, by marrying to attain her freedom— Bonner Maher becoming her faithful husband—Clarrie never saw his brothers again. Today, in his seventies he still longs to meet them.

Word was spreading the caste-police were active again in the area. Ulie heard and was determined to save her son. Some mothers resorted to blackening their children with charcoal trying to make their skin appear darker. Fathers, while not their biological parents, sent them down to hide along creeks. Ulie tried a different method. She sent Ronnie away. Not far, just to Meeberrie, a station adjoining Muggon to the east. She sent him to her close friends Paddy and Laurie Donnelly, a childless couple, who were themselves termed half-caste. Official policy did not insist on removal if both parents had 'Aboriginal blood'. And she was happy for him to stay and live there, close enough for visits, close enough to keep an eye on.

But the authorities moved into action.

30th October 1937

> *Constable J. Clark,*
> *Protector of Natives,*
> MEEKATHARRA.
>
> *On perusing Dr. Davis' list of natives examined during 1936, I noticed that he examined a half-caste child named Ronnie, 8 years old, at Meerberrie [sic] Station.*
>
> *As I have no previous correspondence in reference to this child, I am desirous of learning his personal history and parental particulars, that is, if he is not the child of two half-castes or of native blood on both sides.*
>
> *If he is the child of a white father it might not even now be too late to secure maintenance from the latter if he admits his responsibility and provided the child is removed to an institution for education and training.*
>
> *I shall be glad if you will look into the history of this child, and report to me in due course but even if he is the child of parents with native blood I should also like to have information concerning him for record purposes for future reference if necessary.*
>
> COMMISSIONER OF NATIVE AFFAIRS

The enquiries were made and Leslie Macpherson, the Meeberrie station manager, submitted the details as he knew them. He also added character references and a veiled opinion of his own, hoping to influence the police officer and his subsequent recommendations.

25th November 1937
'Meeberrie' Station
via Mullewa W.A.

The Officer in Charge,
Police Station,
Mullewa.
Dear Sir,

In reply to your letter concerning the half caste boy Ronnie who lives here, I have to advise you as follows:-

Ronnie's mother is a native woman named Eulie [sic] who has lived at "Muggin" [sic] station for a good number of years. Her man is one named Dingo Jim. Ronnie's father is alleged to be a one time employee at "Muggin". The boy is now about seven years of age. If you require further details regarding Ronnie's parents I suggest you write to Mr and Mrs Leeds of "Yallalong" station who is in a position to give you more exact details than I am able.

About two years ago, Eulie gave Ronnie to Paddy and Laurie Donnelly. They have no children of their own, and have adopted the boy, and are bringing him up as their own son. He has a good home, and could not be in better hands. Paddy has been with me for many years, and his character is excellent. Laurie who was at "Wooleen" for many years also bears an excellent character. Paddy and his wife have a cottage at the homestead, and the boy is there with them. I am mentioning the above regarding the child's living conditions in case the Commissioner requires this information.

We take this opportunity to wish you the compli-
ments of the Season,

> *Yours faithfully*
> *(signed) R Macpherson*
> *Manager*

Once again it was a sad and futile attempt, this time from a caring white man. But the authorities didn't seem interested in whether Ronnie was loved or cared for, or had a good home. His proximity to black people was the problem, so the documents go on to show, and had to be rectified. His white father would have had little influence either. There are stories of men who did try to look after their children, but those were still removed. And Alf, even if he had known the course of events, would probably never have admitted paternity. He could have gone to gaol for consorting with an Aboriginal woman. Ronnie belonged to no-one but the state. According to the state.

22nd April, 1938.

Sergeant E Moloney
Acting District Police Officer,
GERALDTON.
... respecting Alf Bond of Glenburgh Station, I desire
to inform you that, as Ronnie of Meerberrie [sic] is now
about seven years of age and too much time has elapsed
to secure a conviction under Section 46 of the Native
Administration Act, there is no need to make a special
journey for the purpose of interviewing Bond on the
question as to whether he admits parentage and is
prepared to pay maintenance for the support of Ronnie
in a government institution.

> When convenient, therefore, I shall be pleased if you will arrange for Bond to be interviewed ...
>
> Meanwhile, I think Ronnie should be receiving some education and as he can receive this at the Moore River Native Settlement I shall be glad if the Mullewa police will arrange with Mr. Macpherson of Meerberrie Station to have him sent in for transfer to the Settlement where he will attend school and subsequently be trained for employment.
>
> I am aware, of course, that Ronnie has been adopted by Paddy and Laurie Donnelly but as Ronnie is a half-caste and possibly capable of taking his place at a later date in the white community I think he is deserving of the opportunity to do so in preference to a life with black people.
>
> COMMISSIONER OF NATIVE AFFAIRS

The Native Affairs department unsuccessfully pursued Alf, seeking an admission of paternity which was not forthcoming, and maintenance payments. Pursuing anyone wasn't easy in this part of the country, as a Gascoyne Junction-based constable knew too well. He had set out to go 110 kilometres to where he understood Alf was working, travelling in a buggy pulled by a camel. But he returned, walking, the camel injuring its foot in the deep gutters washed into the wagon road. When he wrote his report about his failed attempt, the camel was still lame, but happily running free somewhere on Bidgemia Station. He plaintively requested the District Officer to authorise a trip by car.

The chase for maintenance sounds admirable and as if Ronnie's true welfare was being considered. But had any maintenance money been paid by Alf, none would have reached Ronnie directly. The money would go to the running of the institutions which would in effect hold Ronnie. He would have no freedom to come and go, to visit, to ever see his family or Paddy or Laurie again. And certainly no freedom to be Yamatji.

The department finally decided it was useless proceeding further against Alf, having had little help from anybody in the district. 'As a matter of fact, I did not expect to receive any assistance from Mr Leeds, the manager in question,' writes the Deputy Commissioner of Native Affairs, 'for we have evidence that he also is the father of a half-caste woman.'

Many a man with a spotless reputation in the white world was in fact a bunji-man. As a young girl travelling with Ulie in a white man's car, along with two other Yamatji women, Bessie remembers the vehicle coming to a halt. 'Who's first?' was the question, and the man and the two women disappeared behind some bushes. Ulie and Bessie sat beside the car, Ulie stressing that Bessie must look straight ahead, not look around under any circumstances. They sat, statue-like, and waited. The three came back to the car, and off they all drove, Bessie bewildered.

Bessie as a young girl had heard her mother talk about half-castes, and had wondered why some children were the colour they were. She asked her mother, who explained.

When she was older, at one of the many stations she worked, Bessie was embarrassed by a future bride checking up on her soon-to-be husband.

'Bessie, how long have you known Brian for?'

'Since 1947,' she replied.

'Do you know if he has been bunjying, going after the Aboriginal women?'

Bessie had heard, but not seen anything. She didn't know what to say.

'I don't know,' she muttered. She felt for the woman and couldn't believe the question had actually been put.

Ulie was more fortunate than some Yamatji mothers. She was given time to say goodbye. Paddy, Laurie, and Ulie all knew when Ronnie was going away, Mr Macpherson having no option but to do as the department ordered, organising Ronnie's travel to Geraldton. From there he was escorted by the police officer's wife, the policeman unable to go himself, on the train down to the Moore River Native Settlement. To allow everybody their time with him, he was sent to stay firstly with Pearlie for a week at Yallalong, then with Ulie, his mother, before going back home to his adoptive parents. In 1939 everybody said goodbye and cried. Ulie went back to work at Muggon, overseeing all her remaining children. Paddy and Laurie continued working at Meeberrie, childless once more. They remained so all their lives. In 1945, when Mr Macpherson died, Paddy was so overcome with grief at losing his beloved friend he just about threw himself into his boss's grave.

'The half-caste child Ronnie, who was removed from Meeberrie Station ... requires a surname,' said the internal memo to the Commissioner of Native Affairs. 'I suggest that Ronald Meeberrie would be a suitable name for this child ... We have no natives indexed under the name Meeberrie.' So Ronnie, son of Ulie, adopted son of Paddy and Laurie, ceased to exist. Ronald Meeberrie took his place.

Further north, inland from Port Hedland, another family was saying goodbye to their son. The same result, a son taken against their wishes, but not with the same dignity allowed. Iganinni was about eight years old, his brother about four. While the family camped between the stations where they mostly worked, the police rode in. Mother Polly frantically threw a blanket over her

Ulie and Dingo Jim in front of the chaff shed on Muggon Station, displaying a fox catch for the unfamiliar camera.

The family line up in front of Dingo Jim's camel cart. *Left to Right:* Friday, Pearlie with her daughter Olive in front, Bessie in the white dress, young Jimmy in front and Ulie. And, of course, Linda and Keeta the camels.

Ronnie, the Christmas before he was taken away.
Laurie Donnelly, his 'other' mother looks on.

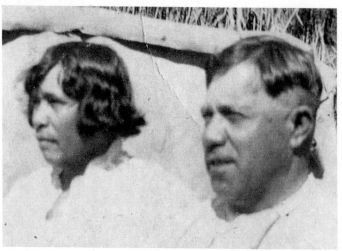

Paddy and Laurie Donnelly, to whom Ulie gave Ronnie, to try to prevent him from being taken away.

Ronnie and his best friend, Bob Chitty and a group of boys at Roelands Mission, where Ronnie was sent after 2 years at Moore River Native Settlement. Bob is the tall boy in front of the window, Ronnie to his left.

Working men's quarters at Yallalong Station where Pearlie and Joe lived in single room when they were first married.

Stone tank (on the ground) at Muggon Station where Ulie fell in looking for planes during WWII.

The horse annex attached to the stable at Yallalong Station where Dingo Jim, Ulie and the boys were housed, and which finally persuaded him to take his family and search for a new life for them all.

Les on Billabalong Station. Taking his own photo out in the scrub, with a string attached to his Box Brownie.

Below: Joe, Pearlie and family going on holidays from Billabalong Station to Yallalong Station.

Les Dingo in full flight.

Peet's general store in Mullewa. It was outside here the kids would hang around Les as he waited to catch the mail truck to Billabalong Station and it was here Mrs Peet used her dustpan and brush to good effect.

Mr Tim Officer amusing his son, Ted.

Bessie with Jane Officer.
'She was my first baby', says Bessie.

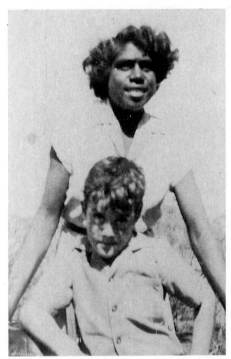

'Gee, the sea's rough,' Friday always said about the kinks in Bessie's hair. Tim Officer Junior looks to smoother waters.

Off to the Murgoo Races, according to the set up magazine shot. Ulie looks out between Jimmy and Bessie at the front, in a Woolgorong Station-owned horse and cart, which was used to cart equipment to the races instead of people.

two boys, telling them to be quiet. Iganinni hadn't seen them coming but knew to obey—until the shots rang out, and he heard the dogs squealing in pain. He ran in terror through the dusty chaos and din. But it was no use. He was escorted with his mother and younger brother into Port Hedland to wait for a ship to come in to take the boys to Fremantle and then on to the Moore River Native Settlement.

The two boys were shocked and afraid. But at least they would have each other. In the few days they had to wait, it was noticed that the younger boy might be just a bit too dark. Iganinni was finally put on board by himself. His brother, it had been decided, could remain with his mother.

At the Moore River Native Settlement, with a flick of the pen, Iganinni became Bob Chitty, his mother and family having no knowledge of the name change. Over time Bob was led to believe his family had all died. He was now without family or identity. The state took it upon themselves to create their own for him.

Bob and Ronald would become firm friends.

Chapter Eight

When Pearlie married Joe blackfella way, her younger sister Bessie was only about eight years old. Pearlie continued working in the house at Yallalong, but now lived with her new husband, returning each night to the working men's quarters, just over from the stable. The one stone room with a fireplace wasn't flash, and she didn't expect it to be. When she needed privacy she nailed a bag over the window. Privacy was indeed called for. Joe was every young woman's dream—good-looking, likeable, with an easy manner, and even temper, and well regarded as a worker. Pearlie had a good catch. So had he with her. It took no time before they were devoted to each other, and no time before she fell pregnant. She had it made.

But temperatures on the remote stations could often become dangerously high, especially for a small baby living in a tiny heat-trap of a room, or out on the verandah which gave some shade but little relief. And water to sponge her down had to be carted. So aged only two months, Pearlie's and Joe's first child died. Clarrie and Cecil helped Joe with his baby's grave, just over from where Mr Mitchell's little girl was buried. Her grave was solid and substantial, the headstone ornate. Pearlie's and Joe's daughter's by contrast was simple and unconventional—to white eyes, that is. Clarrie and Cecil had helped Joe hammer in the four rough posts to which a fence of chickenwire was attached, topped with a row of barbed wire. Colourful shells circled the tiny earth mound within. Both graves were embodiments of the parents' love, the best they could do for their respective children. And both were perfect. They still stand today, but the shells sometimes shift if a willy willy passes through. Pearlie took some time before she returned to the house to work.

While Pearlie was experiencing the sorrow life can bring, over at Muggon Bessie continued to gambol about in all her innocence and joy of living. She was happy there, free to roam, ride horses, run for her life from the camels, collect bush tucker and play. The mugs made from jam tins with hammered out makeshift handles and the flattened down rim to prevent any cuts didn't trouble her. She didn't notice that their only possessions were the station-issued tents, blankets and a few old clothes. She had it all she thought. A life in the bush was for her, and for her brothers and sisters. She was a child, and the world provided for her. The only problem she recognised was dodging the reprimands which insisted on coming her way.

Ulie and Dingo Jim had become reconciled and grown closer

over the years. They had two children after Bessie, two boys, and she and her bigger sister Hilda were often required to help with the youngsters, although what help they were was questionable. Donald, the older of the two—born on a Friday, and consequently now called Friday—was lucky to survive Bessie's baby-sitting techniques.

Wilgarda—Jimmy his whitefella name—was now crawling well, but Bessie and Hilda were too busy playing to notice. By the time they twigged something was missing, and realised just what that something was Wilgarda had covered a fair distance, taken a good position and nestled in. The tucker was good here as well.

'Wilgarda,' they shouted, frantic now. 'Wilgarda! Where are you?'

Bessie and Hilda were in a state. Ulie sure had a temper if aroused, and Bessie's managing to lose the baby she had been given strict instructions to watch could no doubt bring on a display.

Bessie tried to believe the best. He couldn't come to any harm in such a short time, she hoped. She was right, up to a point. Little baby Wilgarda was found sprawled fully on the ground. He had pushed a few of his furry brothers and sisters out of the way, commandeered one of Midget's teats for himself and was happily sucking away, the sheepdog unperturbed with one extra pup, and no washing-up. All was well in Wilgarda's world. But Bessie and Hilda were in big big trouble.

Bessie went out bush with her Dad as often as he would take her. When he was fencing she tried hard to be as helpful as an eight-year-old who didn't understand fences could be. But he didn't mind. The job would get done, he would see to that. Once while he was 'cutting the line' near the windmill called Corktree, Bessie looked up in amazement. 'Hey, look what I found,' she said jumping and laughing joyfully as a miracle appeared before her. From the branches of a scrawny tree straight ahead, oranges and apples, two apiece, hung in rare and juicy splendour. Bessie couldn't believe her eyes. Here, out in the scrub!! Mulga trees had never before borne such fruit. Dingo Jim enjoyed her delight. It wasn't often he had something to give his children. And what better way than to make his daughter laugh.

Ulie was called to Yallalong for work periodically, now that the Leedses had moved over there, and she would take the two youngest boys. Dingo Jim was left in charge of the remaining children, Bessie, Hilda and Les, home for a while from his cowboy apprenticeship. But Dingo Jim still had his own job to do. His windmill run could not be neglected, the wellbeing of the stock depending on such regular checks. All the pumps and troughs, along with the water pressure at each well, had to be examined, cleaned and repaired if necessary, in addition to the workings of the windmill itself. In such dry country stock would soon perish if these essentials were neglected. Dingo Jim would never overlook anything. He knew his job, and did what was needed without waiting for orders from the boss, wherever he was. And he was glad he was a distance away from old Leeds.

He put the saddle pack on Linda the camel, hoisted Les, Bessie and Hilda up beside the food and water, and off they jolted, the four of them. On this windmill run, Dingo Jim detoured to visit the Ryan family at the camp at Mt Narryer Station to the east. They ate their lunch while Dingo Jim talked to Old Man Tiger, and Hilda and Bessie lounged back like old hands against the seated camel as if it was a comfortable chair, thinking what bigshots they were. Hilda perhaps should have taken more notice, because it was this family to which she had been promised. She married Tommy, blackfella way, not too many years on.

On their way back to the Muggon outcamp, Ulie, now returned from the main station, could hear the familiar 'bah bah' as Linda headed for home, loaded with weary children and Dingo Jim. 'Dad's comin',' Ulie yelled to the two younger boys, and they ran out together to meet them. Bessie, showing off, kicked the camel into a trot and they bounced the last few metres home clinging precariously to the saddle. Her cheerful tomboyishness bubbled away. She and her brothers and sisters always found it hard to rein in their exuberance and it was hard for them to stay still and be quiet when they were asked. These requests were not made often, and they were a little out of practice.

'Hurry up tonight,' Dingo Jim said to Ulie early one afternoon. 'Get the kids to go home to bed.'

Home for Dingo Jim's family at this time consisted of three tents—one for Bessie and Hilda, one for Dingo Jim, Ulie and the two young boys, Jimmy and Friday, and the third for bigger brother Les, when he came home, all sheltered behind a bush breakwind. But Polly's mia-mia was no longer nearby. She had left this world not long after seeing Pearlie's baby born, and was buried on the station.

They hurriedly ate their evening meal out the back of the house and scampered to the camp before the sun went down, as Dingo Jim had insisted. The fire burned low in front of the tents, and the sky grew darker. The tent flaps were tied back so the children could see out. However nothing outside held any interest for Bessie and Friday. They sat on their rough beds made of piles of branches covered with blankets and teased and poked one another, ignoring their parents sitting with great concentration on the ground. Dingo Jim and Ulie were waiting.

'You *mayu*, be *birndu* now, hear. Be quiet.'

Bessie and Friday hesitated. What was going on? But they were soon giggling and annoying each other again.

'Be quiet!!!' Ulie and Dingo Jim hissed. Bessie and Friday

snapped to and shut up.

'Have a look at the fire,' said Dingo Jim in Wadjarri.

Bessie and Friday stared. So did Hilda and the other boys. The fire suddenly flared, turning a luminous blue. Bessie was goggle-eyed with fright. The flames seemed to get bluer and bluer until suddenly they turned to a strange milky green. Granny Polly was here. Ulie and Dingo Jim burst into tears.

'We all *barndi*,' they called to her spirit. 'We all good.'

Hilda cried too. She had been Granny Polly's favourite. Bessie remained wonderstruck.

When Polly passed away, none of the children had been permitted to go to the sorry ceremony, the funeral, no children at all. Hilda's granny had come to check up on how they all were doing.

She couldn't come often: after all, her spirit had been told to go home the day following her burial. At night, a firestick had been taken into the bush and held up while Polly was called to. When she called back, as they knew she would, the burning stick was left on the ground, waiting for it to change to the beautiful blue, showing she was fully there. Ulie then called into the night, telling her she could now go, she was on her way home and it was time for her to leave. The firestick would light her way. But Polly, it seemed, insisted on one last meeting before joining the other spirits at the mouth of the Murchison River.

Ulie tended to both Polly's grave at Muggon and Tommy's at Yallalong, and made sure the billycans left out for them were full of water. One time she took Bessie to where Tommy was buried and, following the old way, lay on the grave embracing the earth mound, embracing Grandfather Tommy interred below. She told Bessie to do the same, and Bessie did. But her mind was more on something else. She was trying hard not to pee herself, so frightened she was.

Because Muggon was out of the way and only an adjunct to Yallalong, the station proper, it operated in isolation much of the time. This was in the workers' favour, now that Mr Mitchell was gone, and they appreciated being left alone. Yet it was always a welcome sight when boundary riders from adjoining Mt Narryer would come riding in for a short visit. One poor chap soon discovered just what those visits could mean.

Dingo Jim was a bit of a dancer at times. He would dance by himself, legs shaking, hands clapping, feet stamping, doing *nyumbi loo binya* when the mood took him. It made him feel good. Visitors were always invited to join in and, before they realised what they had done, had placed their destiny in Dingo Jim's hands. Franklyn came from Mt Narryer at various times of the year and like the rest would soon be dancing, sometimes with Dingo Jim, sometimes solo while Dingo Jim sat, clapped and made the music—until Dingo Jim decided it was time. The next time he came, Jim gave him a woman and married him off, without the consent of the girl's parents.

'Why marry my bloody daughter off?' the bride to be's father protested. 'I want my daughter here, working.'

'She can't stop all the time with you,' Dingo Jim retorted, both men speaking in one of the Yamatji languages of the area, different from the Wadjarri Jim and Ulie normally used. 'She got to live with a bloke, got to get married.'

And so it was done. According to the law, parents had no say in arranging their own child's marriage. It had to come from an uncle, or a relative or kin from the side—Dingo Jim, in Franklyn's case, one of the old people who could do so.

When next Franklyn came to see Dingo Jim, he was accompanied by his wife and a baby boy.

Muggon's remoteness meant Dingo Jim and Ulie had been able to retain many of the old ways which had been scorned, forbidden and forcefully destroyed in many other places in Australia, especially down south and in the eastern states. And Dingo Jim could continue to use his powers. He used them many times. In addition to his telepathic skills of 'knowing' what was happening, who was coming, and where he should be, he was also a healer. When they were sick, he would fix them up.

There were no clocks out here, where the only possessions were clothes supplied from the station and a couple of blankets. Yet when Dingo Jim moved forward, his hands cupped, a distinctive Tick, Tick Tick could be heard. *Marbarrn*, magic, Bessie knew. He rubbed his hands over the place where pain was located, wherever his patient felt sick. The healing was then released, put in, and the pain would disappear.

This was not to be trifled with. Whatever had given him the power to heal could not be revealed to others or debased by those not permitted by law to know about it. None of his children was ever allowed to ask to see what was in his hand. There were good reasons for the Yamatji laws to be obeyed and they generally revolved around keeping yourself healthy and out of harm's way.

Bessie felt secure and cared for, in that tent she called home on sandy Muggon, unaware her life didn't fit any of the accepted standards of the outside white world. She loved her family. But that outside world was soon to intrude and the day-long freedom she had known in the bush gone. She would glimpse it again every now and then, but only when she could steal herself some time.

Mrs Leeds had asked for her. So as Pearlie and Ulie had done before her, and countless other Yamatji girls elsewhere, Bessie had no choice but to obey. She left her parents at Muggon and went to live in the big house at the main station, Yallalong.

Chapter Nine

When Bessie was sent to work at the Yallalong homestead, Rita was still there. Bessie was younger, with less direct experience of widpellas. She was scared and therefore more pliable than the determined Rita. And she was sad.

Rita tried to console her. 'Don't cry,' she would say. 'I did the same thing too, cry for my mother and father when I first came here. It gets better.'

But Bessie cried for a long time. She was very lonely, even with Rita with her, and Pearlie in the working men's quarters. She was scared her parents would die, leaving her all alone. Like now. She cried and cried in the night. As Pearlie did before her, Bessie saw her parents rarely, once yearly, now she was in the house. Mrs Leeds softened in the wake of Bessie's endless tears and relented, sending for Ulie, who was far away. Bessie needed that visit. That reassurance and those cuddles had to last a long time.

At first Bessie and Rita shared a bed—foot to foot Bessie calls it—until another one was found. Often they were cold. Bessie and Rita were well aware the widpellas weren't. 'They had plenty of rugs, blankets, sheets and quilts,' she remembers. 'I used to ask for more to cover myself. I got more wagga, bag. They sew 'em up.'

Bessie's chores began as simply contributing to the social aspirations of the whitefolk. Her reward was to be introduced to the fear of displeasing them. In her first week she was dressed in an apron over a dress and required to wait the table when visitors called. She would bring in each dish, soup, vegetables, meat and so on, and put it on the table for the master or mistress to serve, stand quietly behind while they dished it up, then deliver it to the place she was directed. Some visitors said hello, she remembers, and some thanked her. Between courses, Bessie had to stand outside, motionless, waiting. She had plenty of time to worry about getting into trouble. Dingle dingle dingle. The bell would sound again for her to enter and remove the plates. A little black maid. Pretty one too. For no pay.

The pretty maid used to push herself. She had to wait until dessert, coffee and the washing-up were all over, before finishing up, all way past a small girl's bedtime. Sometimes the visitors would come in and wash up, but she was required to stay anyway. She found it hard to last, and occasionally nodded off. Only after Mrs Leeds put the dishes away was Bessie finally allowed to go to her bed.

Soon Bessie was taught that art of washing-up. And wiping. This was all a new experience for her, foreign and not much use at the camp. She was impressed when Mrs Leeds dried two plates together, but couldn't manage it herself. With extreme concentration, she wiped one side first before turning it slowly around to the other. To many people who have grown up with sinks and dishes and houses, wiping dishes would never be considered an achievement. But Bessie was proud. She could do what those whitefellas did.

She progressed from waiting table to polishing floors on her hands and knees, a task which had to be done once a week. It was a large house with the usual big passage, and Bessie would sometimes be there all day. It made her young knees ache. Mrs Leeds showed her how, but the exuberant Bessie was often accused of putting too much polish on. She was in trouble again. It wasn't hard to get into trouble working in the 'big house'. Expectations and experience were cultures apart. 'Come along,' Bessie would hear, and Mrs Leeds would take her to where the Singer sewing machine strap was waiting. Bessie hid the strap at times, but a good country woman knows how to improvise under all circumstances and Mrs Leeds would find something else. Bessie would *yukkia,* yelp, again, in a way that Pearlie never had to.

As Bessie learnt the parameters within which she had to live and work, she figured how to have the semblance of a childhood while satisfying Mrs Leeds' demands. So her playfulness, always evident back at the camp, slowly emerged again. No matter what Mr and Mrs Leeds thought. No matter the risk. But she did try to cover her tracks as best she could.

Her chores increased with time and expanded to include that of cowgirl, responsible for heading bush, finding the milking cows and herding them back to the house for brother Owen to milk. Getting the cows in gave Bessie time she used well—learning to swim, without a teacher. She floated, splashed, then rested on the banks of the Murchison River which flowed straight through Yallalong Station. She'd be up and out, then have another go until eventually she was able to swim along. With water still dripping from her, she'd locate the cows and hurry back, hoping her absence had not been noticed. On one occasion, when she had no intention of getting wet, a young bull in her way persuaded her otherwise. She was shooing it dismissively away until she saw its rolling eyes. They were rolling and rolling. Not a good sign, she knew. She turned and ran as fast as her skinny legs could tumble over each other straight for the safety the water offered, or so she thought. Facing the bull turned out to be the better option, for she ran straight into loose wet sand which she called quicksand. The astute bull decided against following, and Bessie sank lower and lower. She managed to pull herself out, but was now twice as terrified and decided to risk the bull's wrath rather than be sucked to the centre of the earth. The bull could see it was no longer in charge.

One mishap has never tamed any child, and Bessie was always willing to test the boundaries permitted her, even when she grew older and more aware of the myriad ways to attract a scolding. Bessie could now cope with causing displeasure, and indeed was willing to do so. She was Dingo Jim's daughter after all and, despite a natural inclination to be mostly gentle and sweet, still refused to be fully subjugated. She was a girl who enjoyed living too much.

'The cows have gone through. Where's the cowgirl?' Owen asked no-one in particular. His brother-in-law, Joe Egan, Pearlie's husband, shrugged. He looked around, but had no idea either. They had driven to the well on the windmill run, ready to fix the pump in the trough, and noticed the cows sauntering homewards to the stockyards, unaccompanied after drinking their water.

Owen didn't trouble himself with an answer to his question.

'I'll get a drink for myself,' he said, downing half a pannikin and throwing the remainder back into the well.

'Look at those swallows,' he said, puzzled by their odd behaviour. The swallows kept swooping low into the well, returning to their nests inside as they always did, but this time they swooped right up again. They wouldn't stay.

'They're frightened,' Owen continued. 'There's something down the well.'

He peered over the side into its man-made depths. A wide-eyed face framed by bedraggled hair stared straight back up at him. Bessie, clinging to the sides halfway up, and desperately trying not to be seen or heard, had been sprung—and showered, courtesy of her brother. She had already climbed to the top once, but had quickly scampered back down again on hearing the car coming, and stayed there, too scared to move.

'Get out of there, and get goin',' Owen ordered, then asked, 'What were you doin' down there?' But he didn't really want an explanation.

Bessie slowly pulled herself up and out and stood before her accusers, in a very sorry way.

'Go and lock the cows up,' Owen said exasperatedly, with an air of expecting instant obedience.

Bessie knew Mrs Leeds would hear of her escapade. She knew she was in trouble—again. But that was nothing new. The indignity Bessie felt so keenly was her own brother dobbing her in, and showing no mercy.

With trouble so easy to find around the station, and Bessie so innocently careless and censure-prone, it would seem sensible to find someone to deflect it or warn when the mistress's displeasure threatened. But little understanding the secrets of survival in the white world, Bessie and Rita had not thought to cultivate a brother-in-arms. And there was really only the cook, and cooks were generally a breed apart. Frequently they were alcoholics who had taken the job up bush to dry out for a while. Many of them, under their surface gruffness, were lonely. One cook in his late forties seemed perfect for the role of ally, apparently having a crush on Rita. But therein lay the problem. Love can hurt, and wounded suitors rarely wish to protect those they believe have wronged them. This cook would never really be an accomplice.

He bought Rita a small suitcase from the passing Afghan hawkers with their camels and carts, and presented it to her so she could have something in her room in which to put her clothes. He thought his courtship was going well until he spied Rita sitting on the woodheap out the back, talking to men! Rita and Bessie gathered here with the others when they could, the wood providing the only place to sit, since they weren't allowed near the house. If Mrs Leeds caught Bessie she would be in for it again, for she was forever told she wasn't to talk to the men, even though they were her own brothers and Clarrie and Cecil.

When Rita went back to her room later that day, her case had been reclaimed, and her clothes dumped unceremoniously in a heap on her bed. The poor cook's hopes had been dashed, so he believed, and he was miffed. Love was not always easy to find out here.

His attitude changed. 'What are you doin', you blinkin' cows?' became the expression he favoured most. And so he got little sympathy for his stiff leg missing a knee cap.

Fresh produce was a luxury on the station, and as Bessie and Rita were seldom offered any, they had taken to sneaking fruit and vegetables from the garden. It was a dangerous move. The cook had assumed the role of watchdog and applied himself vigorously to the task, especially when Mrs Leeds was resting.

Bessie and Rita sliced the watermelon straight down the middle. Sitting on their beds opposite one another, they sank their mouths into the slabs of lush moist flesh, more than willing to risk the ire of Mrs Leeds for the pleasure. A pair of towels were at the ready to throw over the booty if anyone should come prying. But just as they were beginning to enjoy themselves the cook rushed in and jerked the towels away, jubilant at having caught the girls in the act. He had them, or so he thought. But they weren't about to give in so easily. They wrestled and wrestled with him, both determined this was the one fight they should win.

'Quick, quick, grab his good leg,' Rita called to Bessie. And skinny Bessie, surprising herself with what she could do, did as she was told. The cook had to stand on his stiff one. Over he went, toes up, and off the two miscreants ran.

All the events were funny at the time. But not for long. It would only take a few more incidents before Rita would discover how cruel and heartless some people could be. Whitefellas have shown time and time again there are those among them who don't like blackfellas, especially the cheeky ones, those who refuse to accord respect or fall into line with white middle-class expectations of deference. And Rita certainly didn't.

She had been assigned yard duty, and didn't take kindly to the position she had been thrust in or the stern style of both Mr and Mrs Leeds. One time Bessie heard the thud thud of a stick coming down, and peeped out to see Rita kneeling while Mr Leeds thrashed her on the back and then began kicking her on the backside.

The police came and got Rita, taking her first to Mullewa, where she helped the policeman's wife at home until someone could take her across to Geraldton and on down south. She was sent down to the Moore River Native Settlement, where the whitefellas who'd arranged her removal apparently hoped to teach her a lesson for not knowing her place. She was never given a reply to the question she kept asking on her journey, 'Where am I going?' And she knew better than to ask, 'Why?'

Alone in the house now Rita was gone, Bessie went in search of company as often as she could. She was allowed to stay overnight with Pearlie across at the working men's quarters, and did so whenever she could. Cecil was there now, moved in from Wail, and so was Clarrie. Everything was so different with her own mob, talking Wadjarri, laughing at anything, being all together. Back at the homestead whitefella things were still a real mystery, and nothing was ever simple, like what could happen on race days.

A sweep had been conducted, and the cook—a new one with both legs in good working order—had entered Bessie's name without her knowing. Bessie returned to the house early in the morning after staying overnight with Pearlie, ready to start her chores.

'You've broken a record,' said Mrs Leeds, and Bessie started planning her excuse immediately. But she was confused about the crime.

'I never broke no record down at Junyu's (Pearlie's) place,' she thought. 'I only went down there and sat on the bed. *Next* to Cecil's gramophone.'

By the time the difference between records and records had been explained, the cook had done a runner. Left for a holiday, with the record winnings. But at least when he came back he made amends. He bought some material and on his own sewing machine, sewed Bessie two new dresses—a decent gesture, considering she had not actually entered the sweep herself, although it was not the same as cold hard cash which didn't ever seem to be forthcoming from whitefellas to Dingo Jim and his family. Bessie would not have had any money to enter the sweep in the first place. She had never received any in her life.

Cecil and Clarrie, alone but with each other now that their mother and brothers had been sent away, found life on Yallalong had become close to intolerable. They saw how sick men were left to battle their own way to try to get to town and see a doctor, and they saw how they were treated overall. Not much better than the dogs. Indeed, they ate their meals out the back with the rubbish bins and dog slops. Yallalong under Mitchell had a shed, a dining area for all the men, but now, when no whitefellas were present, the Yamatjis were not permitted to enter. They ate their one dish of food, mainly boiled meat and bread, where they could.

Clarrie and Cecil walked. In 1941 they left Yallalong, took their swag, and walked to Billabalong. Never having left the station before, they found a new world. And they could not believe it. They found work, some money, and a boss, a station owner, who was more like Mr Mitchell. He even let his workers borrow the trucks and go to the Show and to a football match. Clarrie and Cecil saw town for the first time.

They came back to Yallalong after a time, to pass on the good news—there was life after Leeds. Les would join them soon, Owen a while later. Clarrie was in his late teens, Cecil a few years older.

Dingo Jim and Ulie were still stationed on Muggon, still working, still staying near to Polly's burial spot and near to Old Harry, making sure he was doing all right. He continued to work even though he was a fair age. Stockmen out here generally work-ed till they just about fell off their horses, and Dingo Jim and Ulie would always stay while he was still alive. No promised land could lure them away from their obligations to family.

Chapter Ten

World War Two touched Australian soil. Darwin had been bombed, so too the airport at Port Hedland, further down the west coast. The armed forces were mobilised, pouring into northern Australia. Nine thousand troops were stationed around the Murchison area. In Mullewa itself, the town was ready. Trenches were dug outside the school, and the young children participated in daily drill, learning to keep their heads down. Similar precautions were taken at the hospital. Recruiting parties constantly visited the town, enlisting some men, rejecting others, saying they were essential manpower needed to keep the country running. At Billabalong they came past frequently, big mobs of them going backwards and forwards, and Clarrie considered joining for a while. At first he thought he would never be eligible. 'What's the use of goin' if you can't read or write?' he told them. 'That's nothing to do with it,' they replied, 'as long as you can hold that gun.' He decided against it when Cecil was refused. They could take the two together or none at all. He would never leave his brother behind. His labour was needed anyway on the station. Not many whitemen were around, and Yamatji workers, as they had been from the beginning, were crucial. As always.

Some Aboriginal men from closer to the coast joined up, experiencing for the first time what it felt like to be treated as equals. They were even allowed to have a beer, man to man, with their fellow white soldiers. The harsh Australian reality would be waiting once the war ended, and civilian life was again theirs. They went back to having no rights, no real freedom of movement, no acceptance as equal human beings.

The scare caused by the Japanese bombing raids meant the Murchison sky, like much of northern Australia, was now patrolled regularly. Bessie waved excitedly to the Tiger Moths which flew overhead a couple of times a day. Airforce men drove up recruiting a home-grown spotter team among the station people, and distributing posters to them. At Yallalong Bessie, Pearlie and Mrs Leeds had the responsibility of scanning the sky, guessing what type of plane it was and running inside to the poster to check, as did Ulie at Muggon. Mrs Leeds would then report the sightings.

Pearlie, pregnant again and nearing the end of her term, had endured the hot, bumpy and long ride up to Muggon in the workers' truck so she could be with her mother. Only Ulie was ever to be trusted with the delivery and early nursing of her babies. Bessie jumped at the chance to get back home, and announced to a startled Mrs Leeds she was going too.

Ulie was outside the chaff shed at Muggon when she spotted a small plane up high. It wasn't a difficult task out here. The sky was mostly cloudless and was always a magnificent clear blue. A plane could be seen and heard for miles. She decided the rock and cement water tank near the windmill would put her just that bit closer to the plane above. She gazed skywards, hands shielding the sun from her eyes, when she put her foot on a pipe. Over she went as it gave way, toppling her backwards into the waist-high water. Pearlie laughed so much she couldn't stop and Bessie too could hardly suppress her giggles, despite her mother's plight. Ulie was determined not to see the humour at all. Her mind was still on the important job she had been allotted.

'You fellas!' she said indignantly, as she clambered to her feet, sopping wet. 'Never mind for laughing. What about the ack ack ack?' she reminded them with as much composure as she could muster, which wasn't a lot under the circumstances. 'Hurry up. Get that drum and get me out!'

Ulie performed her midwifery duties a few days later—with aplomb—and baby Olive was born to Pearlie and Joe. They were so very happy. And Ulie and Dingo Jim had a granny, a grandchild.

Overhead planes on the lookout for aircraft sneaking over the region meant normal living was suspended for people both in the towns and on the land. All windows had to be blacked out, with no light to be visible anywhere as a target for the Japanese. Clarrie and Cecil were camping out with their workmates over on Billa-balong Station, with nothing shiny allowed and no fires to be lit. They had their feed before the sun went down and shut everything up to settle down for the night. They could hear it, that plane with no lights. 'Here's the Japs comin' from Darwin,' somebody sang out. But the wit had Australia upside down, and the plane was going the other way, on the way up to meet any coming down.

The army wanted information from the Yamatji men. Clarrie told them every little waterhole he knew—which was good water, which wasn't, where all the wells were, and just about every bend and variation in the Murchison River, when it was running, that is. He liked the men from the armed forces. They were all good blokes, he said. And they repaid the openhearted treatment they received by making sure everybody else was given the same respect. On Yallalong, an Aboriginal stockman, Rita's brother, had been thrown and dragged by his horse. He had a gaping wound in his head and a broken leg. Those in charge at the station seemed in no real hurry to get him to help; but an army vehicle fortuitously arrived and the uniformed men all sprang into action. They demanded a mattress for the back of the truck, and refused the one presented as not fit for him to lie on. They asked for a pillow, and again had to demand another. In contrast to what was usual at the station, they treated the injured man as they would any other. The Yamatjis all saw the difference. The injured stockman was taken to the army hospital, and is still doing well today.

The war brought many changes including rationing. Petrol rationing in these remote places had a dramatic effect on the properties. Windmill runs, the essential checks of the wind-powered water pumps on the stations, had been done by car for some time at Yallalong, once a road of sorts had been cleared. A car was faster than a horse, could carry a couple of men when repairs were needed at the wells, and also had space for parts. The car had become the windmill man's preferred mode of transport. Petrol rationing put a halt to that. The bicycle took its place.

Owen had always preferred the fiddly stuff over stock work.

He was a good worker and generally conscientious. But he didn't take to those long trips away. Instead, in his late teens he became a windmill man, with Mr and Mrs Leeds' nephew, John. They were a good team and enjoyed each other's company. Before bicycles were forced upon them and they had a vehicle at their disposal, they would do some shooting between troughs. Owen, like Les, was a remarkable shot. One day John saw a wild turkey, about 100 metres away, and had a shot. He missed. 'Give us the bloody gun,' Owen said quietly from the passenger's side, and standing up, with no time to take good aim, felled the bird. It was nothing unusual and he was indifferent to his ability. He knew many men who could do what he could. A thoughtful and more serious lad than Les, Owen was always careful too. 'Hey, Jack,' he'd call to John, if he saw him carrying a gun. 'You haven't got that loaded, have you?'

On the bicycle round, the new-style windmill run, John and Owen would have to cover 100 to 120 kilometres a day, pedalling in the heat through the sand. They divided the run and took to racing each other, taking different tracks and meeting at the end. It was a good game, but not such a great idea when the aim of the job was to attend to any problems at the windmills on the way and, apart from having a drink themselves, making sure the sheep partook as well.

'I reckon you jokers were supposed to have cleaned out the troughs,' Mr Leeds would say. There were always a couple missed when a race was on. John, Mr Leeds' nephew, got just as many boots up the bum as anybody else.

It was a real battle to keep the fences up on Yallalong and Muggon, and maintenance was constantly required. Out they headed on their Malvern Star bikes with the doctored sprockets to make them go faster. Down they went, through creeks, over rocks, having to push the darned things if the sand was bad. Often they rode a couple of extra kilometres to try to dodge the worst areas. They steered with one hand, the other holding a crowbar on their backs, wire strung around their necks. Somehow an axe, lunch and water had to be carried as well. They pedalled in the heat and worked in the heat, chopping dummy posts to put alongside those already there, then fixing and straining the wire up. Fixing punctures or busted sprockets was nothing after all that.

Although the war brought frequent parties of servicemen to the station, Bessie was still not much wiser about the goings-on out in the wider world. She had never been given any opportunity to learn about it. But, soon enough, the world came to her. And Bessie, sweet innocent, playful Bessie, was struck dumb, at just twelve years old.

The Mitchell family still owned Yallalong and the Muggon outstation, living down in Perth and employing the Leedses from afar to manage the property. Bessie liked Mrs Mitchell and often wished she had her for a boss instead of the sterner Mrs Leeds. With the war seeming so close, Mrs Mitchell's married daughter sought sanctuary at their country property, bringing her two boys and two of their friends—a boy and a girl—to stay as well.

One of the boys had a birthday party, and John Mitchell's daughter, in a gesture which would have pleased the old man, invited the Yamatji housemaid.

Bessie sat glowing at the head of the table, spruced up in a pink floral dress made especially for her by the boy's mother. She struggled to contain her excitement, though not in the least frightened. There were six children at the party, Bessie the only Yamatji, and the only one with bare feet.

She joined in the chatter, pleased to be part of it all. She felt good, all dressed up, sitting at the dining table. The much older

Pearlie peeked through the door and watched for a while. She had never seen anything like it. So much food, so much choice. And Bessie there!

Bessie enjoyed it immensely, especially when after the mothers had cleared away the food, the time came for playing games. However, Bessie was at a disadvantage. At Muggon they had spoken mostly Wadjarri, and like her parents she had never had the chance of going to school. Her English had been learnt through trial and error, passed on from boss to worker, and while never 'pidgin' English, was not extensive. She discovered what a cost this could be.

One of the games involved identifying the voices of the others in the dark. Bessie nominated the boy she was convinced had called out. But she got it wrong and, according to the rules of the game, had to pay the price.

'I'm not gunna kiss you,' she said, brave under fire.

So she was given another chance. But it was as if it had been ordained. She picked the same boy again. Bessie, shy-way now, put her head down and wouldn't move, until someone suggested what seemed to be a way out of her predicament.

'Why don't you just go and give him a peck,' one of the grown-ups said. Bessie breathed a relieved yeah—and found she still had to go and plant one on him. She wasn't impressed, and neither was he.

Towards the end of the war, Bessie was granted her greatest wish. Her parents, Ulie and Dingo Jim, were transferred from Muggon to work at Yallalong after Dingo Jim had an accident. She was overjoyed, although she would have preferred the runaway camel and buggy not to have broken her father's leg. But it had turned out all right. Staying with him in the Mullewa hospital as he mended hadn't been bad. She had been sick then too, but not so that whole new world had gone unnoticed. It was the first time she had been off the station, and even the Native Ward with its fly-wire windows, known to all Yamatjis as the Meathouse, looked new and fascinating.

Now with her parents close by, she could see them regularly again. Her happiness overflowed, and she felt safe, complete once more. And she got to resume watching her Dad, still active, no matter the age he now was. Yallalong attracted more Yamatji visitors than remote Muggon had done, and on a couple of occasions Dingo Jim organised a corroboree at night after work had finished.

There had been many before, while 'on holidays' away from station life, when word would spread and everybody would get together, but now times were such that around the Murchison they had no choice but to stay whitefella way. The Yallalong corroborees were the last ones there.

Dingo Jim kept up his traditional role as much as he could. He showed all his boys and his son-in-law how to dance, even 'the working mans', according to Pearlie. Painted up with the rest, he would join in for a while, then sit and sing, letting the young men have the turf. Les wasn't so good at it, his mind elsewhere. He was planning to join Clarrie and Cecil as soon as he got the nod from his father. Joe, Pearlie's husband, was the fella really putting on the style. Dancing was just something else he could effortlessly master.

Ulie would get up sometimes but mostly left it to the men, joining her daughters at the side. Bessie thought it a great time. She would sit, laughing irreverently, and keep the fire burning, an important job. The fire would be set in place, all the bushes thrown on, and then, to great excitement, it would be ignited. And the men would emerge out of the darkness and begin to dance.

Dingo Jim continued doing the general station work he had

done since a youth, but scaled down. He was no longer a young man. Old Harry, Polly's husband after Tommy, was even older, and now becoming sick.

Dingo Jim was not happy. When he was told to leave Muggon and come to Yallalong itself, he and Ulie knew they had little choice in the matter. However, the quarters—a grandiose term for the deplorable accommodation they were given—were worse than what they had at Muggon, and perhaps contrary to Mr Leeds' expectations, they knew it.

Dingo Jim, Ulie and the two youngest boys were placed in an annex, a horse yard which a long time before had been built on the side of the stable. An attempt had been made to clean it with phenol and it had been painted with whitewash, a real estate trick from way back. The new coat on the unlined walls may have fooled those who didn't have to live there, but certainly not Dingo Jim and Ulie. Ulie slept with their two boys on the old rusty beds above the dirt floor, looking out through the gap where a door should have been while Dingo Jim camped on the floor, the horse hitching rail a vivid reminder that they had been housed with the animals. Old Harry had been given the room on the corner. A tent, a bough shed and a life of their own had indeed been paradise to this. It was time to move on, if only they could. Dingo Jim told his two eldest boys to go and join Clarrie and Cecil. So off they went, to where the bosses were good men, the food was generous, and you could even get paid for your labour.

Old Harry faded and died. With little ceremony he was below ground. There was no morgue or freezer to preserve a body out here in the soaring temperatures. Ulie, Dingo Jim and the children all cried for the lovely old man. But his death set them free. With Tommy, Polly and now Harry all gone, they could go themselves, leaving Yallalong forever.

So in 1945, while the rest of Australia waited the end of the war, Dingo Jim, an old man now, made his move for a new life. He collected Bessie from the station homestead, and together with Ulie, Friday and their youngest son Jimmy, set off on foot, with Friday's shetland pony—a gift at one time from John Mitchell to Clarrie—laden with bedding, clothes, tucker for the road and a waterbag. They were off to reclaim their lives and their dignity—to see the world.

Chapter Eleven

They set out to reach Billabalong station, thirty-eight kilometres away, hoping to join the boys, and hoping to find work. They had to. With virtually no money ever paid them, they left the station with none at all, and few possessions apart from their bedding and clothes. It was risky, this venture. Dingo Jim was almost seventy years old, though with a few musters left in him yet.

Bessie and her brothers nattered as they went. Of the children only Bessie had left the station before, and then only over the boundary to Mt Narryer outcamp, and to spend those few eventful days in the 'Meathouse' at Mullewa hospital. She had not travelled far. Just far enough to know she would soon see and hear new things. She led the dreaming as they talked, wondering what they would find. Although no longer young, Dingo Jim was still robust and held himself well. He didn't walk so much as march, though now with a slight limp courtesy of the flighty camel, and this was one march he had long desired to do. He marched, the kids skipped, and Ulie steadied them all, although she too was keen to see those other stations she had heard about. The poor overloaded shetland pony was unable to join in the excitement, wondering how it had happened to become a mule.

There were many stony patches on the sandy road. Yet Dingo Jim was unperturbed. Encountering the hill country didn't faze him either. Like many Yamatjis all through the Murchison, he thought nothing of setting off on foot. White station workers always marvelled at the distances they would travel. But there was little alternative. With such scant wages, owning a car was rarely a possibility. So they did what they had to do.

Thirteen-year-old Bessie took her turn to carry the extra billy-can of water, changing regularly with her younger brothers. Dingo Jim had stressed careful handling, as he did not know where or when more water would be found. Bessie kept herself in check, understanding there were to be no games. But she had high hopes fun was on the agenda where they were going.

They made camp in the soft sand of the dry creekbed at New Forest Station, ate the specially dried-out bread used on long trips, cooked the raw meat in the fire, and lay back and drank in the magnificence of the night sky. Old Man Moon was nowhere in sight, and the stars glittered in all their brilliance. Before daybreak, they refilled the billycan from the stockmen's well, and kept on walking. The late May weather was perfect. Not too hot. And an unexpected pool of clear water a thing of beauty.

It was sundown when they reached the station where Les,

Owen, Cecil and Clarrie all were. Dingo Jim and his family had walked, with a few billies boiled on the way, for two days. Jim waited at the gate, standing with Ulie, Bessie and the loaded-up pony, while young Friday and Jimmy went to ask if there was room at the inn. Their Dad was looking for work, they said. Billabalong Station's owner, Bob Campbell, was sympathetic, knew of the family ties, but hadn't space for them all. Wanting to help, he rang through to his brother-in-law. The next day, Dingo Jim joined a muster, Ulie became the musterers' cook, and the family went to Woolgorong, the adjoining property, where a young man named Tim Officer was the station owner.

Dingo Jim was happy once more. He was back in the saddle, on new country with new friends, family near, on a station which provided what it could manage for the workers. This was the first musterers' camp he had been to where beds and mattresses were on hand. He stuck with the way he knew, his swag on the ground, but noticed the differences.

Ulie expected her children to help at the outcamp, but with little success. In no time Bessie was in trouble. There was plenty to distract a girl who'd been inside for too long. She'd take off with her brothers looking for gum, wild onions and little red apples, and Ulie would alway have a few words to say.

But Bessie hadn't endured those years with Mrs Leeds without learning a thing or two. Her hide was thick, her hearing selective. Off she'd go, doing exactly what she wanted. And there was much to do around here. At the camp she became friendly with a girl almost the same age, and she and Margaret would rise early, the creek water splashing high as they eagerly threw themselves in. Their routine always worked perfectly. Bessie put her feet on the turtle selected as breakfast that morning, held it in place, and Margaret would dive and retrieve it. Home they'd head to throw it on the coals, Ulie silenced by such a prize.

Dingo Jim, Ulie and the kids moved camp with the rest, on to the next mob of sheep. This was the life they knew. While they were mustering near Slippery Well on the northern Woolgorong boundary, Les and Owen, Clarrie and Cecil all appeared. There was much embracing, plenty of excited laughter, and of course tears all round. Clarrie came with presents, a cooked kangaroo tail for Ulie, and a *guwiyarl*, a goanna, for Dingo Jim. Good times were with them again.

The sheep were all through and they headed in to the homestead, the shearers about to arrive. It was time to finish up and begin the search again, when Mr Officer offered what they had been seeking—a place to properly unroll their swag, a position on the station. But Woolgorong, like Yallalong, had few quarters built yet for their workers, and there was only a building for single men. So Ulie and Dingo Jim did what they had done all their lives—put up the bough shed and erected the tent. But this time it was with a strange new feeling—optimism. Woolgorong Station was different. In contrast to bad-tempered Mr Leeds, thirty-five-year-old Tim Officer was mild, kind, and in Bessie's words, not like the savage-looking fellas they had known.

'I think we got the new good *maja* (Master) now,' Dingo Jim announced quietly to his family, his one small sentence revealing both his powerlessness and his longing. He needn't have said it aloud. Ulie and Bessie had been thinking the very same thing.

Maja was a commonly used word. The Masters, the station owners or managers, claimed the term had lost its original meaning and become innocently interchangeable with 'boss'. But it would always be a loaded word, heavy with decades of meaning and use. And sure looked real enough. There were more than enough stations with bosses who lived the role, seeing themselves as lords of the realm, enduring the colonial path to power and prestige until they could make enough money to acquire the right-sized property in Perth. Their wives relished being the Ladies and fell easily into giving orders, playing the game which delivered such large doses of self-importance, the game of hiring and firing staff.

Tim Officer was not of this set. Like his brother-in-law Bob Campbell, Tim was a man who, when he looked at the Yamatji station men and their families, saw them for who they were, men and women, people, who worked for him and, now their own world had been taken from underneath them, sometimes needed a hand. Dingo Jim was right. He had indeed found the new good *maja*, someone who never saw himself as one.

Mr Officer was one of the new breed, the young ones. In Western Australia, there had always been some good bosses, John Mitchell one, Bob Campbell's father another, mixed in with those who bashed their workers while the others had to stand and watch, who flogged 'cheeky Abos' with whips and who bunjyed as they desired, several boasting of their plans of breeding their own half-caste free labour force. The new young bosses were mostly station owners' sons who decided enough was enough. They had grown up beside Yamatjis, playing together when children, speaking their language. Some had even sucked a black breast as a baby. And when it was their turn to be boss, they knew them as people. One of the sons from Byro Station up north, Simon Keogh, used to swear openly at his father, vowing he would never treat them the same way. He kept his word. The stories of how he stood up for them are still passed between Yamatjis.

Tim Officer shared their view even if he wasn't a station owner's son. Instead his father, originally from Melbourne, was a doctor with a philanthropic bent who had moved to Perth, and

Tim, venturing north to jackaroo when a young man and buying his station not many years after, was never inducted into the local mores and so had few of the attitudes to discard. He could simply carry on the way he knew, gentleman that he was, with a station to run.

Dingo Jim did general station work as required, still saddling up and riding out from their camp over near the house. Ulie now helped in the homestead kitchen, Bessie with the housekeeping, proudly adding making beds to her repertoire. Working was now so different from Yallalong. Part of her duties involved helping with the three Officer children, Ted, Elizabeth and Tim, and Bessie's life was just about as happy as she could imagine. She loved playing big sister, washing and plaiting Lizzie's hair. Tim even asked to have his combed as well, and it was wonderful to be able to take them for walks, all in the line of duty. Ted and Lizzie learnt to recognise and eat all manner of bush tucker including *bardis*, squeezy fat white grubs. Even today, Ted still finds them delicious, preferring them in their natural state, uncooked.

Bessie's exuberance no longer had to be so reined in. She could frolic and carry on as much as she liked after her chores were finished in the house. The only constraint outside was one intended to keep the sheep in. Once when Mr Officer, a man who liked children, drove all the kids, Bessie included, down to the gate to greet the mail, she ran from the car and tried to take a short cut by hurdling the fence. She soared through the air, only to get her foot caught in mid-flight between the two top wires and ended up hanging from them by the ankle, just like the emus who regularly did the same thing. She slid to the ground, tangled and embarrassed, but eventually wriggled free and dusted herself down to join in the laughter.

Life was good here. Soon Mr Officer built Dingo Jim and his

family a one-room 'house' with a bough shed verandah all the way round. It was small, but more than they had ever had and they knew it was well intended. Ulie fussed over it and planted a creeper. Dingo Jim was pleased to have his own place to sit, yet every night he still unrolled his swag and laid it out either on the verandah or often under the stars. For seventy years he had slept with the hard ground beneath him and he wasn't about to stop now. Anyway, Bessie and the boys made too much noise, he said.

Dingo Jim was slowing down, as old Harry had slowed down before him, and his work was accordingly lightened. But he still was headman of his camp, his family, and unquestionably ruled the roost. So when Bessie wagged wood-collecting, leaving young Friday to do all the work by himself, while she climbed a tree and rode a dangerously slender branch like a seesaw, there was little chance her father was likely to greet her with open arms.

'You gunna get a hiding,' Friday predicted when she finally came down and wandered over to the house.

Sure enough, her father was sitting in the cool of the verandah fiddling with a strap. Bessie winced, thinking she had seen stirrups too. She tried to edge her way past him, but came too close and he grabbed her and whacked her hard with the strap. But at least the stirrups hadn't been meant for her. 'You fellas don't like me!' Bessie cried, and went off to lick her wounds.

Dingo Jim hoped she had finally learnt just how dangerous trees could be. He didn't want to lose his daughter, and certainly not the very same way he had lost his son in his first marriage.

He took Ulie and the children over to Billabalong Station to visit the boys when he could, Tim Officer doing that which was unthinkable under Mr Leeds. He lent them a vehicle, a horse and a four-wheeled cart, station-made but indeed serviceable. They would camp and stay for a while, one mob again. Getting to the cart provided a wonderful spectacle for young Ted Officer as he stood watching in wonder as the family moved out, Dingo Jim striding in front, head up, arms swinging, with an emu egg gift to give held firmly in each hand. Several paces behind struggled Ulie and the children, somehow lugging bedding, battered suitcases and parcels of food for the road on their backs and shoulders and under their arms. Dingo Jim, a tribal man whether in whiteman's clothes or not, adhered to the way he knew, and his family role was never as packhorse. He was out front again, as in days not long gone, as hunter and protector—at least all the way to the wagon.

Yamatji ways remained strong with Dingo Jim, and many others. There were important cultural elements still alive, having survived with—and because of—the numbers of Aboriginal people necessary in the pastoral industry from its very first days. So when Dingo Jim was summoned to a tribal meeting, a ceremony, he had to go. Tim Officer readily agreed, and lent him the horse and cart, and Ulie, Bessie and the two young boys went too. They travelled quite a distance through four stations before arriving at the meeting ground, Bessie having no idea what it was they were to attend. She had heard about the law ceremonies, but always been afraid. And now, here she was, about to go through, and take the role of guardian for a nephew as well.

Dingo Jim, Ulie and Bessie did what was required for the many days they were there, Friday and Jimmy being looked after by other families in attendance. Bessie learnt endurance and for-bearance, and came through with extreme self-respect. Dingo Jim, a fully initiated man of power, a Clever Man, did not do so well. He made an error, a serious one. And the Law would deliver the consequences.

Apart from his wrong-way marriage, a social transgression,

Dingo Jim had always taken his responsibilities as a lawman seriously. He treated his duties and his knowledge with gravity and respect, maintaining the mandatory secrecy. He knew how important that secrecy was, how powerful those forces were, and he knew the damage they could inflict. They were not to be revealed to people not strong enough to cope, and among those who were, the same forces were not to be flirted with or treated as a plaything to impress or amuse. Any lapse would always invite punitive action, for any lapse revealed lessons to be learnt.

He knew all this well, and had always done what was right. Throughout his life a parcel in his keeping had always been near, but never on show or displayed to his children, never left out in full view. One time Bessie glimpsed something under the bed, and it was quickly removed—so she would be out of harm's way. She heard veiled references and whispered conversations about it, but rarely was it mentioned openly—and even then only when necessary. When it was removed from under the bed, Bessie, Friday and Jimmy were told where it had been placed, but never to go near it. The tree where it was kept was left alone for years and years, and even passing by it metres away could put the fear of the unknown in Ted Officer.

At the ceremony, Dingo Jim was moving to where he should be, when he looked back and noticed something on the ground. He was horrified, and Ulie even more so. She had seen him drop the sacred object and a young girl was nearby. He kicked it aside and then grabbed it, shoving it out of view. But it was too late. It had been done. He could do nothing but wait for what would come.

They returned to Woolgorong, back to the station, Bessie so proud, so gratified, and a 'member', someone who had been through the law, part of an affiliation of people who would look out for her. More importantly, she now had responsibilities. Bessie had become a woman.

Out fencing one day it happened, even though his two spirit dogs had been on guard as always. Dingo Jim had been caught, Ulie said, by that which descended from a cloud. He became sick, and Tim Officer took him to Mullewa hospital. 'They got him,' Ulie claimed.

He was there for several months, and Ulie worried, visiting when she could. But it was hard, with no car, children to look after and work to be done.

'You better go down and see him,' she announced after one visit. 'Go and see your Dad.' She said nothing more. Mr Officer drove Bessie and the boys in, waited while they sat with their father all day, and late in the afternoon picked them up again, taking them home to Ulie. She didn't ask much about their day. And she was quiet and caring.

Word came Dingo Jim was worse. Ulie made sure they all packed enough and, with bedding under their arms, they caught the mail truck, getting off at the edge of town. They set up camp by the windmill to be near water, had a wash and set off for the hospital.

Bessie and the boys watched as a man rode towards them on horseback, and wondered who he was. Ulie knew.

'I ... I came too late?' she asked in Wadjarri, pleading for a denial she knew in her heart would not come.

'Yeah ...' he finally forced out, choking, tears in his eyes. 'Yeah.' He could hardly be heard. Ulie and her children stood stunned, crying, wondering what to do.

'You better go to the police station,' he said softly. 'I'm going up to the cemetery now to dig the grave.'

They walked, sobbing and empty, but they weren't alone for

long. Arthur and Jack Comeagain knew they were on their way in and had come out to meet them, with their mate, Frank Phillips. They grabbed Ulie, supporting her, and held Bessie and the boys. Together they all went on, Frank Phillips hurrying ahead to find a taxi.

The policeman showed them to where Dingo Jim was lying, covered by a blanket in the unrefrigerated morgue out the back. Bessie flung her arms around him and cried and cried. They all did. They loved the man lying there with the blanket still over him, but they did not look at his face. Dingo Jim, with his snow-white hair and beard, his dark black skin, his little limp and his funny proud ways, was no more. It was time for him to leave the earth. And time for him to be of it. Bulthargardu was his creator. Now Bulthargardu called his name. It was time to go home, at last.

Outside, Frank Phillips was waiting with Horrie Peet and his taxi. Servicing the town and all the nearby stations, Horrie knew everyone in the district. Now he looked after Ulie and the kids, waiting with them at the cemetery next to the freshly dug grave. A van arrived bearing a rough-and-ready pine coffin, another instant burial by the government contractor about to happen. Out bush in a different time, Dingo Jim would have been surrounded by ceremony, by language, by family, by friends coming from all around. Here he was laid to rest, with just his wife, only three of his children and a few of his old mates to say goodbye—a forlorn little group which had arrived too late, but just in time.

His mates filled in the grave, making sure it had a good enough mound to do Dingo Jim credit, neatened it and marked it with rocks. His body now firmly below the soil, Ulie, Bessie and the boys stepped forward to say their goodbyes. Ulie and Bessie stood close to where his head would be, sobbing endearments.

Then they turned, held each other and walked away. The following night, the night after the burial, as custom decreed, Ulie sent his spirit away, told Dingo Jim to join the others.

His death certificate said that Jim Dingo, the new name a public servant somewhere had just given him, had died of emphysema, on the eleventh of January, 1948.

Chapter Twelve

I t was nearly dark as the truck pulled into Woolgorong Station, the last home Dingo Jim had known on this earth, and where he had been happy. Ulie knew she had to return here, knew there was something she must do. And she needed to see Mr Officer to arrange time away. Her grief had to proceed properly, with kin and friends throughout the Murchison given the opportunity to express their loss as well. She was required to 'meet' them, to cry and grieve in the prescribed way, until all had been allowed to voice their sorrow.

Joe and Pearlie, now with four children, had collected Ulie, Bessie and the boys from Mullewa as soon as they heard the news.

Pearlie and Joe had come to live and work on Billabalong too, Joe to join all his brothers-in-law, Pearlie her brothers. The mail truck had taken them from Yallalong to their new home, complete with meagre belongings, and Pearlie, like all who had gone before her, was grateful for the change. In so many ways. Billabalong delivered undreamed-of amenities for the workers, one of the most important being the loan of a vehicle when Yamatji business needed doing. Pearlie could be with her mother at this sad time.

Les, Clarrie and Cecil were also in the truck from Billabalong, the family all together as they should be. Only Owen and Hilda were missing, Owen having moved north to another station, Hilda married and now with two children on Wooleen Station. The rest had piled on the back, a little crowded but of no matter. It was all there was and did the job, taking them where they needed to go. They appreciated it—and had earned it.

Mr Officer walked over to Ulie when he saw them arrive. They talked for a while, and he placed an arm around her shoulder.

'You've always got a place here, *Winja*,' he promised, speaking with great tenderness, and calling her by the name he always used, the respectful Yamatji name for older people. 'You can stay as long as you want.'

More tears welled in Ulie's eyes. Dingo Jim had left her. But with good people.

Pearlie's four-year-old daughter Ilyama—Joan her whitefella name—unable to wait any longer while the adults talked, got out of the truck and ran straight over to the house, the little one-room hut with the verandah. She didn't get far. Suddenly she was back, howling.

'Something hit me,' she yelled. 'Something hit me.'

Too late Ulie realised. 'We shouldn't have let her get out,' she sighed. Both she and Pearlie, lost in their sorrow, had forgotten the need to keep the children back until she had cleared the way.

'We have come back now,' Ulie called in Wadjarri. She spoke, it seemed, to the air. 'That's our *gumbadi*, our grandchild, Junyu's *mayu*, Ilyama, and look what you did to her. Don't be so cheeky.'

It was as she suspected. Dingo Jim had come home. To Woolgorong. Back to his family and turf. Back to where he wanted to be, regardless of her endeavours the night after the funeral to send him on the journey he should take, telling him to go, go with the big white dog who was waiting. She, and everyone else, would catch him up soon enough. Dingo Jim, it appears, thought differently and decided to stay right there. And he wasn't having any kids coming and upsetting him. Joan, Ilyama, copped the full force of his irritation. Ulie chastised—and soothed—her husband, then went to her granddaughter, rubbing her to make her come good, and making sure she kept down low in the truck, well out of his way.

Ulie now did what she must. She placed the green leaves and small branches her family had collected in a drum and lit them. Smoke came easily and headed skywards.

Les and Joe dragged the drum into the house, watching as the grey fumes snaked about. Every corner had to be filled, every crack. Then out all around the house, and into the bough shed where Dingo Jim had preferred to camp. The house was being smoked—cleansed and purified—giving Dingo Jim's spirit no choice but to leave and go where he should. Everyone walked through, rubbing the smoke into themselves, silently saying goodbye. And Dingo Jim was satisfied. He knew it was now time. The blue *mili*, blue light, shot into the sky. He was on his way.

Ulie gathered his clothes together, packing them ready to give to a friend on Wooleen Station, handing them on, as required, as soon as possible. Somebody else could use them, after they waited a respectful cycle of the seasons.

Ulie and her family camped overnight at Woolgorong, in front of the hut but some distance away from it. It was January, and hot, and sleeping outside was sensible anyway. In the new light they left, Ulie now to begin 'meeting' everyone she should. 'After her bad luck' would be the explanation, rather than some harsher term. The word death spoke of a finality, and did not acknowledge that Dingo Jim had moved to a different plane. Other terms would be used, mostly 'gone now', 'passed on', or 'passed away'—but they were not mere euphemisms. They were, instead, descriptions.

Joe dropped the family at Billabalong Station, and together with Les took Ulie to Wooleen to see Hilda and her family, then on to Twin Peaks and Meeberrie stations. From now on, Dingo Jim's name would not be spoken aloud, out of respect for both him and those left behind. Instead he would become 'my husband' to Ulie, 'my old Dad' or suchlike to his children, 'that one that belong to Ulie', 'Owen's Dad', 'Pearlie's Dad' and so on to friends. Or more simply called *Nyaji*, which means sand. His own name, both his Yamatji and whitefella name, would not be spoken again for many years. And even then, only if there was no possible way of avoiding it.

Ulie returned to Woolgorong to live and work, Bessie and the two youngest boys still with her, but with her life dominated by her husband's passing. There were traditional procedures to be followed, and Ulie, who had been through the law, would observe them. Whenever the family now gathered at Billabalong, Ulie always sat with her bread or maybe some tinned corn beef, looking on as everyone happily ate not only the kangaroos they hunted, but also the *guwiyarl* and echidnas, all cooked in the coals, the way to really bring out the flavour and all the juices. The family would tuck in. But not Ulie. All three meats were forbidden her, because of her bad luck, and she must wait until her eldest child proclaimed the time over.

About twelve months later, on a visit to Billabalong, while they all sat around the fire, Pearlie stood with ceremony and faced Ulie, kangaroo fat in her hand, but did not speak. No-one spoke. She rubbed Ulie's face slowly, spreading the fat evenly. Ulie knew the import of Pearlie's actions and burst into tears. Her mourning may now be declared at an end, but it was hard to let go. Bessie saw her mother hesitate when the male kangaroo meat was offered, saw how difficult it was for her accept it. To eat meant leaving Dingo Jim behind, once and for all. But Ulie had no say in it. It was already decided. She took a piece, only a little, but enough, as she was merely required to taste. Her compliance had been duly witnessed and would be reported to all who should know. Ulie was to begin a full life again.

Les, Clarrie and Cecil, and Owen were now all in their twenties and had grown into fine men, healthy and fit. Life in the saddle had served them well. When boys, they had listened to what Dingo Jim had to teach and noted it, coming through mature and capable. Owen went to work at Byro Station further north, while Les was content to stay at Billabalong. In his flash riding boots, quietly cowboy shirt and jeans with the fashionably turned-up cuffs, he had become what he had always wanted to be—a horseman, a stockman, just like his father. He could ride with the best of them, each muster testing and revealing his ability. He loved the thrill of it, the freedom and challenge it offered, whether breaking in the wild ones, the brumbies, and becoming their friend, or riding flat out, him and his horse together, partners in adventure.

Sometimes he didn't achieve the harmony he sought, and sometimes in his youth, his calculations were out—not often, but even once was more than Clarrie would have liked. Not long after arriving at Billabalong, he and Les had been stationed at one of the outcamps for a six-month stretch, the two of them alone, except for the fortnightly visits when rations were delivered. Back at the homestead, they had made enough mud bricks for the workers' houses they helped build, and now there was not enough doing, no horses to break in, no mustering to organise. And so they requested this work. It suited them. They had a small house to live in, and here there was plenty that needed to be done. They looked after a few thousand sheep, fixed fences—the constant problem on any station—and had a line of windmills and troughs to oversee and upkeep. As well they had to look after themselves. Both Clarrie and Les were always well turned out, keeping themselves neat and clean even out here. The six kilometres to travel to good water to do their washing were nothing.

'I'll drive,' Les announced as they set out one morning for the spot. Clarrie finished harnessing the cart-horse to a small rubber wheeled buggy and got up beside him. They went tearing off along the roughly formed track, Clarrie grimly hanging on with his *marnda*, his rump, feeling every bump along the way. After a while he decided to grab one of the bags of washing to use as a cushion, but just as he stood up to shove it under himself, one of the wheels hit a rock on the side of the track and the cart tipped right over, sending him flying among the trees.

'Are ya right?' called Les, from somewhere in the middle of the upturned buggy and the washing, trying to contain his mirth. He could always see the humour of a situation, no matter how serious.

'Never mind about right,' Clarrie shot back, his hip skinned and sore. 'Go and catch the horse!'

They resumed their trip, Clarrie staring straight ahead, refusing to talk. Les realised some diplomacy was called for and refrained from speaking as well, although he had trouble suppressing a chuckle or two.

On the way home, washing complete, he could contain himself no longer. Clarrie only had to say one word, his first, and out it came. Les burst out laughing—and laughed and laughed.

'I knew you wanted to do that!' Clarrie exploded, 'but I was too wild with you for skinning my hip bone.' Each was as good-natured as the other, and Clarrie could not maintain his annoyance for very long. At least he had the satisfaction of making Les suffer as well. Les, who sometimes seemed to laugh all day, had had to restrain himself for quite a while.

But there were times when Les considered things to be a bit beyond a joke, particularly when it was simply a question of doing the right thing. Once on the return trip from visiting his family at Woolgorong in the down-time between mustering and shearing, the mail truck he was in hit trouble. Steam poured from the radiator, accompanied by an almighty hissing. Out there water was scarce, and few vehicles drove past each day. There seemed few options on offer. Kelly, the driver, waited for a while and then decided to drive on, with the idea of trying to hedgehog to where they might get water.

'You're not driving any further,' Les told him bluntly, standing out in front with a crank handle in his hand. 'You're hurting the truck.'

The startled Kelly stared at the iron bar. It was a good persuader, even if Les never intended it that way. It was what was needed to start the vehicle, but of course it wouldn't work with the radiator bone-dry. Having made his point, Les volunteered to carry out the most obvious and sensible course of action, the one rarely considered by the widpellas in these parts.

'I'll go and get the water,' he said, and trudged off down the road in the heat, jerrycan in hand.

Les was like that, a decent kindly bloke, comfortable with himself and at ease with anyone. He was well liked, by whitefellas as well as Yamatjis, and a hero in Mullewa to all the kids. Whenever he came to the town on the mail truck on a break from Billabalong, they'd hang around him while he joked and chiacked, breaking into laughter at it all. He had a lot of time for the kids, and they all wanted to be just like him. And even though he had good reason to be, he was never a bragger. It was no big deal he had ridden and conquered Chain Lightning, the famous buckjumper, when the rodeo had blown into town. But it was to the kids. Just to talk to him was something.

It was 1947, the year before Dingo Jim passed on, when Les became the town hero. It was always them and us when any home-grown boys were pitted against any out-o'towners. And the rodeo, with wild beasts to conquer and cowboys to better, was a ready-made myth-maker. Chain Lightning, the unstoppable and angry bay, was coming to Mullewa. Everybody knew about him, Clarrie, Bessie and Pearlie. You name 'em, they knew. The posters dared any pretenders to line up for the showdown, offering ten pounds for ten seconds to any who could last the distance. Les, well practised not only from breaking in horses but also riding wild cattle while he was yarding, got the money. His reputation was set. He was the man the kids wanted to be. Ulie, ever sensible and determined her son should remain so too, was not quite as impressed.

'Don't be so munninge-munninge, silly' she would always warn when she thought it might be going to his head.

130

But her advice was unnecessary. Les was never seduced by the adulation, his unassuming manner making him even more popular. He was merely confident, healthily aware of his own capabilities and unafraid of life. He knew who he was, as always. But nonetheless he was beginning to change, though not in the way she suspected. Les had enjoyed his moment of glory in the buckjumping ring, but rather than puffing up with pride, he began to contemplate his world. It could perhaps be a little wider. There were a few things he wanted to do.

A year later, much to Ulie's horror, it looked as if Bessie planned to imitate her brother. If he could, she could, it seemed. Bessie always was full of surprises.

Mr Officer had taken them to the side of town where Yamatjis were permitted, dropping them off to join Les near the tree the family would all sleep under. They had nowhere else to stay, and it would do. Mr Officer, who never failed to help Ulie build up her camp, made sure the makeshift windbreak to shield her bag mattress was in place before leaving. He always let Ulie and Bessie know when something big was happening and took them in to it, and Bessie, ever a thrill-seeker, had been unable to think of much else after hearing the Buddy Williams Buckjumper Show was on its way. She still remembered the electrifying night the year before when Les had suddenly appeared atop that bucking bronco and won. She had been so frightened, so awestruck. Her brother had been out there. And done that! Her brother had a great time. She wanted some too.

She and Ulie went early in the afternoon to look over the horses, taking it all in. The workers, men who would appear that night in costume as sharpshooters and daredevils, were busy pegging the big tent, assembling the scaffold seating and putting the centre rodeo ring and two-gate shotgun chute for the buckjumpers in place. It was all so exciting.

At eight o'clock the show began. Lights, music, rope-spinning, shooters, tumbling clowns on trick horses, donkeys for the kids and plenty of thrills and spills—the travelling show, here for one night only, had it all. Bessie and Ulie sat in their new winter coats the Officers had ordered for them from Perth, feeling quite grand and very cosy. The gift of the coats at the station a while back had been a special event in itself, and they were so delighted that they took turns to pose for the camera, standing stiff as a board as if to say 'this is me and my new coat', in the heat. Bessie's ankles had never looked skinnier. Those same ankles were soon called upon to support her centre-stage when Buddy Williams asked for a volunteer to step forward.

'I'm goin',' Bessie finally said, when it was obvious no-one else from the audience was going to take up the entirely resistible offer of holding a gold ring between their thumb and forefinger while Buddy shot a bullet through it.

'No you're not,' Ulie snapped.

'Yeah,' Bessie continued, 'I'm gunna go.'

Ulie could see her words had little effect. 'Oh, all right then,' she said. 'Go and get shot.'

She paused to see Bessie's reaction, and as her daughter was obviously undeterred she tried another tack.

'If you gunna go out there, I'm takin' off. I don't want to see you droppin'.'

Bessie took off her coat, folded it with care and told her mother to look after it.

'I'm not mindin' it!' Ulie retorted, and off she flounced. Bessie handed the coat to somebody else and, to a mixture of applause and hooting and hollering, made her way out to the centre of the ring. She was braver than the brave. Just like Les.

Buddy's assistant, in full cowboy dress, escorted her to the front of the target and showed her how to hold the ring between her fingers. Bessie, a slim, tall, striking girl dressed up to the nines, looked as if she belonged in the limelight. She took the ring, her eyes sparkling and beaming with confidence until she saw Buddy standing with the gun aimed right at her. Ulie, peeping through the scaffolding under the seats from the other side of the tent, knew it would come to this. Oh, what a foolhardy daughter! Bessie suddenly began to shake uncontrollably and she dropped the ring into the dirt.

The cowboy unconcernedly retrieved it and walked over to reassure her, and offered to hold her arm. Bessie surrendered to her fate. Gold ring held high with the cowboy's help, eyes tightly closed and head down, she waited. Bang! She screamed. So did the audience. Ulie sucked in air. The balloon in the target behind Bessie burst as intended, the sound magnified in the tense still air. The crowd went mad, clapping, cheering and laughing in relief and admiration for the local girl who had dared when they would not.

Bessie was delighted. She'd done it, been out there, been as game as her brother. Les and she got together, laughing and comparing experiences, Bessie so proud she had conquered herself.

'I dunno what you're gunna try next,' said Ulie. 'You get up to all sorts of silly things!'

Testing himself was nothing new to Les. He had been doing it since he was a boy. Independent, and self-reliant, he had always striven to master challenges. But life was not without disappointment for him, even though he was a man among men doing a job he loved on a station which treated him with some decency. He held his head high and always tried, but capable as he was, he was up against the whiteman's standards of worth, measured on a different scale from the one he set himself. Many things were denied him, his life never really his own. Any freedom he felt was illusory, and could be taken away at somebody else's whim. He could be ordered out of town, or out of anywhere if the whitefolk and police wanted it. He needed a permit to work, and to join in the simple mates' ritual of having a drink together at the pub, he needed state-approved citizenship, something automatically granted to any white person born on Australian soil, but not to blackfellas. Instead it was only available when Aboriginal people were considered to have made themselves somehow white, when they had been, in accordance with requirements of the 1944 Natives (Citizenship Rights) Act 'deemed no longer a native or aborigine'. And he could not move about freely, having to be out of town and off the streets by nightfall. He and his mates who set out to have a life comparable with the whiteman, yet retain who they were, did not realise how hard those standards were to attain. No matter how hard they tried, it never seemed to satisfy those men of little heart who sat in judgement.

Les's reading and writing had come along well since his days with the sauce bottles and jam tin labels at Muggon Shed, and since the days when he and Owen used to eavesdrop occasionally outside the room when Mrs Leeds instructed her nephew John Macpherson. Over the years, he had continued to practise. He was immensely proud of his beautiful script with its swirls and plenty of capital letters, as good as any schooled man. He was competely self-taught and his achievement under such circumstances remarkable, no matter the inevitable spelling errors and grammatical slips. At Billabalong he wrote most of the letters for his

Yamatji fellow workers, and used to order all the cowboy gear from the R.M. Williams office in Adelaide—the belts, hats, stock-whips, shirts, pants, boots and even chaps, which to an outsider could sound a fancy affectation imported from America. But to a stockman chasing cattle and sheep through wild scrub country, the loose-fitting cowboy-style chaps were a necessity, ordinary trousers being ripped to pieces in no time. The parcels would come back, cash on delivery, and much pleasure derived from them.

Les was not the only Yamatji to have taught himself to read and write. Many had pushed themselves against the odds to learn what the whitefellas said was useless to give to 'natives'. One of Pearlie's husband Joe Egan's workmates at Billabalong, doing his utmost to be correct and proper in the whiteman's manner, had written a letter for him to the Commissioner of Native Affairs, seeking some compensation Joe had understood was owing after an accident on Yallalong. He penned it in a style almost as floral as Les's, but not so neat and tidy in execution. To Joe, any letter written for him was wondrous. Skilful, talented and illiterate, he was one of the many capable and intelligent Yamatji workers never given the opportunity of education.

> *Billabalong Station*
> *August 9th 1947*
>
> *Mr Macbess*
> *Dear Sir I am writing to you abut a count of a year 1936 when I was a boy the age of 17 years old was working at Station Yallalong for Mr Mitchell I was working with a windmill man and the cogs of the mill crushed my two fingers at the first joint from the neal So I was taking to Mullewa Hospital and the two fingers*

was cut of at the next joint and the convanchion of the two fingers was sisted on by the department and said that I was not to get it till I was in the age of 21 years old and I have been looking out for the convanchion from that time till now and never heard any thing about it So I think I should get something for it so I am replying to see if you can get me any thing or ward for it as you are the Prinsabell man to ask about it so if you can let me know about it I would be verry thankfull to you and will be waiting for your reply soon thanking you Sir I am the age of 27 years as now So I will Remain yours fathell

    Joseph Aggens Billabalong Station Via Mullewa

A letter came back, addressed to Joseph Aggens, and Les, attempting to make good the mistake that had been made, got pen and paper out, and answered with all the manners he could gather.

    Billabalong Station
    10 Jan 1948
    Dear Sir
    I recived your most wellcome letter quite alright Well I never change my name. My right name is Joe Egan and the bloke what wrote the letter for me he the one who put my name wrong
    from your faithfull
    Joe Egan

Trying hard to present in an acceptable manner never seemed to work, however. Life for Aboriginal people in a culture not their own was hard in too many ways. Little goodwill seemed to be present when the manager of Billabalong decided he knew Joe's motives. He wrote to the Commissioner of Native Affairs:

> *... I have questioned this native and as far as I could discover, he was under the impression that he could claim on your department for compensation for the loss of two finger joints. Who advised him to write to you I have not been able to discover.*
>
> *Egan has not put in a claim through my insurance company, and I conclude that his letter to you was a 'try-on'. ...*

In time widpellas discovered who Joe Egan really was, and he became much sought after, known as a good hard worker. 'Honest as the day was long,' said Norm Armstrong, manager of several stations, including Mt Narryer Station, who worked with Joe for many years. 'Joe was a good man.'

Almost a year after Les's triumph at the Mullewa buck-jumping show, a year after he became known to just about everybody in town and out, a year after he began wanting more, Les did the unimaginable, according to those in authority. He applied to be officially declared equal with white Australians, to be given citizenship rights, rights denied all Aboriginal people by the 1905 Aborigines Act. Les not surprisingly considered himself the same as any man, since he could do just about anything asked of one. And everywhere he went he was accepted, or so he believed. Yet when he applied for those rights, his true position was made clear. Those people with the power to decide one way or the other argued the merits of whether he was fit for acceptance into their world, the now dominant society. There were no merits, they agreed. He was no man, they determined. Les was denied, with a haughty 'how dare he'.

He had written, as always presenting the very best he could manage with no formal tutoring and English as his second language. And aware that Yamatjis frequently made errors in white eyes, he wrote in the manner he spoke when attempting to do as the whitefellas. He added 'h's at the beginning of words which didn't require them, a result of being unclear where they should go as there was no 'h' sound in his own Wadjarri language.

> *Billabalong Station*
> *Via Mullewa Post Office*
> *Sept 11 1948*
>
> *Dear Sir,*
>
> *I am Just Writting you this few Lines Just to Ask you hoe Do I got to see so I Can get hunder the White Man Hact so hoe I got to see you or hoe. So Please will you Noater fiear me About it Please or Do I got to go Down and see you about it My Sealf that will be the Best go Down my sealf and see you About it. So Noater fiear me Please.*
>
> *hopping to hear from you soon*
>
> > *from yours faithfully*
> > *Leslie Dingo*

But Les was to be disappointed. He was notified, but not with the answer he expected. The way he lived was not in keeping with the requirements of 'the white man hact'. He loved his family and friends and still visited, worked and stayed with them, whereas the Act required, if he were to be accepted as a citizen, that he should sever all 'tribal and native' associations. The state required Les to cut himself off from everyone he knew and loved, required him not only to deny his race and who he was, but also to reject Ulie, Bessie, Pearlie and the rest of his family, required him to sell his soul for a ticket of dubious worth. If he had done as the authorities wanted, he would have found himself utterly isolated. There were few white people who invited Aboriginal people fully into their homes or lives. 'You're the only white lady who invites me in for my cup of tea,' Les said to Norm Armstrong's wife Val, in the 1950s.

Moreover, in a telling mistake in the letter the misnamed Protector of Aborigines in his local area forwarded further up the lines of authority, he identified Les's 'caste' incorrectly, perhaps presuming that only half-castes would have the nerve to apply. 'Full-bloods', those of full Aboriginal descent, would surely know their place. And it would never be beside the whiteman.

Re application for Citizenship Rights
Leslie Dingo Half caste
Attached hereto please find a letter received from Leslie Dingo native of Billabalong Station seeking information to procedure to obtain Citizenship Rights.

This native is employed at the station as general station hand and very seldom visits Mullewa he lives among natives at the station and has native tendencys [sic], *and in my opinion there would not be any advantage served in the native obtaining citizenship rights.*

Signed R McDonald
PROTECTOR OF NATIVES

Les, the man with many friends, was without a friend where and when he needed one. The Protector of Natives had not seen him as a man but as a 'native', and two whitemen decided between themselves that Les Dingo, the man who set himself standards, was of no worth.

9th November, 1948

Constable F.J. Wass
    Protector of Natives,
      MULLEWA.

re Leslie Dingo

Constable McDonald's memo of the 22nd October last regarding the procedure necessary for this native to apply for Citizenship Rights is acknowledged.

As you are well aware Citizenship is designed for natives who had adopted the manner and habits, and living conditions of white men. As stated by Constable McDonald this native is a station hand living among the natives at the station, and is therefore wasting the time of the court, the Protector and my Inspector.

However, should Dingo insist on making application for Citizenship Rights he can complete the enclosed forms and furnish them to the Clerk of Courts at Mullewa who will advise him of the complete procedure.

It is not the intention of the Legislature that natives of this type should qualify for Citizenship as they are essentially natives to heart and their living conditions and traits are such that Citizenship is of little benefit to them. It is the general practice to discourage applications of this type, but I am leaving it to your judgement as to whether you forward the forms to Leslie Dingo.

S.G. Middleton
COMMISSIONER OF NATIVE AFFAIRS

Les didn't mention the rejection to many people, didn't mention he had been judged less than human. Because he seemed so calm and confident, the whitefellas who knew Les thought nothing ever worried him. But Clarrie knew. After all, the same restrictions applied to him. Clarrie, a gentle moderate man, blamed not the whitepeople who worked beside them but those who ruled from above. Nonetheless, they all had their limitations. 'We had a lot of good white friends,' he says, 'yet they wouldn't let you mix up and that. Didn't want you to have the same as the whitefella. They want to keep you as low as they can, all the way along the line.'

Les determined never to be as low as it seemed they wanted and maintained his dignity as ever, despite his disappointment. Regardless of what the state and those in power had decided, Les knew his real worth as he had from the beginning. Dingo Jim and Ulie had seen to that. So had all the white station hands and Mr Mitchell who had treated him well as a boy. As a result, he never doubted himself or gave in to despair. In this, in Australia, Les Dingo, the 'native' who wasted the time of the big white boss, was one of the luckier ones.

Chapter Thirteen

At Woolgorong Station, Bessie's only worry was the occasional nagging from Ulie. Her chores were manageable, leaving plenty of time for merrymaking. At the homestead her main job was to clean the office, hallway and bathroom. At night she cleaned shoes, Mr Officer's and all the kids', and in the early morning when she went down to the house to be with the children, she would survey her work, polished beautifully, lined up and waiting.

Young Ted Officer had gone off to boarding school now, but Lizzie and Tim junior still accompanied Bessie on her jaunts in the bush, along with the Officers' new baby, Jane, well tucked into her big-wheeled cane pram. Bessie had much to teach, and they enjoyed the bush tucker and the stories she told them about the animals they came across. Bessie explained quite a bit, especially to Lizzie, helping her put two and two together. Later, at boarding school, Lizzie was able to pass on what she knew to the girls at the Perth Presbyterian Ladies' College. Those sex education classes had been a real eye-opener, Bessie's influence reaching further than she ever imagined.

The children were always permitted to go on those walks, but the line was drawn at going to the Yamatji camps. During mustering time, there were several Aboriginal families on the station, their tents and bough sheds dotted through the scrub, all to one side of the station, away from the white workers. Kept apart like pepper and salt, says Bessie. Dora and Joe were there at one time, their bough shed built away from the homestead, as prescribed by law. They knew not to go against the strict conditions it imposed. Prison sentences or hefty fines made all Yamatjis afraid and aware of the way their lives were controlled from outside. As well as forbidding any Aboriginal person or family from camping too close to a station homestead, the same Act of Parliament—the Aborigines Act of 1905—declared it illegal for any white person even to visit a place where Aborigines were camped without the written permission of a Protector, usually a district policeman. White people were not to socialise with Aborigines or expose themselves to 'native' tendencies, and white men were not to co-habit or consort with black women, for fear of contributing to the ever-increasing numbers of children of mixed race. In other words, white and black were meant never to freely interact. These instructions were duly passed on to the Officers' children at home. After all, this was the law and the law must be obeyed But not by these kids, they decided. There was too much they might miss.

Ulie's camp was endlessly fascinating, no matter how strange at first to their Anglo sensibilities. At sheep-killing time, Bessie would collect the runners, the intestines, and take them home to cook on the coals.

'Ergh! How can you eat that?' the kids would say, until persuaded by Bessie to eat and discovering it was indeed as good as she said. Lamb tails were equally delicious.

'How many times do I have to tell you not to go out there?' their mother would chide, nothing but innocence lined up before her.

It was never just the wood smoke which gave them away. Greasy smudges on faces were always a good indicator, and so were all those black bits in their teeth.

Ulie would sometimes still go with the musterers as the cook, but now she mostly worked back at the station. After the men had finished at the two camps, Mudbelong and Slippery Well, and gone further out, Ulie came in, her job to cook the bread and meat for the men's lunches in the homestead kitchen, Mr Officer riding in every second day to collect it.

'Would you do something for me?' he said to Bessie, on one hurried visit. 'You can use the bike.'

So Bessie became the killer collector, while the men were working. For the muster's duration, she was to find and bring back the luckless sheep chosen as upcoming tucker and accordingly known by the inverted tag of 'killer'.

Out she rode into the scrub, Tim and Lizzie in hot pursuit on their own bikes, Lizzie's plaits flying. Woolgorong Station was a wonderful place, with so many unexpected patches, small gullies and changing vegetation, so many miles to cross and explore. And so many places for sheep to be concealed. Yet without fail Bessie always led her charges right to where that killer was resting.

'How did you know the sheep were up there?' the children would ask, amazed.

'I know,' she'd say, in that Yamatji way of never explaining too early, in the way of making it clear any further questions would also be ignored. It was up to the kids to watch and work it out, learning on the job. They would be told, soon enough, but after the lesson had been fully imbibed.

'You've got to watch the wind,' Dingo Jim had told Bessie when it was her turn at Muggon. 'Watch where the wind is coming from. That's where the sheep always head.'

'When you old bushie, that's what you used to do,' Ulie confirmed for the children when they decided to check up on what Bessie had told them.

But she didn't mention—or perhaps didn't know—that Bessie had amended Dingo Jim's method, taking advantage of a pretty tinkle to listen out for. When doing her work at the station in the mornings, she always noted the wind, waiting to hear that one sheep with the bell on. Then in the afternoons, when they journeyed out, even though the sheep was now sitting still after eating, bell silent, Bessie easily led them all straight there.

Ulie gradually assumed the role of matriarch. Now acknowledged as head of the family, she ruled completely and was accorded absolute respect, though not always the obedience she required, much as she tried to discipline and protect her children. Sometimes her persuasive procedures appeared slightly odd to outsiders. Lizzie Officer watched agog one day as Bessie ran for her life from their hut, a three-pronged pot stand soaring through the air after her. But Bessie knew all about ducking and weaving. And Ulie, anyway, would have been devastated had the missile actually connected with its target. Quick to scold and quick to comfort, she was all about bluff. And her kids were all wise to her bluster, though not so everybody else.

The windmill man, a whitefella with a liking for alcohol, was targeted after an altercation with her two angelic boys. 'You get out of my workshop, you kids,' his constant refrain to the Officers' children as well as Ulie's, had been said once too often. Jimmy and Friday spoke back, Jimmy never known to be short of a word. The windmill man countered and threatened them. Ulie, ever loyal to her family, was incensed. While she was in the homestead garden cutting some salad vegetables for lunch, she spotted him and her anger rose to the surface. The large kitchen knife she was using became a means of sending him a warning. She bent down and slashed at a lettuce at her feet, savagely detaching the head from its stem, then turned and glared at him, brandishing the knife in front of her. In case he hadn't got the message, she repeated the exercise several times, until Mr Officer appeared on the verandah, anxious to avert any trouble, and she marched triumphantly into the kitchen to practise the gentler art of ripping the salad apart and preparing the midday meal. Mr Officer enjoyed Ulie's performance, as always, but didn't let on. Ulie and her clan always provided good entertainment and in addition, knew how to laugh at themselves, passing on the mood. Ulie and her mob were never dull.

Grandchildren also needed pulling into line, Ulie was now discovering, Hilda and Pearlie providing seven so far. As a Yamatji grandmother she had an important role to play. It was her duty to make sure all the grandchildren, the grannies as they were called, were looked after and cared for as they should be. And like grandmothers anywhere it was also her place to have the little blighters to stay. Hilda, her husband Tommy and their two boys, Michael and Larry, came for a while. Young Michael—

Budgerunga his bush name—was six years old. Born in a bough shed on the flats near a windmill at Muggon, his birth was typically Yamatji. So too are his major concerns these days—keeping the stations in order. It took no time at all for him to try to whip Woolgorong into a shape of his liking. No sooner had he arrived than with the help of his four-year-old brother, he was rounding up and yarding those recalcitrant turkeys running loose, draughting them into similar sizes, big ones in one yard, small ones the other, just like Dad did with the cattle back at Wooleen. Turkeys were jumping everywhere, mostly through the wide stockyard fences, and there was a mighty ruckus happening. But a budding stockman's got to do what a stockman's got to do, and he wasn't having livestock running loose under his nose when he and his offsider were on hand and the job was begging.

Tommy heard the commotion and came to check on his boys. It was an opportunity he found hard to let slip by, so he didn't. When Bessie and Ulie came home from the station house, the pot was boiling and the smell enticing. Hilda sat in a corner mulling over the possible consequences, but fearing none quite as much as that which could come from her mother. Ulie would be furious.

'Oh, shame,' she groaned when Ulie appeared. Without regard for the Australian tenet of never ratting on your mates—or in her case her husband—and speaking as if he were in no way related, she pointed right at him. 'Tom Ryan did that! And with the widpellas right there too!'

There was nothing else to do but quickly eat the poor bird. Indeed there was not much else you could do after it had received such an unexpected knock on the head. Hilda helped, her embarrassment so acute she was willing to down a few mouthfuls to destroy the evidence. The taste wasn't so bad, anyway. Ulie ate up big too.

Michael and Larry had a ball, chasing young calves, going swimming in the river, rolling around on the claypan. Wherever there was a slippery place, they'd do the sliding. And the old perennial, making mud pies, was a favourite.

'Look at all these kids comin' back!' Ulie would say as they finished a hard day's play, coming home to her hut, wiping the backs of their hands across their noses, pushing the dirt around. 'They might as well live in the mud like a frog.'

Ulie knew all about frogs. When Jimmy, her youngest boy, had been a baby back on Muggon Station and the rain would not let up, she had stripped him of his shirt, taken him out into the downpour and held him up high to the sky.

'*Meeunga, meeunga,*' she said over and over, imitating a frog call at the end of the rain. '*Meeunga,*' she repeated, in her attempt to stop the deluge.

Invoking help, she uttered the sound which, when it was heard, signalled rest for the land. It was the sound of the exquisite time just after the rain, when all things looked new, when frog calls rang out in the stillness giving thanks to the sky, and when people could move about again. The rain stopped soon enough, but no-one was sure exactly who had been responsible.

Water and cleanliness always seemed to be on the agenda for the youngsters, Jimmy, now about ten, included. At night-time when Bessie finished her work and returned from the station house bearing an apple or an orange for each person, the fruit became incentives in the clean-up-the-kids campaign.

'These boys never washed themselves,' Bessie would sing out to her mother. 'Got an apple for them, but they not gettin' them till they get cleaned up.'

With Ulie brought in as adjudicator, to scrub or not to scrub was quickly resolved. Fully scoured, wet hair combed, dark curls stuck down flat, the boys would sit and have a bite or two, then save the rest and leave it on the table, waking in the middle of the night to creep over and have another couple of munches. An apple lasted a long time back then. And boy, did it taste good.

Jimmy and Michael were great friends, never far away from mischief with Jimmy, only a few years older than his nephew, ever the instigator. There were so many satisfying ways to get a giggle on a station.

'Michael, hey Michael,' Jimmy called.

'What we gunna do, Uncle?' Michael replied, knowing that tone many times over.

Friday rode back into the station, his work finished for the day. 'Puppy, puppy,' he called even before he dismounted. The pups were his pride and joy, and he was still choosing which one he would train as his own sheepdog. It was a hard decision. He wanted to make great working dogs of them all. The pups scrambled over one another, their little tails wagging frantically. Friday bent to grab them.

'Who's been bloody shearin' these pups!' he cried. Jimmy thought his scissorwork beautifully crafted, the crutching around their bums as good as any shearer could want. Friday didn't agree. A mêlée then ensued. Michael watched.

Michael enjoyed these times with his grandmother, collecting bush tucker, taking the horse and cart to go fishing and swimming in the river, fooling around with his uncles. But like the rest of the family, he learned quickly how to stay in line or dodge the consequences. Ulie was determined her children and their families would grow up to be adults she could be proud of. She had done her best to have it so.

Some people, however, all of them white, thought her parenting and the morals she passed on were not all they should have been. Her children, after all, led lives flagrantly lacking in respectability, according to white morality. Why, two of her daughters, with children of their own, remained unmarried, their Yamatji unions unacceptable in white eyes. At Billabalong Station where her eldest, Pearlie, lived happily with Joe and their four children, the boss's wife, Mrs Campbell, decided she could have it this way no more. Marriage whitefella way was necessary. The Yamatji children would then have a name and everything would be in proper order, with the added bonus of saving their souls and rescuing them from the sin their heathen native ways had led them to. Marriage would fix it all nicely. Pearlie, unaware of the anxiety her living arrangements created until Mrs Campbell enlightened her, yielded. The boss's wife had spoken. Pearlie, then, was to be a bride.

Mrs Campbell had not always been so devout. It was only when station life had all but defeated her that she had turned to a fire-and-brimstone style of Roman Catholicism for support— along with a drink or two. Pearlie's soul, plus a few others, then came within her sights.

Mrs Campbell was an Englishwoman, a nurse who had come to these parts when she was young to care for old Mr Campbell. A pretty girl, she had won the heart of one of his sons and married him. With little preparation she was now of remote Australia, and there were few compensations for those so ill-prepared. Even the satisfaction and prestige of being a pastoralist's wife could disappear in an instant behind closed doors. Station life was difficult for those unable to appreciate the strange attractions it offered—the open spaces, the big skies, the tough but friendly people. Instead those who couldn't cope found emptiness, oppressive silence, boredom and in the end, loneliness.

Mrs Campbell's predicament was shared by a handful of

women in the area who came to rely heavily on each other, the opportunity for a wider circle to ease their isolation blocked by their wish to preserve the exclusivity of the social status and class they claimed for themselves. These women lived the role of squatter's wife to the full and reduced their lives to issuing orders to domestic servants. In the vast quantities of remaining time then, what did one do? Whom did one talk to?

Their husbands who were out and about with the workers did not seem to be so gripped by the need to keep themselves separate and, with real work to do, did not suffer the same way. These men, like Mr Campbell, were even known to invite the lowly mail drivers indoors for a cup of tea when they called each week. The Peet brothers, Bill and Eddie, grateful for any consideration shown them on their long hot run, knew whenever such an invitation was issued on such stations that the missus was away. It would never happen otherwise. On others, where the owners struggled to make a go of it and the wives worked as hard as their husbands, where leisure was unheard of and where delusions of grandeur could never be entertained, the Peets were offered real hospitality, even though there was often little to give. Bill and Eddie saw it all. They also noticed the change in attitude as soon as they entered the Gascoyne area further north. There the stations were even more remote and consequently more mutually dependent. None of the whites could afford to consider themselves better than the next: after all, no-one knew just when they would require help, or from whom. Up there the mail drivers were treated like one of the family, especially on Dalgety Downs.

In the Murchison, the group of wives so afflicted propped each other up with the few diversions available to them. The party telephone line was in constant use, with conversation and gossip shared as if they were all together partaking of a civilised morning tea. And for free too, callers only being charged when requesting a number through the exchange. Of course there were problems with this system. Anyone else could listen in simply by lifting the handpiece whenever the phone rang as it did in every connected home, with a particular code—such as two short rings followed by a long—for each household. A click could always be heard whenever anyone tried to eavesdrop, but that didn't stop those who had difficulty reining in their curiosity. 'Get off the bloody line, Ethel,' had been Mr Leeds' constant cry back on Yallalong Station. To alleviate their boredom, the women also waited for their weekly parcels of books, four at a time, to arrive from the Perth Literary Institute, sent by train to Mullewa and then on further with the mail truck, the books then discussed over the phone. But with not much else on offer, apart from the infrequent party organised by an acceptable family, or a trip to Perth for a couple of months of the year, life could indeed be bleak for someone craving society or ready amusements. Mrs Campbell, in Aussie idiom, was not cut out for it, did not have the internal fortitude for the life she married into. And station life devoured her. In her attempt to survive, she found something to occupy her time and interest. Pearlie and the morality of the women on the station were it.

Not all station owners' wives were of this ilk. Some of them were known to seek the Yamatji women out for company and a chat, and some even joined in digging for yams, looking for all manner of bush tucker together. Mrs Officer of Woolgorong was always friendly and caring, and understood enough to respect the differences between her ways and those of the Yamatjis on her station. So when she heard about the forthcoming wedding, she was horrified—and even more so when she heard that not one but two were planned. Cecil Whitehurst and his promised bride

Shirley Boddington were to share a ceremony in a double wedding with Pearlie and Joe, two Aboriginal couples fulfilling white requirements in the one go. Mrs Campbell had been busy, very busy, and the coerced foursome duly submitted to her arrangements. Mrs Officer could not believe what her sister-in-law was doing. She knew Pearlie was already married and had children, and knew one culture was being imperiously and ridiculously imposed on another. And she could not believe the white wedding dresses either.

Pearlie and Joe, Cecil and Shirley travelled into Geraldton a week early—plenty of time, it would seem. But all was not as ready as believed. Mrs Campbell, as well as the Catholic priest, had been unaware marriage for 'natives' had been declared a matter of state. There were certain preconditions to be met. In accordance with the requirements of the 1936 Native Administration Act, the individuals were to be assessed and permission to marry either granted or refused, like a parent to an underage child, as if they were not to be trusted to handle their own affairs. Pearlie, almost thirty years old, Joe, about thirty-two, and Cecil and Shirley, both of similar age, were all to be paraded before the Native Welfare representatives and judged according to the whiteman's standards. In complying with the wishes of the widpella who had pushed them to marry, these four people, who were happy to remain as they were, had now been placed in a position where they could be ruled unfit and unworthy. And at the end of the day they could be sent away, the department denying them approval.

The couples were split and taken into a room, their partners waiting outside, Pearlie interviewed first with Cecil, Pearlie's husband Joe with Shirley. Pearlie was scared, all this so strange and intimidating. What did they want to know, and why? Question after question came, about the way they lived, the work they did, their answers influencing whether they were to be allowed the privilege of marrying like a white person. Pearlie really only heard the questions about whether there was another boyfriend or girlfriend lurking. She answered truthfully, incredulous anyone should ever need to ask. There had never been anybody else but Joe.

She was even more stunned at one of Cecil's answers, which he gave without a hint of shame. Had he ever lived with a woman before, he was asked. He simply said no. Pearlie turned away, astonished at his brazenness. Cecil, more experienced in the ways of the white world, knew too well what the reaction would be if he answered yes as he should. Knowing he had committed no wrong, he felt no compulsion to inform them of something he regarded as none of their concern. Outside, Shirley wanted to know what had been asked, and what they said in return. Pearlie wouldn't tell. The Murchison district inspector for the Department of Native Affairs gave his provisional approval, notifying his superiors in Perth in case those fellow white men at head office should disagree with his recommendation.

GERALDTON
5th July, 1949

The District Officer
Central District
PERTH.

Re marriage of
Shirley Boddington and Cecil Whitehouse
Joseph Egan and Pearl Dingo
Enclosed please find Notice of Intention to Marry
duly completed by the above.
Mr Campbell of Billabalong wrote Rev. Father

O'Connor arranging for the ceremony and reception to take place on Friday, 8th July, at Geraldton, and enclosed the relevant forms required by law to be completed. The couples concerned were allowed to proceed to this centre a week prior to the date fixed for the marriage. Mr. Campbell and his wife hope to be present.

Evidently Mr. Campbell and the Rev. Father O'Connor were unaware of the provisions of the Native Administration Act as regards marriage which has since been explained to the Rev. Father.

Being satisfied with their conduct, industry, financial circumstances and housing arrangements tentative approval on behalf of the Commissioner has been given to the marriage subject to advice to the contrary being received by cable from the Commissioner. This action was taken in view of the distance travelled by the two couples, the elaborate arrangements that have been made and the inconvenience that would be caused should another date for the ceremony have to be fixed.

Should the Commissioner dis-approve would you kindly arrange for notification to be sent ...

(Signed)
Inspector
Murchison Sub District

Ulie and Bessie had never been to a widpella-style wedding before, and they both liked any new experience. This was exciting. They were collected from the outstation where Ulie was cooking for the musterers and stopped in at Moorhead's Fashion Centre at Mullewa on the way. A hat apiece was in order, Ulie determined to appear as she understood one should on such an occasion. They changed fully into their best clothes at the reserve when they reached Geraldton.

In the Catholic Church a small group gathered, mainly Pearlie's family, to watch the nuptials. Pearlie, mother of four children, wore a white dress, a little cream hat with a bow, flat shoes and no stockings. A corsage was pinned on her chest. Shirley, who had no children, dressed as a traditional bride, complete with veil. A dress code in keeping with one's circumstance had been arranged by Mrs Campbell, as had the bridesmaid each. Marriage over, they headed to the grand-sounding reception described in the letter to the Native Affairs department. They went to the reserve, the only place they had to go. The two couples and their assorted guests spent the night in tents and under makeshift mia-mias, Shirley folding her veil and placing it carefully in a box, in case it rained. They were soon back at work on the station. Pearlie had been persuaded being married like this was for the best. She still thinks that way, glad her children took her husband's name. There were too many Dingos she had been told, even though the name Dingo had only come into being when her father died one year earlier. She was confused. And she never could fully accept that as the real reason she had to marry. After all, the brand-name Dingo was on every bag of flour she saw, and nobody seemed to object to its frequency there.

Marriage was merely another facet of life decided upon by others. Ulie, her family and all Aboriginal people were subject to the state's control, not their own. Ulie might have the appearance of all-powerful matriarch, in accordance with her people's culture, but not where it really mattered, with her life, or her family's. Any white official could wrench it all away. There were so many state-authorised methods to interfere, so many means to remind her she was utterly without power. She and her children lived in dread of 'Welfare' calling.

Clarrie Whitehurst holding his first child, Patrick, standing with good friend, Les Ryan. Clarrie and Les were both born on Wail, the Yallalong Station outstation.

Left to Right: Ben Boddington, Eric Boddington, Onslow Franklyn, Clarrie Whitehurst, Cecil Whitehurst, Bob Boddington and Colin Boddington, workmates at Twin Peaks Station.

Mrs Peet and her sons with the mail truck. Bill on left, Horrie on right, Obbie and Doug in the cabin.

Horrie Peet's Mullewa taxi.

Les in a photo which appeared in the
Australasian Post in the 1960s.

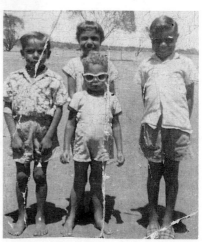

Left to Right: Kevin Taylor,
Marion, Ernie (in the Elton John
glasses) and Bruce all freshly
scrubbed at 'Between the Lines'.

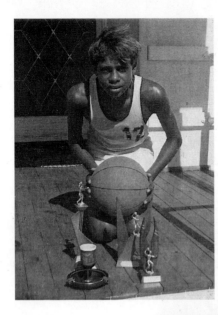

Ernie proudly displaying his basketball trophies.

Ernie wearing a pink and white shirt with purple and white flared trousers while playing cousin-brother Gavin's red guitar. Today Ernie still plays the same three chords for whichever song he sings.

Bessie had her first direct experience of Welfare on Wool-gorong while her father was still alive. They had come calling, checking on parentage, asking for birth dates for herself, Jimmy and Friday. Bessie had heard her mother talk many times of the children they knew had been taken, and Ulie and the kids had all been scared. Ronnie had gone, and they feared they could be next. Bessie had come to their notice, during the war, and they now had time to follow up. When she had been with her father at Mullewa hospital while his leg was mending after his camel encounter, a fellow patient, a deranged father suffering overwhelming anguish at his son's internment in a prisoner-of-war camp, walked past Bessie over to a small rise where he hacked at his neck with a razor blade and died. Bessie saw a crow peering from a tree, desire and hunger in its eye, and gave directions to where the man lay. The police in turn directed Welfare. And Bessie had heard for the first time when she had been born, in whitefella terms, and how old she was. Now they came again. And Jimmy, the youngest, was to go away—sent to school, but still away. He was sent from his family to the Roman Catholic Mission near Tardun, south of Mullewa. Ulie was so very sad, Jimmy in shock, unprepared. He never fully recovered from the unexpected separation.

When Jimmy went away, Ulie was overcome with memories. Two sons gone, so hard to bear, with one taken forever. Where was Ronnie, and would she ever know? Most didn't, but Ulie heard. News came, not from the department or from official sources, but by chance, brought by one of the few who managed to return from down south. 'You belong to that boy who was taken?' she was asked. And Mrs Officer phoned, as Ulie request-ed, to find out if what he said was true. Ronnie was dead, at eight-een, dying suddenly from meningitis. Ulie went to meet and cry with Paddy and Laurie. And cry they all did. But they never knew where he was buried, or even how his life had been. And they were never officially notified of his death. Nearly fifty years later in 1996, in the course of research for the family story, Ronnie was found again, the family hearing about his short life and seeing photos of him, and Bessie met his close friend Bob Chitty. Bob, Bessie and her son Ernie placed flowers and cried together at Ronnie's burial place, the grave marked with a number only. Ronnie was taken home, in their hearts.

Chapter Fourteen

Station life in the Murchison, for those in charge, was always dominated by the prices cattle or sheep could bring in the market place. In years gone by there had been serious droughts, with devastating floods in between. So when good prices came, rejoicing came too, and if you were on a good station, one with regard for people who worked it, sometimes those workers, Yamatjis and whitefellas both, were able to share in the benefits. In 1951, when wool reached a pound a pound—a phrase which still rolls off many an old timer's lips—Ulie felt the effects. Mr Officer built her a new home. Her first real house. And she could not believe it. It had three rooms, one with a fireplace which she commandeered for herself, and Bessie and Friday also had a room each. There was a fence all around to keep out any wandering livestock, with two gates for access, and Mr Officer prepared a garden bed for her around the fence edges and against the house itself, digging and fertilising it with manure in preparation for the seeds he bought and gave her. Directly in front of the dwelling he pushed the rim of a water tank into the soil, just the right height so she could fill it with flowers, achieving the same formal landscaping look favoured by the homesteads in the area. Ulie was thrilled. This was hers to do with as she pleased, given as soon as Mr Officer could afford it. Her garden was a profusion of stocks, sweet peas, carnations and calendulas. And she planted a tamarisk tree, the first of many. Mr and Mrs Officer would come and visit, looking in admiration at what she had done, chatting and seeing what else was needed. Ulie had indeed found herself a home, one she would never leave she thought to herself. She was so very proud.

She spring-cleaned on a regular basis. They all did, Bessie and Friday too, but always to Ulie's schedule. With great purpose, she would hurl everything out of their rooms, out of the house, and the dust would fly. Her domain would be as she wanted, and that meant spick and span. With a bush brush she made herself from twigs and twine, she swept inside and out, no errant dirt or pebbles allowed on her patch.

The magical wool price, a pound for a pound, meant marked prosperity for those with sheep. And benefits even for those without. There are stories of people ripping open their woollen-filled mattresses to get to the fleece and earn a few quid. And stories as well of raids on creekbeds to get the wool which in past times had been thrown down to smooth the bumps at a car or truck crossing. When wool wasn't worth much, a dead carcass was an ideal filler and provided an invaluable commodity in the scrub. Good tyre grip. A dead sheep could still be a good sheep. You just had to use a bit of bush ingenuity.

On Woolgorong, Mr Officer struck a deal with Ulie and bought her a second-hand bike. If she were to go looking, combing the station and collecting what was called dead wool, they would evenly divide the proceeds of the spoils. This was an opportunity Ulie would not miss, and even without his generous offer she would have agreed and delivered. She'd have done anything for young Mr Officer. Bessie and Friday, while certainly pleased and appreciative of what they now had, were not quite so amenable or indebted, being too young to fully understand what Ulie's life had been till now. Ulie had seen enough whitemen come and go in her time to know Mr Officer was among the best, one of the few who tried to give her every freedom and happiness that he could.

The three of them set off over the property, concentrating around the windmills, Ulie the scout on the bike, Bessie and Friday her lackeys, going off at her bidding when she located the remains of some poor sheep who had lain down and died. They were to pick up all the wool, stuff it in the chaff and oat bags they carried, then burn the bones and clean the area up. Ulie, meanwhile, continued her reconnaissance.

She could cover a fair distance, could Ulie, determined and thorough as she ever was, her bike solid and serviceable. And big, twenty-eight inches according to the old measurement. It was also what has always been known as a boy's bike, with a horizontal bar between the front and back of the frame, so that even with the seat lowered as far as possible, Ulie needed help to get on and off. Her legs were never long, anyway, as she was only about five feet three inches tall (161 cms) when stretched. This bike gave her problems.

Bessie and Friday threw the bones onto the fire, following their mother's instructions to the letter, until it lost its allure and they no longer wanted to play, at which point the valuable good wool often ending up in the flames with the bones as a result. It was so much easier than sorting and separating, so little trouble to simply toss it all in and watch it burn away. That's what Bessie liked—few complications and a straightforward life filled with fun and laughter. Collecting dead wool didn't fit the bill.

They heard the panic in the shrill ding ding of the bike bell, but such hysteria was by now routine and predictable. And they were well used to the 'Grab me, grab me, quick quick', which Ulie sang out whenever she rode. Her call was always the same, as she knew from experience her aides were not always reliable. And she needed them. If they weren't in time, that sideways crash to the ground was uncomfortable and scary, and had been known to hurt.

Bessie and Friday took their usual places like rodeo clowns ready to rescue a rider should a horse or bull go mad, and ran in from both sides, seizing her before the wobbles took hold and she fell in a noisy heap. No matter how many times Ulie had been through this routine, she was still relieved when it passed off safely. A competent horsewoman and camel rider over the years, mistress of those four-legged beasts with their changeable moods and behaviour, it was only now on that new mechanical contraption that she felt she was really risking her life. Her children, who cycled with typical youthful ease, smothered their tittering and assisted their brave mother, catching her with an appropriate gravity, of sorts.

On firm soil again, her breath back and mind on the job, Ulie explained exactly where the next sheep were, her part of the mission completed satisfactorily, and now awaiting the ground patrol to move on in.

'What are you doing?' she realised she should ask of the ones with the sheepish faces.

'Oh, we burning the bones,' they replied with a sudden faith in miracles and a silent plea for clemency. But Ulie, never fooled in the past, was unlikely to be now. Good wool, saleable wool lay in full view, singed and ruined. She got a stick and pulled the charred mass out, holding it aloft for Bessie and Friday to see.

'Well, you want the money,' she said grimly, reminding them of the gramophone and clothes they were so anxious to buy.

This was all the prompting they needed. They collected three bales in all. Bessie bought her gramophone, a wind-up one, Friday some shirts, and Ulie treated herself to a wireless. And there was some money left over for later. Dead wool could come to life with the right resuscitator.

That shiny tortoise-shell Bakelite wireless opened Ulie's horizons right up. It brought the world to her. But Ulie wasn't overly surprised by much these days, as just about everything was new after her closeted decades on the one station. In the early fifties when talk about a space race was beginning, Ulie heard mention via the airwaves of a possible event which she decided to keep an eye out for.

'We gotta be watchin' the moon soon, Missus,' she announced at the homestead one day. The surprised Mrs Officer naturally wanted to know why.

'Cos they gonna be putting a flag on it,' Ulie said. That momentous event didn't happen for about another fifteen years, but Ulie was ready for it and didn't doubt for a minute that it would come about nor that she would be able to see the pennant fluttering.

The same wireless gave Bessie a new sense of community, of brothers and sisters together, all the Yamatjis throughout the

Murchison region, glued to their sets at the same time, speaking to one another through the announcer. On Saturday nights, the local station 6GE broadcast a hillbilly music program, playing requests if two or more letters asked for the same song, a condition easily met. The same person would simply write two or more letters. Cheerios were included too, the lists so long the listeners seemed to be sending their regards to every man, woman, dog and even the odd sheep in the region. Bessie loved to hear all the names and be able to recognise them, and to eavesdrop on the messages they sent each other, waiting to see if her own letter and song would come up. Lizzie wrote for her, week in, week out, Bessie telling her word for word what she wanted said. One time Bessie laboriously copied out the letter Lizzie had written and added Lizzie's name to the list of cheerios herself. She was so pleased she had managed to do that, proud she could write, even if just a few words. It was always an unbelievable moment when she heard her own name, and more so when the very song she wanted was played.

The wireless and all it brought were just one aspect of the new life Ulie had stepped into since leaving Yallalong. She had been places and seen things she had never imagined before. In fact, all who had left there trod the same path. When they first got to Billabalong Station Pearlie and Joe were in awe at what they encountered when they were allowed to go freely into town. 'Oh gee, we seen some things then,' Pearlie says, that initial excitement still evident in her voice fifty years later. 'Mullewa show and all!'

Everybody dressed to the nines for the Agricultural Show at Mullewa, the bustling nearby town which operated as the social and business centre for the region. Ulie would wear one of the dresses the Officers got her, sometimes from Perth, sometimes Melbourne, a floral print her favourite. With her dress she teamed a cardigan, scarf, handbag, shoes these days, and white socks turned down at the ankles, always making sure she looked neat and clean, and always achieving a look of regality, rather like the Queen Mother. Other bosses ordered dresses for the Yamatji women on their stations, but there were some even after many good years of wool sales, who rang their orders through to Moorhead's Fashion Centre, specifying 'Send the cheapest you've got'. Clothing their lowly paid workers was required by law if their keep was part in lieu of wages. But unfortunately the law didn't concern itself with how adequately that requirement was carried out or how well. Some bosses didn't seem to, either.

Coming in from Billabalong, Pearlie dressed up all her children, the show an important event with such a big crowd present, and she wouldn't take her kids in their station clothes. She would not be shamed, she made sure. The men still wore the stockmen's clothes they favoured almost as a uniform, but only ever their best. 'No rubbish. Nothing!' says Pearlie, her head high. Those lucky to be from good stations were the ones who stood out above the rest. The Yamatjis from Wooleen Station, it was noticed, were always well turned out.

The Mullewa show was an important event in Pearlie's life. 'That was our first freedom!' she remembers with passion. It was 1947, and the first agricultural show held since the middle of the war.

'I think you fellas had better have a bit of a break, go and see the Mullewa show,' said Bob Campbell, the boss. 'Ever been to one?' And he gave everybody a wages cheque.

Pearlie worried when Joe told her where they were off to. She knew nothing of town, having only been there with Mrs Leeds, with the Missus firmly in charge. And then she had kept her head down, shy and unsure. Now she worried about them all going in, worried there was no-one to show her what to do. And she worried where they would stay, but needn't have bothered. There were no options. The bush it was to be, on the outskirts of Mullewa. Pearlie didn't mind the tent. She was just happy to be seeing what happened out and about, something new and different from anything she had seen before.

Pearlie walked through the crowds with her family, marvelling at all before her, especially at all the people. So many—and a big mob of Yamatjis, some of whom she had met already on the station. Her youngest daughter Betty, one year old, had gone to sleep in the truck Mr Campbell had lent them for the trip in, and Pearlie sat with her watching the sideshow ride in front, going round and round, the chains swinging the seats so fast and way up in the air. Pearlie wondered why anybody would ride in it, although the screams of delight appeared to answer her question. Suddenly the screams turned to terror. 'Prtaay,' was the strange sound Pearlie heard. 'Prtaay' was the noise others heard as well. A poor Yamatji teenager, a girl, lay on the gravel, bleeding and broken. She was already dead. They stopped the merry-go-round straightaway, and everything else as well. Everybody left. As always in those times of no refrigeration, the funeral was held immediately. The ride was left in place, the chains hanging limp, no pleasure to be had from it now. It was many months before it was taken down. The rumour persists she was pushed, her boyfriend playing a game.

There weren't many events in the Murchison to break up a year of hard work. Apart from the Agricultural Show, the Wild West Rodeos and the circus, everybody waited for the race meet at Murgoo Station which had been held almost annually since the 1920s. The Murgoo races were loved by everyone, even though it was a time when class and race divisions were openly on display.

The squattocracy, the self-appointed local 'royalty', were in attendance, mingling in a separate sort of way with the workers and with 'the natives', who, not accepted as citizens in the country of their birth, were not accepted on any rung on the class ladder yet. At night there was a Ball where a Belle was chosen, but not surprisingly Ulie, Bessie, Friday and all the other Yamatjis were not invited.

As pastoralists and leaseholders of a successful station, Mr and Mrs Officer were accommodated in the homestead, but Mr Officer came down to Ulie's camp to help put up the tent he had arranged for her, a miniature version of a de luxe circus-like big-top.

The Murgoo race meetings were lively, understandably so, with few times per year given to stop work and let loose. There was plenty of drinking—and then more drinking—until many of the racegoers passed out, high jinks among the young whites ramming the bumperbars of each other's expensive cars, and one year a two-up game organised by the local police sergeant disrupted the races so effectively it was henceforth banned. Thirteen heads straight had been thrown, and the punters deserted the main race in droves to watch and wager, the puzzled jockey who crossed the line in triumph trying to figure why the crowd which had been there only a few minutes earlier had so rapidly disappeared.

The drinking at Murgoo was par for the course in the bush—for the whitefellas, that is. For the Yamatjis it was still against the law, bringing a mandatory prison sentence. Yet they had plenty of examples to follow, with large numbers of whitefellas getting drunk in front of them, making a mockery of the reasoning for such a law. Some Yamatjis wanted to join in, and risked gaol to sneak beer of their own. They got drunk too. Ulie and Bessie did not want to be near either lot, keeping away from them all.

In 1951, the buckjumper show again came to town. Pearlie, in hospital with a minor ailment, could still hear the crowd roaring, the music and the announcements from her ward. She heard her brother Leslie Dingo introduced and hailed over the loudspeaker, and wished she was there to see those teeth shining and hear his triumphant cowboy yell as he rode that horse the distance, with no saddle or bridle and only a single girth strap to cling to. Ulie came to see her the following morning in distress.

'He's gone. He's gone,' she said, tears streaming down her face. Pearlie, knowing immediately what had happened, put her head down and wept too.

'I told him not to, not to, not to!' she said, blaming herself for not trying harder. And she blamed her mother too, having pleaded unsuccessfully for her to intervene. But Les was a grown man and did what he wanted. He had upped and gone, on the spot. With his mate Basil Jones, he had joined the Dusty Rankin Wild West Buckjumper Show to travel Australia, something no Aborigine in the area had ever done or dreamed of doing. It was the only way the two of them would ever get to see the big land they lived in. They went when the Yamatjis and most whitefellas as well stayed put. Ulie and Pearlie were devastated, Bessie in awe. They all waited for news.

Pearlie and Joe had shifted workplaces. The overseer Norm Armstrong was impressed with Joe's work and had persuaded him to come to Dalgety Downs, Don Scott's station further north. Bessie, on a holiday from her duties for the Officers, caught the mail truck up and went for a visit.

'Norm's got you a horse,' Joe said, when he came to meet her. Bessie, Norm, Kelly Hawkins and Joe did a good day's riding. It was exhilarating, but Bessie was sore all over, feeling every bone and joint in her body. And there was still the rest of the week to go.

'I can't go riding this time,' she said to Joe the following morning when he told her the day's route and the work they would be doing. But Joe was a persuasive type and Bessie was back on her horse again as soon as breakfast finished. Despite the initial pain, she really enjoyed each day in the saddle. This was the life her brothers all led, this was what it felt like to be a stockman. She was grateful to Norm for his generosity and his thoughtfulness. He was another whitefella boss known for his fairness and his decency.

On her final day, they travelled by station jeep towards Mt Augustus, Joe shooting several wild turkeys. Pearlie roasted them, sending them back with Bessie on the mail truck down to Ulie at Woolgorong.

Bill and Eddie Peet were the mail truck drivers Bessie joined up with for her journey, and she knew them well. Most people in the Murchison knew them, the mail truck carrying everything needed for the stations, including the workers. It was the only way most had to get around and they piled on, sometimes twenty people at a time, with the wool, fuel, machinery parts and stores, or found a place somewhere in the mountain of dried kangaroo skins. Sometimes there were the embarrassing incidents, like the time the new cook was on the way up as the sacked one was heading down, the meeting between them at the station a mite icy. And sometimes the bizarre, as when Hilda, Tommy and family sat on top in a picturesque silhouette, three wool bales high, with swags and a cat and Michael and his pet emu. They were on the move, no doubt about that. The Peet brothers' arrival was always eagerly awaited. Old Bringo, on Wooleen, came in by horse and cart from the outstation every mail day to collect his personal order of fruit and vegetables sent up by one of the Mullewa greengrocers. After Bill and Eddie unloaded the station's supplies and equipment and caught up with him about a kilometre or so further on, without fail half his case of food would be gone, devoured on the way. By this time Bringo was always one very happy man.

Bessie was lucky on this trip. There were no other passengers, and almost an empty truck. She got a seat in the cabin, riding in the front in style. Byro was the station where Bill and Eddie always camped on their run, and as soon as they arrived, at about ten at night, they prepared to turn in, ready for the five o'clock morning start. However, Bill spotted a kangaroo and couldn't resist taking a shot at it. He wanted the tail, the favoured eating part, and brought it down, only to discover a joey in the dead mother's pouch. But he could play parent, he was sure.

They unrolled their swags, one of the brothers taking the ground, the other the back of the truck. Bessie was given the front seat, a luxury and a privilege, promising a good night's sleep. However, the single room suddenly became twin-share, with the orphaned kangaroo stuffed into a bag as a pouch substitute and placed in the front as well, on the floor. But not for long.

'Have a good night's sleep?' Eddie, ever polite, asked in the morning, unaware Bessie had spent half the night being jumped on and the rest shoving the joey back in the bag. She had finally given up on the sweetness and light, and closed the top securely.

Back at Woolgorong there had been a call from Les. In the many months he had been away, he had never phoned but always written, his letters creating great excitement. Ulie would sit and listen while Mrs Officer read and reread the pages, her face and eyes reacting to every new bit of information or mention of a place where he'd been—to Adelaide, to towns all through South Australia, Victoria, New South Wales and right up to Queensland, all such a long way away. What a grand life he was leading! He even went to Kingaroy, and wrote about the peanuts they grew around there. Bessie, who'd never seen any, hoped he'd bring some when he came back.

But Les, when he wrote, didn't tell the full story, omitting all the difficulties and trials as per usual. The travelling buckjumper show game was hard, 'shockingly hard' as one long-time player, Happy Gill, described it, and not for the faint-hearted or those lacking in stamina. It was a life of labour which tested everyone who tried it. Many failed, leaving as soon as the reality of the hardship and the daily grind sank in. The Gills, who owned most of the travelling shows across Australia, would sometimes wake in the morning to discover their staff had absconded with nobody but family members left to do it all. They could do nothing but wait until more men who could stick to a horse offered themselves at upcoming towns, lured by the bright lights, travel and romantic notions of being a rough-rider.

And they always did. The buckjumper shows, with the noise, the clowns, the country singers and sharpshooters, carried every-body away with the thrill of it all. And the spirited horses arching high, with the rider as god, one arm in the air, giving a yell of sheer exhilaration and triumph, got the blood racing and the adrenalin pumping. It was hard to resist, especially for those who saw themselves as horsemen.

Many who tried the chute and came through, who conquered their fears and glimpsed the wild unrestrained sense of raw power they could achieve, lost their heads and failed to recognise the brief wonderful experience as only part of a job basically filled with tedium, repetition and hard work. But the chute would always work its magic, blinding riders to the hard and uncomfortable slog. In the chute there was nothing like it. The atmosphere was charged and electric, the concentration intense. Nothing else seemed to exist. The rider lowered himself astride the horse, shifting his weight and locking himself into position. He seized the leather handpiece connected to the one rope around the horse, the strap around the girth, placed his gloved balance-hand underneath and wound the connected leather strap tightly around his hand, punching the fingers in, pausing to make sure it took the tension, then wound and punched some more until there was no more movement in the rope. Old timers issued last-minute instructions.

'Remember when he pigroots high, he'll twist his head to the left, and when his feet land, you know his body will follow like a whip.'

All eyes were on him. And he was the centre of the universe. Everybody waited for eye-contact, for the sign all had been checked and he was ready. Nobody moved until they knew. The blokes on the rails watched, eyes narrowed. And the men at the chute front were frozen. Nothing but silence. The rider finally locked eyes with the official, raised his arm high, and nodded. 'Let him loose!' came the order. And the gates opened, horse and rider coming out sideways. The ride began. And so did the addiction. Ten seconds in the centre were all it took.

But life on the road would never suit all who hankered for it. It was only for the most resilient men and women, demanding perseverance and a strong will to see it through, no matter the circumstances. The nightly rides on the bucking beauties meant jolted bodies, backs done in, legs bashed and bruised against side rails, and of course cracked ribs and broken bones. And injuries did not mean any time off, only that the rider would be in considerable pain when he rode again in the show, which must go on. Each town meant new ground and a variety of surfaces, all firm, with no sand ever scattered to cushion a fall. In some towns the show-workers first had to rake the rocks out of the yard. And then there were the regular requirements of the job. As soon as they arrived in the day's new town, all hands had to work feverishly to peg and get the tent up, then erect the seats, set up the lighting and the buckjumping yard, and if they finished in time, a short break to shower or swim before the audience began arriving at seven. Then the big moment, the performance at eight. No food before a show, an empty stomach sensible for rigorous riding, and after the applause finished it would be out of the costumes and on to immediate dismantling before supper, then bed in a caravan, well after midnight, to start all over again at dawn the very next morning—in rain, cold or heat, six days a week, no matter how many aches they had. And some rider-workers had to double as bouncers if the boss saw they could throw a punch or two, ejecting rowdy or drunk patrons creating a nuisance, and even fighting them if they had to.

Les wasn't bothered by the daily rigours many others fled from. He'd grown up in far worse conditions and was as tough as the lifestyle required. He was determined as ever to enjoy himself and find something to smile about. Wherever he went he still found time to joke with all the kids who used to hang around.

'How's your *boogoo*?' he said mischievously to one lot, presuming these eastern state youngsters would never understand the Yamatji in-joke, 'backside' being just about the naughtiest word they could find to say when children. Even when they were older, Yamatjis invariably rolled around laughing at its daring in a culture so conscious of appropriate behaviour.

'Good, how's yours?' came the reply. Les and Basil recovered from their shock and laughed at the joke being turned back on them.

Les and Basil enjoyed the freedom and the new experiences the travel to other States gave them, and they were readily accepted by their fellow riders and workmates. They all even went to some cafes. But not the pub, the time Les was most reminded of the social place he had been assigned. Mates together, according to the law, applied only to whitefellas, and Les and Basil had to sit outside and wait.

He and Basil could have gone on travelling for a long time, but after nine months Les's body felt the strain of the nightly rough-riding. After being injured one night, he made the call to Ulie. He was coming home. He had lasted longer, nine months longer than most men who tried the same game. So he left Basil to go on without him, across the water to tour Tasmania, while he himself headed west to the Murchison, back to his country and his family. They were overjoyed at his return.

Ulie and Bessie waited for him at the homestead gate, but Bessie found it so unbearable she climbed the windmill just as she and the Officer kids did every Thursday for the mail. She peered into the distance to see the dust rising and the overloaded vehicle slowly approaching. He was here. As thrilled as they both were at his coming, the Yamatji way meant both Ulie and Bessie were to take their positions and wait. Bessie was champing at the bit, but had to stay, standing formally next to her mother. Ulie stood as tall as she could manage, her face composed, masking her joy. Les stepped from the cabin and embraced his mother, both of them weeping with happiness. Then it was Bessie's turn. The proper greeting over and restraint no longer required, Bessie and Ulie could look at him fully. He was back, back where he should be, but in a bad way. Les was battered and sore, walking in obvious pain. And he looked so thin. He'd come home just in time, Owen thought, when he saw him. Bessie liked the posties he brought back, the postcards with photos of places he'd seen. And he did bring those peanuts. He was the bravest and best brother she could imagine. He'd bounce back in no time, she was sure. He always did.

Bessie and Ulie had their bags packed ready to join him and travel up to Dalgety Downs, the station where he was headed, his former workplace where Pearlie and Joe were living, together with Owen and his wife Sylvia.

Bessie and Ulie stayed at Dalgety Downs for a couple of weeks, the Scotts—the station owners—welcoming and warm, and pleased to see Les again. His job was waiting, held open if ever he returned. Les met everyone he knew and reacquainted himself with his nieces and nephews, chuckling at one three-year-old niece who insisted she'd been 'poijoned' after raiding the garden and chewing a chilli. Overall, though, he was subdued and in constant pain, but insistent on working as he did before. In time his limp, and the occasional wince he tried to hide, disappeared, Ulie collecting and administering bush medicine, determined to help him to his former good health. Les was home. He had seen a lot.

He was finally granted citizenship in 1954, the papers to prove it required to be on his person at all times. Les had not changed. The requirements had.

Chapter Fifteen

Bessie was like Les in many ways. They both grasped life and delighted in the pleasures people and new experiences could bring. They both were easy-going and quick with a smile. And they both never doubted they were the equal of any other Australian. But Les, ten years older and male, had more opportunities to follow the life he wanted, Bessie still a teenager and required to stay with her mother. Every now and then she bucked against the restrictions, and did as she liked, but never yet with anything like Les's maturity and dignity. Bessie was too young and high-spirited to see any virtue in this. She was a rollicking youngster and life now was safe and secure. She would do what she wanted.

· Back on their home turf, from Dalgety Downs, she and Ulie were pleased once more to see the Officers, the family they regarded as almost their own. Bessie's enthusiasm, however, didn't always extend to the governesses, the young women employed to teach the Officer children in their primary school education. With a governess on the station, Bessie's sphere of influence seemed to recede somewhat, and it rankled. But Bessie was never short of ways to solve such problems.

When Mr Officer was out mustering, only three horses were available for casual Sunday riding. Bessie, Lizzie and Tim were in the habit of going off together, and Bessie regarded herself as the boss of her horse, the one Mr Officer had specially arranged to be at her disposal whenever he was away.

'You know, I'd like to go riding,' said the governess to the yardman, who knew Bessie was the one to consult. Bessie agreed, for one day only she thought, and the governess and her son rode off with the yardman for an enjoyable Sunday outing together— and the following Sunday, and the next. Bessie was put out, convinced her wants were not considered at all. So were the Officer kids.

'When's our turn?' they asked.

A new Sunday arrived. Bessie rose before dawn and waited in her dressing gown in the bushes to see which of the three pads the horses would come in on. At last she heard them coming and prepared for action. When they were almost on her, she leapt out in front of them. 'Waahoo,' she shouted. The startled horses turned and galloped off, Bessie chasing after them until they were safely out of sight.

She slipped home to find Ulie just out of bed and demanding to know where she'd been. Bessie was a bit uneasy about the lie she told, but her plan worked. Down at the house she tried to look troubled when the horses failed to show and commiserated with the yardman, who looked at her strangely, obviously wondering. The following Sunday Bessie and the children rode off as they had before, Bessie considering herself victorious.

But she was mistaken. All she'd had to do was ask. The yardman had realised what she'd been up to and, sensing that she was unable to talk to him about it, had decided to put things right. The Yamatji custom of never disagreeing and resorting to all manner of diversionary tactics to avoid causing embarrassment or offence had been at work. Bessie got what she wanted, but only because the yardman had figured the puzzle.

Not all governesses threatened Bessie's dominion. One became a good friend, and introduced her to the pleasures of late night walks. They would take off after the children were asleep and go birdhunting, peering in the nests, and seeing the country in its moonlit garb. Often it was the early hours of the morning when they returned. Ulie was unsettled, concerned that the girls were going off for a rendezvous, and worried for her daughter. She needn't have. Not yet anyway.

Mr and Mrs Officer had decided it was time for a well-earned holiday, their first since Tim had taken on the station. The good wool prices meant some of the pressure of servicing the debt he had with Elders, the company who had financed his venture, had lifted, and extra money was available. He was in his early forties now, and had worked non-stop since coming to the Murchison as a young jackaroo in his teens. Back then, determined to learn all he could, he worked first on Billabalong before being appointed manager at Woolgorong, the station he still ran after buying it in his late twenties. A holiday would do him good—after all, it hadn't been easy. As a first-generation landholder who had bought the lease with his mother's help after his doctor father died, he had been debt-ridden for years, joking when his first-born Edward (Ted) arrived that the baby should be given the name Elder, because Elders owned everything else he had.

Tim Officer had acquired the leasehold at the end of the depression in the middle of a drought, and times were often tough. When the good years came and wool prices rose, he was still only slowly turning the station around, while some pastoralists, those whose families had been on their properties for several generations, were sitting pretty, debt-free, their only discomfort being to tally up all those wool cheques. He deserved this break, which they had decided to take in completely different surroundings. Tim Officer and his wife Jean went by ship, bound for the eastern states.

He'd had time away from work the previous year, but it certainly wasn't a holiday. He'd been unwell, uncharacteristically complaining of aches and pains, and had undergone a complex chest operation.

'No boss, don't you do that,' the Yamatji workers had protested when, just four months later, he was lifting heavy slate at Muggon to take back as paving for the Woolgorong garden.

He recovered and was looking forward to his sea voyage. 'See you when I get back, *Winja*,' he said, the same as he always said whenever he went away, even if just to go mustering. Ulie was glad he was going, knew he needed a rest, and was happy to oversee the homestead until his return, under the direction of Mrs Officer's mother. She stood at the gate and waved them both off.

One hot afternoon a couple of days out to sea, Tim and Jean Officer played an enjoyable game of deck quoits and went into the bar for a drink. Personable and friendly, they had made friends quickly and there was no shortage of people to talk to. Tim was sitting contentedly while Jean joked with their new acquaintances at the next table. She turned back and froze, faced only with an empty chair and her husband lying lifeless on the floor. It was 1953, and Mr Officer, Ulie's new good *maja*, was dead, just forty-three years old.

Mrs Officer took some time before going back to the station. She saw to Mr Officer's cremation in Adelaide and spent a few weeks with her brother, recovering as best she could, stumbling through the numbness and shock. She had never expected this. They were both still young, working hard for each other and for their children. And the holiday was intended to revitalise him after the operation the year before. But she could avoid it no longer. She had to go back and confront what was so hard to accept. Wool-gorong was now a different place. Her husband would never be coming home.

Ulie knew she was in the kitchen and walked slowly through the garden with Bessie to the back door, over the slate Mr Officer had only recently laid. Mrs Officer heard them come in and turned quickly to the pantry, a shelf needing an immediate rearrangement, so too it seemed, the next one and the one beneath that as well. Ulie waited, her throat tight, her sorrow fighting for release. She didn't know how to approach her or what to do, but wanted to meet her in the Yamatji way. Mrs Officer kept tidying, clinking cups, straightening the already straight, avoiding Ulie's eyes. But at last she turned, and gave in to the terrible sadness. The two women held each other, sobbing uncontrollably. Little Jane, six years old, looked on, and so did Bessie. They both cried as well.

Mrs Officer stayed on for a while, but found it necessary to appoint a manager. She left her treasured station life, the only life she had known, the life she had loved since her first hesitant steps when still Jean Campbell from Billabalong next door. When she'd married at twenty-eight, she'd only had to move forty kilometres up the road to her new home. Now she went to live in Perth, where Ted, Lizzie and young Tim were all at school, and became a townie, permanently of the big smoke. She missed the station terribly, hating to go back when managers were there. Its soul had gone. Her true home had gone. But there was no other way.

And so the Lanagans came to Woolgorong, with their two children. They were at a disadvantage before they started. They could never be Mr or Mrs Officer. Loyal Ulie found it difficult taking orders from people with whom she had no relationship, from newcomers who could never take their place. Inevitably clashes occurred. Ulie knew her cook's job thoroughly, having been patiently trained by Jean, just as Bessie knew the house-cleaning procedures taught her by Mrs Officer's mother. And now they were told a new way, not regarded as capable, it seemed, or trusted to simply do the job. But worst of all, told the new boss was boss.

For Ulie, Bessie and Friday, Woolgorong without the Officers was empty and the work pointless, proving how hard life could be without a paternalistic benefactor. They could stay, demoralised and disheartened, or leave with next to nothing. For Yamatjis, a decent living had come to depend on having a decent boss. Social security payments were not extended to 'full-blood' Aboriginal people, and Murchison Yamatjis, while paid more than most Aboriginal pastoral workers throughout Australia, still were paid well below the award wage, still below what fellow white workers received for the same work. At the end of any job they had little, or nothing at all. Their choice of an abode to move to was almost nonexistent, and dismal anyway—usually just a tent with bough shed in the bush somewhere close to town. Ulie, Bessie and Friday talked about leaving, trying to make up their minds. It was a big decision, and Dingo Jim was not here to march them along. Just like that time they left Yallalong, they had nowhere to go. So they hung on, at least for a while.

To Bessie's dismay, the new bosses even came complete with a governess, the Lanagans' two school-age children requiring a tutor. This one threatened the status quo, calling for swift action from Bessie, and she brought her own style of arbitration into play. It was quite a sight to see.

Pearlie was staying at Woolgorong, waiting for the birth of her fifth child, Ulie once again to be her nurse and midwife.

'Coming for a ride?' brother Friday called. 'Motor car here. I'm goin' for wood.'

'I'm coming too, Goobunge,' cried the governess, out to impress by using Friday's Yamatji name.

Without waiting for an answer she jumped in the front and climbed over Pearlie, seating herself in the middle, right next to Friday.

'I'm coming with you, Goobunge *mardong*,' she said, looking right at him.

Bessie was appalled. *Mardong* meant 'boyfriend' when used this way, and stated a clear intention. Friday, she decided, was definitely not available. She jumped on the back of the truck, an instant bodyguard for her brother, whether he wanted one or not. Her family, she considered, was under attack. The winter rains had been, and the spectacular wildflowers which sprang up from nowhere every year were so plentiful they fought for space, the few clumps of sorry dry grass now an uninterrupted mass of colour. When the truck stopped, some of those healthy flowers were flattened in no time. The governess, insistent she had every right to be there and ignoring Bessie's hints that she should leave Friday alone, snatched the truck key so no-one could go anywhere and put it in a place she evidently considered unassailable, one that was guaranteed to taunt. She put it in her mouth. And in so doing called a battle forth. Bessie and the governess rolled over and over, wrestling in the everlastings, the blooms swaying and shaking as the two combatants floundered through them. Pearlie watched in amazement. Friday continued his work, every now and then looking up from the fallen dead tree he was chopping, rolling his eyes at the behaviour of these crazy women. There were no prizes for guessing the winner.

His job finished, they got back in the truck, this time Bessie firmly in the middle, the governess now relegated to the back with the wood. At the house, no-one said a word, as if nothing had happened. Bessie was relieved. If Ulie had heard even a whisper, there was a strong possibility those everlastings would have danced again.

But the governess's timing was out anyway. Friday had made his decision. He left to look for work elsewhere. And only Ulie and Bessie remained. Woolgorong, for all its searing temperatures, was now a cold place.

Except when shearing time came and people appeared, and activity and busyness carried all with it. Bessie, twenty years old, vivacious and attractive, noticed the men. And they noticed her. It was her turn now. Indeed, she developed a crush—which was reciprocated, it appeared.

Reg was a rouseabout, a city boy gone bush for a while, in search of the all-Australian experience, in search of adventure, a twenty-year-old who enjoyed living as much as she did. She noticed him as soon as she fronted to watch this year's shearers in action and he collected his first fleece off the floor and delivered it to the table to be tidied up, classed and bagged. He was tall, strong and handsome, with curly hair and a smile, a big one, for everybody. Pearlie and Bessie stood watching, the noise and activity intoxicating in its well-defined purpose. All the men worked together, each knowing his job and what was to be achieved. At smoko they lounged about indolently, as if they couldn't care less or ever be bothered exerting themselves, until the boss of the board said time was up and they sprang into action again and the hubbub resumed—shears hissing, rouseabouts moving feverishly to clean and clear, more men picking up and throwing the fleeces on the table so the classer could assess the quality and fling them into the appropriate bin ready for the presser to do a lot of stomping, then work the lever and screw the wool down into compact square bales.

Bessie watched them admiringly. Reg and a couple of his mates chatted with her in the breaks as she sat with her legs dangling from a bale, kicking nervously while a newly discovered coyness tinged her banter and her laugh. Bessie was *mardong* for him in no time. Besotted. Hopelessly. She was flirting. So was he.

'What time do you knock off?' he asked.

She went home to the house Mr Officer had given them to get ready for her evening chores. Up at the homestead she did as she always did—had her meal, washed all the dishes after the boss and his Missus had eaten, then put them away and swept the floor.

'When you see the light go out, I'm coming home,' she had told him.

And he was waiting. He walked her home, past the wool shed and the shearers' quarters to her house. Ulie liked her daughter's new friend a lot.

'Ahh!' she would say, a joking inference, along with approval and permission, contained within. Bessie brushed it aside.

'He's just a friend,' she insisted.

Reg and his two mates all had eyes for Bessie. Sometimes the two mates waited together for her, intending to see her safely home themselves. But Reg would appear and cut them out. When he took her hand, Bessie thought life could never get any better. They spent every spare hour together, happy just to be with each other. And at night they would climb on top of the piles of bales in the wool shed and sit talking until the morning. And, in Bessie's words, loving up. Reg took to snoring in his tea breaks at work. After all, a bloke's got to get his sleep sometime.

All three young men were welcome at Ulie's house and often turned up in the evening together to play cards with Ulie, Bessie and Pearlie. But Ulie couldn't join properly in this whitefella game, unable to understand its intent or how to get a result. It didn't help that she could neither read nor write, her daughters having the advantage of acquiring enough knowledge to slowly read the numbers, and Bessie even managing a few words elsewhere as well. However, she did manage to win a few games when Reg put her in, tossed five bob on the table and helped her play her hand.

'*Ah Wabiji*,' she said gratefully whenever he helped.

'Don't be silly,' Bessie shot back, 'oh my son-in-law' not being her idea of small talk. Reg always looked quizzically at Bessie, seeking a translation. Which was never supplied.

For the most part, though, Ulie watched and talked, this card and gambling business not for her. Instead she liked the company.

The shearing season came to an end, as Bessie knew it would, and Reg left, on the way back to his city life after this final wool shed on that run. Bessie didn't cry—she had known it would probably be like this, a come-and-go one, a romance with a time limit, destined to finish with the last fleece bagged. But she hoped and hoped, wondering when she would see him again, always on the lookout, dreaming of another shearing season or a chance meeting. Which came, in a fashion, when Bessie saw his photo in the Perth paper not long after. No more wool sheds for Reg. He had won the lottery. Bessie knew then she hadn't. But she treasured the memories. Any mention of Reg would always bring out the giggles, bashful ones. Even forty years later.

Shearing over, Pearlie's baby Gavin now born with Ulie's assistance, the station quiet again, and with the Officers' absence sadly obvious once more, Ulie and Bessie finally made up their minds. They would risk it all, risk never finding another home, leave the security they had and chance it, like all Yamatjis not permanently connected to stations had to do. They departed Woolgorong, their home, Ulie leaving the little house which had always filled her with pride, the bloom-filled garden which she had lovingly tended, the place she thought was hers forever. Young Bessie was not losing as much. She left with happy times to remember and an eagerness at what she would find somewhere else. Ulie and Bessie went, abandoning Dingo Jim's promised land.

Mr Lanagan drove them in to Mullewa, the car loaded with bags and bedding. And Ulie's wireless carefully wrapped, along with Bessie's gramophone and her few records, the Slim Dusty one, the Dusty Rankin and Buddy Williams.

'I'll take you in for a holiday,' he said. 'If you want to come back, you can.'

But the spell had been broken and they had come down to earth, their dependence again laid bare. Their move was a determination to have some say in their lives, to choose, even if they did have to leave the cherished house behind, even if they did lack money, and even if, as 'natives', the state-imposed regulations and restrictions always loomed. Ulie went to stay with the Comeagains in their combined bough shed, hut and tent, an improvised dwelling on the southern side of town, the area the Yamatjis were allowed to be, before heading out to where Pearlie and baby Gavin were camped in the bush while Joe worked on farms nearby. She missed Woolgorong, missed her home, the contentment and constancy gone. But there was little she could do. She existed where she had to, where she could, with no income at all. And like all Yamatjis, she knew tent life well. Bessie headed to Agina near Northampton, to a cousin who borrowed her gramophone and went up the scrub to work. She never got it back. But she didn't worry since it was with family. She could get another, she thought. Ulie guarded her wireless carefully wherever she went. She understood what the chances were.

The following year Bessie gave birth to her first child, Marion, an adored and welcomed baby—but Reg was not baby Marion's father. Bessie, too innocent and unworldly to know how to counter pressure, had been seduced by another man. This was not the only time it would happen. It was not long before her attractiveness was noted and she was persuaded again. And a second baby was on the way.

Chapter Sixteen

'I don't think I'll be making it to the hospital,' Bessie said to her mother around daybreak, on Bullardoo Station.

'Ah, the boss comin',' replied Ulie without a hint of panic.

And she began preparing, a bucket of warm water ready, some Dettol which she now always had on hand, an old mattress and some freshly washed sheets.

Dorrie Cameron's husband Siddy was enjoying his breakfast in the sun at the side of the small three-roomed tin hut, but as soon as a few screams made it obvious what was happening inside, his meal had been scoffed. He was gone.

'He's not gunna sit around here,' laughed Dorrie, making

light of what they all knew. This was women's business, babies were women's business, and Siddy could never have stayed, even if he did normally live there, he and his wife sharing the hut with Ulie.

'It's a little boy,' Ulie announced.

'Ah,' said Bessie, happy. Her son Ernest, soon to be known as Ernie, had been born, 31 July, 1956.

'No-one will ever know,' her new baby's father, a married man Yamatji way, had whispered to Bessie when he enticed her that one time. But he was wrong. Even if his name would never openly be mentioned. Even if another man's name had been given to the authorities who insisted on one. The outcome was her son, Bessie's own source of joy, and later in life she enjoyed the irony, the clanging error in the man's utterance. Her son would indeed become known. By many, throughout Australia. But she bore the man no malice, was never bitter, bitterness at the creation of a child never a Yamatji mother's response. She had her son, whom she loved dearly. She just smiled, always smiled. Bessie, twenty-four years old, and no longer with the freedom to be giddy whenever she wanted, was assuming the same stoic dignity as her mother, as her brother, as her father before. With two children now she had responsibilities she had to learn to meet. Bessie simply moved on, had to get on with scraping a living. But she did think of Reg every now and then, glad to know how tender a man could be. And a good daydream would always help.

Mr and Mrs Jenson, the station owners, came running, alerted by Siddy going the other way. They fussed and peered, excited that a baby had been born on their property, and paid for a taxi to take Bessie in for medical attention to nearby Mullewa.

Bessie didn't go back after her stay in hospital. She wasn't employed by Bullardoo and had no claim on their hospitality, having only been visiting her mother, waiting for her time to come. Now she had to find somewhere to live. Leaving Marion with Ulie, she stayed in the town, joining the women living on a small hill on the side where all the Yamatjis had to live, a small band of women with children, all living in tents. Bessie settled in, sharing a tent with baby Ernie, enduring the bitterly cold winter nights and when the rain came, the mud. One of the women, Mrs Thompson, had somehow managed to erect a tin breakwind for her camp. Tottie was there now Bonner had passed away, with five children, her grandchildren and a nephew, sending them to school every day, battling to make sure they could learn to read and write, the children's parents, Clarrie and Cecil among them, working on the outlying stations and sending money every month. The older children carted water from a tap down the road, and a fence and nearby trees were decorated with clothes hung to dry whenever the rain stopped. Yet when Margaret Moorhead came to pick Bessie and baby up, Bessie to help in her house, she noticed how tidy and clean it was. There seemed an affinity between Yamatji women and home-made bush brooms in and around Mullewa, many a station yard so swept the men chuckled and wondered if any gravel would be allowed to remain in the whole of the Murchison area. But the cause of such obsessiveness gave no opportunity for any real chuckling, resulting as it did from the need to be acceptable to the white people. If they weren't, all Yamatjis knew the consequences. Women lived under the constant worry of being labelled unfit, of Welfare calling and the children being removed, Tottie with first-hand experience of how they could and would do that. And the men knew spells in gaol if termed troublemakers, usually after crossing a whiteman, leaving their families vulnerable to more interference from the authorities because of their absence and alleged bad influence.

'Hey, coon, come here, coon,' the whiteman said, as was his habit, to Johnny Comeagain, the local champion boxer who, it always appeared on the surface, was accepted in the town. And he had no choice but to comply, presenting himself without comment, knowing what cost it would be to resist or to answer back. His only means of retaining some self-respect was to go away muttering under his breath, 'I'd like to punch that bloke one day.' But he knew he never could. He knew what it would mean, for both himself and his family.

Johnny Comeagain and his fellow Yamatjis knew the pressures to be one of the tamed-down 'good natives', knew they were to remain silent about all such treatment or sub-standard conditions or wages. Most did, recognising the risks if they did not. They had few options. And they knew the pressure didn't ease even if they were genuinely sick. Yamatji men with families to support who were living at the reserve, the only place on offer, and who managed to find seasonal work at the wheat farms, worked even when ill or injured, scared of losing their jobs and of being labelled unreliable with no chance of further work. Fellow Yamatjis knowing the score tried to cover for them, did double, let them rest if the boss wasn't about. It could happen to any of them, any time. Mullewa and the Murchison regrettably weren't all in Mr Officer's mould. Eddie Peet, one of the mail truck drivers, was always saddened when he brought a Yamatji worker into town from an outlying station, the man having worked for sometimes as many as six months straight and only ten pounds in his hand, the wage he had earned over and above his 'keep', his food and board for the time. The Yamatji could not complain, or his job would be gone, and so did not. Eddie would bring those workers to town, where they were expected to have a nice time staying at the reserve.

Mail truck drivers constantly travelled between the stations and Eddie Peet and his brothers saw much during their contract time. They knew all the Yamatjis who rode the truck with them, chatted with them, got the family histories, the latest news, knew them all as people. The prevailing town attitudes were not for them. Margaret Moorhead was a member of the Peet family as well. Bessie enjoyed working for Margaret, having known her ever since she was still fancy-free and living on Woolgorong. Back then, Bessie had come into town accompanying Ulie, who was in hospital for a couple of weeks, and after buying a few necessities and chatting at the general store Margaret's mother Mrs Peet owned, Mrs Peet offered her work for however long Ulie was in care. Bessie even helped in the shop.

Mrs Peet was a woman of strength, hardworking, steadfast and kind. Originally from Scotland, sent as a teenager with just a brother to make a better life for themselves, she had struggled, knowing loneliness, loss and tough times. She now extended her hand to others. When any Yamatjis waited outside her shop early in the morning, ready to catch the mail truck back to their work on the stations, she would appear with a steaming jug of tea in her hand and a plate loaded with toast topped with sausage meat and tomato sauce, knowing they had walked a distance from the reserve or camps nearby and had not eaten. She would never let anyone go hungry, even if she was struggling herself. And once when she saw a poor Yamatji gone silly from laced alcohol being attacked, kicked to the ground and cruelly booted, she marched out of her shop onto the footpath and belted the attacker, a local whiteman, on the back with her dustpan and brush until he stopped. No-one would be kicked, no-one would be pushed into any gutter, irrespective of race or colour or sobriety, while she was around.

Margaret had inherited her mother's generous nature. And Bessie, in town without an income, suddenly had some work to do, every second day, until she could find a station job. The pay wasn't much, Margaret's husband Harry still establishing his clothing business in the town after starting out hawking clothes around the stations from the boot of his car, and they were not overly flush themselves yet. But it was enough to feed Bessie and her son, enough to keep going, and she was able to wash and dry the baby clothes while she was there, Ernie treated like a visiting dignitary. Margaret always lifted her own new baby, Julie, out of the cot, her place taken by a very contented young boy. Comfort like this was unknown, Bessie not owning a pram or even a bed for him to share.

Margaret and Bessie's arrangement worked for both of them. Margaret, in line with the times and with the other white women in the town, would never venture down the street unless immaculately dressed and coordinated, in a smart frock, mostly home-made, and accessories, her children equally well attired, matching ribbons, shiny shoes, the works. It was a lengthy undertaking to get ready, especially with two children, and therefore attempted only once a week, mainly on Tuesdays, clinic days. Bessie, then, was much-needed company and a friend for as many of those housebound days as Margaret could arrange. The two spent a lot of the time just yarning.

Mrs Peet's shop, the mail truck depot for the many years her sons had the contract, was an unofficial employment office. Word always passed through there, brought back by Bill, Eddie, Obbie or Don, about which stations had jobs going. Mrs Peet told Bessie, and Bessie, with baby, went off to Mt Narryer.

It was a big station, with a magnificent homestead built of local stone. With its arches, verandahs, timber panelled fireplaces and high exposed beams inside, and sprawling wings to either side of the main rooms, Mt Narryer was the embodiment of just about every squatter's dream, and therefore had a staff of eighteen people to keep it functioning smoothly. Mt Narryer was now owned from afar and managed by Mr and Mrs Shean. Bessie liked the new Missus and, knowing her job, quickly had the house organised her way. Baby Ernie, though, did his best to spread a little chaos. Seated in the pram lent by the station, he would drain the last few drops from his glass baby's bottle and casually fling it away, Bessie's lunges not always ending in a save. On the stone floors and the slate verandahs outside, Ernie managed to smash the four bottles Bessie had for him, as well as the dozen Ulie had sent up when requested.

As he grew bigger and started pulling himself up, Bessie would find him out on the flat, pushing the pram through the sand over from their quarters in a modified hangar heading into the Never-Never. Sometimes she left him with Boomer, an old Yamatji man who had worked on the station for years. Boomer loved to take him, and sat patiently talking and playing with him, feeding him pieces of damper fried in emu oil.

New managers came, Norm Armstrong and his recent bride Val. To be in charge of Mt Narryer homestead was a daunting task for the inexperienced. And Val, at first, was terrified at the responsibility which confronted her on the sprawling station and the unfamiliar world of organising staff. Norm, who had worked on stations with Yamatji people for years, breezed into his role, and immediately demanded the city-based owners pay the Yamatji stockmen under him the same as the whitefellas. He was successful. Val took a while. There was the cook she had to deal with, the gardener, the girls in the house. And then there was Bessie, who had a system in place and didn't want it altered. They had words. And Bessie decided to depart, heading back to her mother who was now living on the outskirts of Mullewa on the way to the reserve, in a patched-up rough and tumble structure on a block of land Les and Cecil had bought between them for their Mums, for the women who had been friends since small girls together on Yallalong Station and for the children the women looked after. Bessie and Ernie joined them all there, Bessie taking little notice of the contrast with where she had been. Family was what mattered, where she belonged, kin and a sense of self always more important than fancy buildings, especially someone else's. Ulie was here in search of permanence, Woolgorong not her only recent heartache. And she'd done enough grieving in her life.

After giving up the much-loved house Mr Officer had said was hers for as long as she wanted, Ulie had accepted a place with the Scotts of Dalgety Downs in the Gascoyne, where Joe and Pearlie, Les and Owen had all worked at one stage. She liked warm Mr and Mrs Scott and had gladly gone, meeting again those who had been kind to Bessie when she had visited on her holiday. All the people there helped to ease the loss she still felt after leaving Woolgorong. She became happy again, part of a family and treated as more than just the help in the house, the help with the children.

But the Scotts were only co-owners in the property and, seeking a station of their own, bought one at Winton, Queensland, asking her to go too, wanting her to stay with them. Ulie, forced to make the most painful of decisions, decided to stay near her own family. She was torn, and the deep sadness she'd felt at losing the Officers returned. As the loaded truck moved out on its way east, she once again cried. And went to Bullardoo Station after Mrs Peet found her the job, then moving into town as soon as Les and Cecil bought the land. They wanted both their mothers to have their own place, Cecil wanting to free Tottie, his mother, and his own and Clarrie's children from tent life, Les enabling Ulie to finish up station work, after all those years. She was tired, getting on, and now able to carry out only the lightest of duties.

The scrappy structure which Ulie had largely erected by herself, with some help from Tottie, and Les when he was in from the stations, was all her own, no-one else's, no matter how unappealing or how far short of many white people's standards. Her home, which was to become Ernie's home for the next seven years, was merely a humpy, a dwelling with three sections, one of them without a roof and another a bough shed, with no water or electricity and warmed in winter by a firebucket dragged inside. Water for washing and drinking had to be carted, as well as wood for cooking. Floorboards didn't exist, bare ground fulfilling that role, covered with a patchwork of different linoleum pieces recovered from the rubbish tip. And the furniture consisted of an old double bed and a couple of cupboards given by white ladies from the town. But Ulie didn't see poverty, although she knew times were now very tough. What she did see above all else was some certainty, a permanent home which, if they were left alone by the authorities, could not disappear before her eyes like the others. The land and the dwelling, which both families referred to as 'Between the Lines', would make sure Ulie would never have to start all over again, unless it was a move of her choosing. And she could stop working so hard, rest for a while.

Bessie went back to work, Mrs Peet passing on the word to people who came into her shop. Bessie walked into town every day and did the washing, ironing, scrubbing and polishing floors, whatever the townspeople wanted, a few hours here, a few there, leaving Marion and Ernie in Ulie's full-time care. Sometimes she worked at the farms nearby, working away from home. Ulie didn't mind, a Yamatji grandmother always having responsibilities towards the grandchildren. But if Bessie's job was in town and she was late returning when her work had long finished, Ulie knew her daughter had been simply yarning and visiting. Ulie would quickly remind her of her role these days.

'Why didn't you come home,' she would say. 'You got kids home.'

She taught Bessie to leave the last vestiges of her girlhood behind. Life was different now, as Bessie was becoming well aware. She was a mother and had to provide for her children somehow. Her meagre earnings and a small payment of child endowment were all she had, with the hourly rate paid by the townspeople who didn't have much themselves was low. With gramophones now a vague memory from another lifetime, she would sometimes buy small luxuries to take back to her mother and children—tomato sauce, jam, camp pie—and they would feel wealthy for a couple of days.

Ulie continued as she always did, never fully allowing it all to drag her down, even if she did occasionally think back to how life had been on Woolgorong. But times were sometimes too hard, the land and dwelling not enough to sustain her. Once again she had no income. Les and the boys sent a little money each month if they had work which paid them more than just their food and board. However, sometimes destitution seemed too close for comfort. So she walked into the Welfare office in town and applied for a pension, ignoring how the law and the official white world viewed so called full-bloods. They were not to be assisted, not to receive what every white person born on Australian soil received. Aboriginal people of full-descent didn't make it on the scale which determined acceptability.

A sympathetic Welfare officer wrote on her behalf several

times, notified in reply that Ulie must first be 'exempted', by applying to be excused from what she was, Aboriginal. To receive a government pension, even though she had worked since she was ten years old and even though cheap Aboriginal labour had indisputably built the pastoral industry in Australia, she had to apply for a Certificate of Exemption. She would then be released from her Aboriginality, from the jurisdiction of the Native Welfare Act, 1905–1954.

A report on her suitability was duly submitted. Her character was listed as excellent, her social behaviour unreproachable, but her degree of assimilation as only satisfactory. The section for remarks must have redeemed her:

'Mrs Dingo is an exceptional type of native, well spoken, well mannered, clean in her person and her camp,' the Welfare officer wrote.

So she passed the test, pronounced acceptable by the lofty condescension of being deemed 'an exceptional type of native'. Ulie, the acceptable, exceptional native, was granted leave from her nativeness, Certificate of Exemption No. A1391, and was allocated a widow's pension of six pounds fifteen shillings a fort-night in September 1957.

Between the Lines was about two kilometres out of town, an open expanse of dirt with little vegetation no-one else was in a hurry to own. Ulie had her camp one side, Tottie the other, and a small area was left in the middle for sitting around the fire. On the southern side was the railway line to Perth, taking the region's wool and wheat delivered to the town by station trucks. To the north, over the Mullewa–Meekatharra line, was a creek, then a patch of ground in its natural state known as the common, a rifle range, and then the best bit of all for Ulie's grannies, a salt flat, with a windmill and a tank stuck in the middle. To the east was thick scrub, a small rise with gum trees, then a slaughterhouse before the wheat fields began again, and to the west, way past the stretch of dirt, the road to town. Marion and Ernie, and Tottie's grandchildren and nephews, thought it paradise, their own adventureland.

Tottie's grandsons—Clarrie and Cecil's boys—Patrick and Crummy Whitehurst, had built a cubby house up the back in the bushes, a boys' retreat. Owen's young son Bruce was there too, in Ulie's care now that Owen's marriage had ended. The girls were obliged to build their own shaky fort, from which they sallied forth to raid the boys. Little Ernie was allowed to sit with the bigger boys, watching the important business going on. When they all set off to the common, boys and girls together, to get *bimba*, the hardened toffee-like sweet sap from a gum tree, Marion and Ernie went too, carrying empty powdered-milk tins ready for good pickings of the bush lolly which hung tantalisingly from the trees like dripping honey. Then there would be the inevitable fight over the division of the spoils, with whatever happened to be left over eventually taken home where the adults ignored their tales of conquest as they began eagerly munching away themselves.

'You mob have to share, share it around,' they would say. Nonetheless, the kids thought it was a bit unfair that the grown-ups, who hadn't been on the *bimba* hunt themselves, seemed to end up with the biggest chunk.

In springtime there was always lots of tucker around. The kids went out after *gogolas* (bush bananas), *gulyu* (yams) and wild onions, all eaten either raw or cooked in the coals. They also dug up the seed which when crushed and mixed with water became a vivid red ink, used by lawmen for body-marking. The kids painted many a rock red and wrote their names on trees, the rain washing it all away so they could start over again.

Once a fortnight, they were scrubbed almost to the *jhullo*, the marrow, dressed in their best and taken into town, a big playful group with Ulie and Tottie rousing on them and urging them to be quiet because the widpellas would be watching. Ernie was still a little fella, about eighteen months old, when he first decided to branch out and leave the security of his mob, his likeness to his Uncle Les showing early. He had first been dunked at the enamel basin with the cold soapy water and then, fully spruced and polished, put into the short-legged yellow bib-and-brace number which Ulie kept in a tin trunk out of harm's way with her own good town dress. Both were reserved for days like this. Most Yamatji women had one best dress, the men one good shirt, and as always before any special outing, Ulie carefully washed the garment and hung it out to dry with a minimum of creases on the wire strung between the trees. Cherubic Ernie, with his shorts, big tummy, dark skin and golden curly hair, looked a treat. He was ready. The others weren't. So off he went, setting off a major search-and-rescue operation when his absence was noticed.

'Baldy, Baldy,' they called, using the nickname Clarrie's son Patrick had given him as a baby and which had well and truly stuck. Bessie, Ulie, Tottie and the string of grannies spread out and looked, peering into bushes and all the other places the kids normally went.

Way up the road outside her house, Mrs McArley, a white woman, waved a hanky high above her head, the signal country people mostly used to attract attention. On her hip sat a little boy in a bright yellow suit wondering why his solitary trip to town had been so abruptly curtailed. After all, he was clean, and he had sixpence. But it was merely a temporary setback, and certainly didn't stop further attempts.

'Where that boy now?' was the constant refrain.

Bessie couldn't watch over him as much as she wanted. Work was necessary wherever it could be found and she was frequently away. It was the same for all Yamatji people who relied on the stations for their existence. Family life was disrupted. Bessie did what she had to do, but missed her children and would take them with her for short spells when she could. She took young Ernie for a time on Mellenbye Station, where he went off by himself again, an intrepid tracker after a pet joey which had escaped the yard. Bessie followed his trail through the sand to arrive just in time. Ernie, upset the baby 'roo wouldn't wait for him, was standing above it with a stick held high in both hands, all set to clobber and capture it, his interpretation of a rescue.

'Baldy!' Bessie yelled, scooping up both hunter and hunted before any damage was done.

Bessie enjoyed her children's antics, though she was grateful that Ulie was there to share the load, ever willing to take over when her daughter had to leave them with her. But one day Bessie was alarmed to learn that Ulie had had a stroke and was being treated in the Meathouse at Mullewa hospital. Despite Mrs Broad, the wife of the Mellenbye Station owner, phoning the hospital daily for her, Bessie was unable to calm down, the memory of her father's decline in the same place still vivid after all these years. She finished her job and hurried back to town.

Ulie was sitting up in bed, looking out through the wire-mesh windows. She looked alert and healthy, but Bessie's heart almost caved in when she spotted her mother's crooked mouth, saw the slack facial muscles and watched as she struggled to drink without spilling any. Bessie broke down and started to cry.

'Don't worry, I'm right,' Ulie whispered.

In time she was allowed to go home and her facial muscles gradually recovered. But she was obviously not well, although she persevered as ever, the poverty she was caught in not giving her much choice. Ernie and the other kids raced around together, unaware of their grandmother's condition, life a breeze when there were so many playmates at hand. Tottie, now also old, looked after seven of them, while Ulie was in charge of a shifting number as various relatives left their children with her, sometimes for years at a time while they worked. Ulie bore it all, her Yamatji duty to love and to guide her grannies, with a good dose of strict discipline when called for. For several years she looked after a boy whose mother claimed he was fathered by Les but who later took him back, introducing him to another family as their relative instead. And now she looked after Audrey, a new sister for Marion and Ernie, who in time became her favourite.

Ernie, older now and able to join in all the play, was brought up fully aware of where all the children and visiting adults fitted in the Dingo family structure, hearing the complicated relationship terms used so often. Bruce, his first cousin in the European interpretation of family, was his brother. And Bruce, four years older, became his protector and mentor, able to do anything according to young Ernie. Sunshine Bruce called him, though Ernie didn't know whether it was because of the powdered-milk tins they all carried or his sunbleached hair. Bruce had nicknames for everyone. They walked together up the dry creekbed, on their way to the rubbish tip over on the northern side of town where there were so many wonderful and useful things to be found. The kids would spread out, holding their booty high for the others to see, sometimes toys or sometimes just scraps of lino to help cover the dirt floor at home. The towns-people's discards were always handy, with many items serving to ease the burden of living for them. They found a set of pram axles and wheels and constructed a cart to carry water to the camp from the government well they relied on some distance away, the one where the sheep and cattle used to come. Ulie and Bessie taught Bruce how to bail the water out into a drum, and when it was loaded on the wagon Marion, Ernie and the other kids would all strain and push it home. Sometimes they wondered why they did it when they felt that cold water at bath time.

'No good singin' out,' Ulie would say.

They made other carts just to muck about in and hare across the flat, but the tip provided the best fun when they collected the components to make the most universal of boys' weapons, the shanghai. It took only a piece of rubber from an inner tyre tube, cut with a piece of broken glass, the tongue from an old shoe for the pouch and a shoelace. Ernie thought he was really a bona fide big boy when the others allowed him to carry such a potent implement. But Ulie, Tottie and Bessie wouldn't allow the weapons in or near the house, confiscating them immediately. The boys kept a secret stash and got them out to use away from the camp. Out bush on the stations the shanghais were called *guwiyarl* (goanna) guns, so accurate and effective were they at felling those big lizards, as well as rabbits and birds. In town the boys made old jam tins jump across the flat, denting them until they were shapeless. Further away they couldn't resist taking potshots at galahs and pigeons, such good tucker and Bruce in particular such a good shot. The kids all plucked and gutted them, cooking them in the coals and enjoying the feast.

There were many areas to explore around their house. Sometimes they'd walk to the slaughterhouse and help pen up the animals or just stand and gawk. Often they'd be sent to buy tripe, the workmen cutting the cow's stomach lining from the carcass there and then, the kids carrying it home to Ulie in a hessian bag for her to either boil or fry for them all to eat.

For the grown-ups, days weren't always fun-filled. Each person had to eke out an existence somehow, and Bessie still continued to work wherever she could. But work was not continuously available on the Murchison and Gascoyne stations and often depended on mustering and shearing times, for women as well as men. So Bessie branched out and, like her mother before her, took a few turns as a musterers' cook, away from her children for longer periods of time.

Les also did as most Yamatjis, moving from station to station when the word was passed a job was going. Having bought himself an old truck, he now had the means to go dogging for a crust if other work wasn't on offer, as well as kangaroo shooting, sending the meat to the big towns where it was used as pet food. His skill in whatever he did was always admired. During one of the mustering seasons on Byro Station, Harry Moorhead had been doing his rounds selling clothes to the workers, hawkers always welcome in these remote places as shops were too far away. Les, Owen and Joe offered to take him with them over the desert-like plains scattered with fossils and rocks resembling inverted ice-cream cones. Eager not to miss this rare chance, he rang his wife Margaret back in Mullewa to postpone his daughter Helen's christening, saying it could happen any old time whereas watching the Dingos and Joe in action out there was a chance in a lifetime. 'The buggers could shoot, you know,' he says. He looked on in admiration as they casually lined the kangaroos up with their .22s and dropped them, then sharpened their knives on the pads of the animals' feet to get a decent edge, before gutting them and stacking them ready to send off. The christening took place when Harry finally got back.

Times in between Les spent with his family, helping Ulie when he could. He would often bring them much-welcomed kangaroo for tucker and, knowing the condition of their mother's hut, he and his brothers were constantly on the lookout for any spare pieces of tin from the stations. They all took their turn at hammering them up. Ulie too would bang away and often nursed sore fingers and thumbs. But despite the add-ons, the partial roof still leaked from the mass of old nail-holes in the tin. They patched as many as they could with road tar, but somehow the water still came in. Ulie sighed, erected a tent inside, dug a ditch beside the lino and battled on. Nothing else could be done.

The open-air picture theatre in town was always a special night for everyone and Les decided to take a couple of the kids along. A cowboy movie was playing. Jimmy, in from Yallalong Station where he now worked, came along too, together with Les Clayton and his young son Big John. They walked into town and joined the other Yamatjis in the segregated section where they were forced to sit.

The camp was quiet, the kids asleep inside, many to a mattress, and a small fire burned low between the two dwellings. The family was sitting around talking after sharing their evening meal. It was a full house, even if they were mostly out in the open. Les Clayton's wife Marge had come over with the rest of her kids and new baby Barbara while her husband was at the pictures. He was a whitefella who had married Marge, a cousin of Ulie's from Mooney Mia, some time back. Joe and Pearlie were there also, together with another station hand named Bob, having come into town to deliver a mob of cattle. Joe, who had obtained citizenship rights in 1951 and was therefore now permitted to drink, had a carton of beer on the back of the truck. He and Bob started drinking, but Bob, unused to alcohol, quickly got drunk and, desperate for tobacco, climbed a tree to get some leaves to chew which would give the same hit.

Shortly afterwards, Les and company arrived back from the movies.

Les was concerned to see what was happening, particularly Bob's unwelcome behaviour at his mother's place. His mate Les Clayton sat down on a stool beside Marge, unknowingly taking Bob's seat. Drunk out of his mind, Joe's fellow worker went berserk, swearing profusely and wanting to fight them all. Les told him to cut out the bad language in front of the women and children.

But his command didn't penetrate and the profanities continued, the man still wanting to fight and Les twice refusing the stoush he was after. Tottie, Pearlie and Ulie sat looking at the fire, attempting to ignore the fella's silliness. It was only when Les saw the bottle in Bob's hand raised ready to come down on his mother's head that he moved and, deflecting the blow the crazed man swung at him, flattened him with two powerful punches.

After Bessie and Pearlie sponged the unconscious man down, Les checked to see that he was all right and breathing easily. Then he and Les Clayton got him into his swag, and put him on a mattress to sleep it off, next to the truck. Deciding the disturbance had signalled an end to the night, Les and Marge Clayton went home up the track, not far from Ulie's camp.

'He still asleep,' said Joe appearing the following morning. 'That bloke Bob—and all this black stuff, everything, is comin' out his mouth.'

Their whitefella friend Les Clayton, who was more familiar with all the ways of the white world, might know what should be done. Pearlie had sponged him down again, but something wasn't right. They were concerned, though they had done all they could, they thought.

'You'd better go and get a taxi,' Les Clayton ordered, even

though Bob seemed to be snoring evenly. With only one taxi servicing the town, it was an hour before Horrie Peet turned up and by the time they got over the railway crossing not far from the camp on the way to the hospital, the man's snoring suddenly stopped.

'He's finished,' Les Clayton said to Horrie. They were all in shock. Les Dingo saw the implications immediately.

'Well, I gotta tell them the truth,' he said. 'I gotta tell them like it happened.'

'Oh. What happened?' Horrie asked.

'I hit him,' he said.

'You better not say that,' Horrie advised the man who through his rodeo riding and pleasing manner had become liked by just about the whole Mullewa community, the man with the laugh they were now calling the Kookaburra. Instead, the cab driver suggested what he considered a better course of action.

Les detoured into town to buy shaving gear, then presented himself to the police.

'Mullewa Native Committed on Killing Charge,' said the 1961 headline in the *Geraldton Guardian*.

Les Dingo, the man who valued holding his head high, was in gaol. Ulie was in torment—and fearful.

Chapter Seventeen

The *Geralton Guardian*'s report of the case was brief but dramatic.

After lengthy evidence had been presented at a preliminary hearing in the Mullewa Police Court on Monday last, a thirty eight year old native laborer named Leslie Dingo, of Mullewa, was committed for trial at the June sitting of the Court of Sessions at Geraldton on a manslaughter charge.

He will stand trial on an accusation that at Mullewa on February 25th he unlawfully killed a native station hand aged about thirty five years of Mt Narryer Station.

Ulie visited him every second day when he was in the Mullewa lockup, thinking up interesting things to say, wanting to help her son. Clean-shaven through it all, Les was holding up well. '*Barndi*' (good), he would shout back to Yamatjis who sang out to see he was all right, as they went by. He was determined to stay calm and appear cheerful. But he was soon moved away to the coast, to the Geraldton gaol, and visiting was harder. In the two months he was there, Ulie only managed one trip.

In Mullewa at Between the Lines, 100 kilometres away from where Les was, Ulie broke down several times thinking of her son locked up and all by himself. It was true he had always been independent, but she knew his singular stance was solidly rooted in the knowledge his family was forever available, not too far away. Now she worried that she couldn't be there, that no-one was.

But she thought even more about the frightening ordeal yet to come, the trial where her son would be judged and a decision handed down and the white police could take another son from her. For the two months she waited, she moved mostly in a daze, finding it hard to think of much else. And what she did think about was grim. After all, he was a Yamatji in the widpellas' court.

The trial was looming and the prospective witnesses were worried, scared just like Ulie, and Les Clayton had to keep emphasising they were all to tell the truth and not to go changing the story, not to think they would be able to save Les by giving a false version. Things had already gone wrong when Les had taken Horrie's advice, going against his initial desire to simply tell the truth. The taxi driver urged him to claim he had ducked Bob's punch and the fellow had consequently fallen over him and hit his head on the ground. But it didn't convince the police. They seemed to think they had a cut-and-dried case. Two different stories, and surely only the guilty with any cause to lie. But for those not fully familiar with the whiteman's processes, yet who knew how a Yamatji's treatment could swing either way and how the white-man's power could be applied, there would always be doubt at receiving fair play. Les wavered for an instant, then regained his courage, determined to face the consequences whatever they were.

And the consequences, it appeared, were more time in gaol. Announcing Les's committal for trial on the charge, the stipendiary magistrate set bail at two hundred pounds with an identical surety also required, a huge amount for the underpaid Yamatjis.

'Leslie Dingo has been known to me for some ten years,' the letter from the District Welfare officer to the head office of the Department of Native Welfare stated when setting out Les's application for legal assistance, 'but has had very little official contact with this Department as he is completely capable of managing his everyday affairs, and takes a pride in doing so. Indeed, his mother, brothers and sister are all outstanding in this regard ...'

Yet the application submitted for him by the Native Welfare department to the Western Australian Law Society showed he had cleared only fourteen pounds over and above his keep in the previous six months. His assets were listed as one half-share in a two-acre building block, the 'Between the Lines' he co-owned with Cecil Whitehurst, with a full value of approximately one hundred pounds, a twenty-four-year-old 1937 Ford truck, valued at fifty pounds, and a .22 rifle, worth five pounds. Not nearly enough to buy his freedom. And he certainly could not borrow the bail from Ulie, his mother having worked totally without pay for the major part of her life. Les, it seemed, would have to remain in custody.

However, he was lucky. He would not have to do the same as most Yamatjis in his position and remain imprisoned after all. The Shanahans, who owned the recently burnt out Crown Hotel in Mullewa and were temporarily trading from a shed, paid the money and put up the surety, a gratefully received gesture but one set to confuse. When some years later all Aboriginal people were permitted to drink, the Shanahans still segregated Yamatji men in a separate bar from whites, and refused to serve any Yamatji women inside, including those merely wanting soft drinks. The Yamatji women were allocated an area outside and served through a small hole in the wall. Les was free because of the Shanahans' generosity, at least for a while—but it came at a price, one the widpellas would probably never have understood. Les, who longed to be seen as a man equal to any other, as well as remain what he was, a Yamatji, had been assisted because he had been excused from his race and allocated quasi-whitefella status. Because he was personally known to the hoteliers, Les had become in their eyes one of the 'good' natives, different from the others, different from all they didn't know and wouldn't accept.

The happy party sat together in the shed, Ulie, Bessie and Les, talking and grinning, with the Shanahans sitting in for a drink. Ulie was out of her element here, but she wanted to be anywhere with her son. She sat in her good town dress, sipping a lemon squash, and hardly spoke, just looking at him. Having him with her felt so good. But she knew there would be more to face. The trial by jury loomed. And so did a trial of different sorts.

The two months passed and the jury was in place. Les's family watched the proceedings, knowing what had really happened, but unsure they could convince these whitefellas in charge. They were tense. Pearlie was hardly able to breathe, the strain having taken its toll in the intervening time. Like Ulie, she had worried constantly and when giving evidence in the morning session she collapsed in a dead faint in the witness box. The courtroom was cleared to allow her time to recover and she then continued, but had to see a doctor as soon as she finished. Bessie too found it terrifying, never before having been called in front of 'the policeman'. She choked, she said, swallowing many times, trying to make the words come.

Some of the evidence made it look as if Les had indeed done what was claimed. Jimmy's acting out the fight, as requested by the prosecution, was almost too painful to watch. One brother, they worried, was helping convict another. And when the detective quoted Les as saying his hit was a good one—'Kid Brearley taught me to fight and said never to pull your punches'—they hung their heads in fear until Les's lawyer, Mr Franklyn addressed the jury speaking on the question of self-defence, and highlighting the fact that Les had used his fists rather than grabbing an object, such as a log or a brick. The jury retired at 4.10 p.m. and returned, with hardly time for discussion. At 4.32 p.m. they announced their verdict—not guilty.

'Joyful Scene as Native is Acquitted of Killing,' reported the *Geraldton Guardian*:

> *Blinking hard to keep back her tears, an elderly aboriginal woman joyously embraced her son minutes after he had been acquitted of a manslaughter charge by a jury of eleven men and one woman at the Geraldton Court of Session yesterday afternoon.*
>
> *The Chairman at the Court of Session … formally discharged Dingo from custody. With a dignified nod of his head, the free man left the dock and walked into the arms of his joyous mother.*

'I was real happy for that. We all were,' remembers Les Clayton. But only time would tell if there were to be lasting celebrations. Les Dingo headed straight up the bush, to the Gascoyne area, ready for the other people he would have to face. He was Dingo Jim's son, and even though acquitted, he'd been involved in a Yamatji's death. Yamatji business would now travel. There would be meetings and possible consequences. At Between the Lines, Ernie and the kids continued their play-filled days, oblivious of the drama. People came and went, some staying longer than others. Uncle Les had gone back to the stations, just as he always did.

Some of those who came were white. Welfare was checking if Ulie and Tottie were raising the kids in accordance with whitefella expectations, and sometimes the Seventh Day Adventist Church people came calling, bringing hessian bags of weeties, apples and oranges, and clothes. The kids would all peep at them in the bough shed, Ulie and Tottie, Bessie if she were there, and the white people talking together, using what seats there were—kerosene drums, or the beds the bigger boys and any visiting men always used. Ulie liked their company and appreciated them coming, as well as the honesty with which they approached her. As a result, she started to attend some of the get-togethers they organised in town at the church hall. Ernie went too. He loved waving the broom handle with the long coloured streamers.

'Who made the beautiful rainbow?' the line of little swaying, arcing rainbows sang, each brandishing a broom handle. 'I know, I know. Who made the beautiful rainbow? Because God loves us so.'

And he tried his hardest to be the first of all the kids to find the checkpoints around town in the treasure hunts. All their games were good, and the Yamatji women, some from the reserve, some the town fringe, shy but willing, talked to the white church people, eating the cakes and goodies and enjoying the outing. They were treated as people. It meant a lot.

It was time for Ernie to start school. Ulie made sure he was dressed like the others in the grey shorts and shirt uniform, and walked with him to the Catholic school in the church grounds. Tottie's grandchildren went there and it seemed the logical place to send her charges as well, Bruce and Marion having already enrolled as well. Ernie had seen the nuns in their black habits in town, so eased in without a fuss, none of it strange, except for a fleeting thought when he wondered why all the nuns were short. Still small himself, the new schoolboy was with the bigger kids properly now, and very pleased they would no longer take off and leave him during the term as they used to.

Bruce came checking on him each break, as Ulie had requested, and satisfied that everything was okay would return to his friends. And so he missed hearing most of the taunts Ernie received.

'Nigger, nigger, pull the trigger. Bang, bang, bang,' the older boys from the wheat farms sneered, feeling powerful, this new black kid all alone and an obliging target.

The puzzled Ernie could only grin, not recognising the strange words they were saying. He wanted to get on with playing, kids together, as he had always done. Bruce came round the corner, this time in time, big brother to the rescue. He king-hit them all and copped the blame when they went crying to the teachers.

The three Dingos, Bruce, Marion and Ernie, were taken from the school, Ulie not wanting trouble, and she sent them to the local government one. Ernie was happy. There were so many Yamatji kids at this school, and most of them like him. He took little notice of the shoes all the white kids wore.

Home from school they would still run as a pack, the Whitehursts, Dingos and a few strays. Patrick, Nancy, Lizzy, Robyn, Margaret, Crummy, Ian, Kevin, sometimes Pearlie's son Gavin, sometimes Hilda's children the Ryans, the occasional Boddington kid, Pearlie's eldest daughter Olive's children, the

McIntoshes, McDonalds and Marion, Ernie, Audrey and their new sister Donelle—so many they frequently formed teams, playing skittles with the milk tins stacked up, or spider, drawing huge webs in the dust, running and screaming, trying to elude capture. Even though they were all family, each team was desperate to win, no courteous holding back for your 'lations. When the winter wildgrass grew, sometimes a metre high, they crawled on their bellies in a line, making tracks, heads bobbing up, playing hide and seek. They walked in the common, watching willy wagtails building nests out of spider webs, and mudlarks busy packing mud for theirs. And in spring, such bounty was on offer. Every one of the kids would head out and return after checking on the little chicks, with armfuls of wildflowers, belly buttons, pom poms and wild orchids, and Ulie's and Tottie's falling-down tin huts, for a short while at least, looked almost like somewhere flash, despite the powdered-milk tin vases.

Each day gave the kids more time, there were games to invent, constantly renewing bush tucker to locate, and plenty of opportunities to frolic. But for Ulie and Tottie, both elderly, time was not so pleasurable. Life in a pitiful hut well out of town was hard. Both needed regular medical attention, and Ulie, who had suffered another stroke recently and was now a diabetic, had to walk to hospital each day, five kilometres there and back, in the heat, along the side of the road.

A district officer with the Native Welfare department began corresponding with head office, seeking housing for the two families closer to town. Native Welfare, now strongly alerted to both Tottie's and Ulie's plight, was just beginning to recognise that Aboriginal people, displaced and dispossessed, were in need of decent accommodation, the same as all people. Ulie signed the application with an emphatic but tilting cross, the unfamiliar pen awkward to hold. The form also stated that Jimmy, Owen and Les had all promised to help with repayments 'in the event of the applicant being in financial difficulties'. Ulie, who somehow made her money last the distance, was now receiving an age pension of ten pounds ten shillings a fortnight, with the rent for the house two pounds ten for the same period. But while they waited, Tottie passed away in the Mullewa hospital. Ulie mourned deeply for her lifelong friend. Cecil and Clarrie were grief-stricken as well. Their mother who'd found her way back had gone again.

Old Papertalk's rickety trayback truck was loaded high and pretty jampacked, even if most of the stack was *gooninye*, sad and sorry in appearance—the beds, a couple of cupboards, pots for the kitchen and clothing all not much value to anyone else. But it was the best of what they had, everything else left behind. Ulie and Bessie got a lift in, the kids all walked. They were off to town, nearly, the fringe being closer than most blackfellas had yet been allowed. It was 1964, and Ernie would soon be turning eight. The kids were excited, Ulie and Bessie glad too, proximity to services a luxury that for the most part only white people knew before.

The new house with three small bedrooms, even if thin tin on a cement block and even if the walls inside stopped twelve centimetres short of the floor, looked nothing less than a palace, those small louvre windows, one to a room, having real glass. Ulie and Bessie were relieved to be in a home where the roof didn't leak and the tin didn't require road tar. Here there was even a tap which spurted running water—albeit cold—electricity, a toilet out the back, close on an indulgence after Between the Lines, where they had used the one Ulie dug in the bush, and a wood fired copper in the combined bathroom-laundry to provide hot water.

They moved in the few pieces of furniture, Ulie lifting her precious wireless, unused but never forgotten all those years, out of her tin trunk, and carefully placing it in the fuse box, a handy built-in cupboard if ever she saw one. And the kids explored the street, noting the vacant blocks with patches of long grass shooting out of the red dirt, the ideal place for team games. They hadn't bothered to stay back selecting bedrooms, Bessie now with five children, her new daughter Virginia just crawling added to her mob, as well as Ulie and Bruce all to be accommodated in the three rooms. They understood sleeping arrangements would be as normal, many to a bed, foot to foot, Ulie sharing hers as well, Audrey always in with her.

Their new house was one of four which backed on to each other, and the block soon became known as Four Corners by all who lived there. Ulie and Bessie knew the three other families. Cecil and Shirley Whitehurst were allocated one, and the Dingo kids were glad to have playmates nearby, especially the Whitehursts again next door. The Between the Lines pack had transferred, and there was always room for more. The games would go on.

There were older houses up the other end, the street now turned into an all-Aboriginal one, the poorer white families who used to live there moved away by the Housing Commission, on to better things. Selected Aboriginal people from the reserve and outlying areas were then permitted to shift in, Welfare officers assessing and recommending who would, the need for Yamatjis to be seen as acceptable to the fore again. Welfare officers had absolute power on the making of such decisions, all of which would affect the Yamatji families for life. Indeed they could whisk children away and have them declared wards of the state for the smallest perceived infraction—or even if they didn't like the living conditions, a Native Welfare officer told me, even though the Yamatjis were living as they did, like Ulie, because they had nowhere else to go. Some Welfare officers understood the Yamatjis' plight, but many did not, a number recruited to the department because they had been patrol officers in New Guinea, their experience with 'natives' regarded as a suitable recommendation for the job. Bessie, and as a result Ernie and his sisters, had been unutterably lucky the officer who came to Between the Lines had been on their side.

Ulie continued her daily visits to the hospital, the walk now less of a struggle, the shorter distance even leaving time in the afternoon for the rest she was told she should have. But she was on hand whenever Bessie needed her, her daughter wearing herself out with kids and work around town, walking to ten houses a week, two a day. At home they worked together and the kids grew well, emotionally secure, the absence of a father unnoticed and unremarkable. There were many families the same. But every now and then Bessie did notice—and she allowed herself to long for a man who would stay, someone to be there for her kids, a longing she would let pass, no point dwelling on what wasn't. She kept on, as her mother had always done, accepting what was, doing the best she could for her children, and making sure they did what she called the right thing, just as Dingo Jim and Ulie had always tried to do for her. But they would try anything, her kids, lively, imaginative and determined as they all were. Bessie, though, remembering her own youth, was nearly always their match, and now with the new house in town, able to keep a close watch.

Up the back of the class Donald 'Ducko' Papertalk and Lexie Maher were talking when Ernie decided to play prefect, disregarding his own tendency for an attention-grabbing yarn. He turned around to shh them and Mr O'Connor summoned him to the front of the classroom, whacking him across the knuckles with a technique designed to sting. Ernie, scandalised at such injustice, strode from the classroom and up the street, bound for home, Mr O'Connor right behind.

Bessie, sweeping the yard by the gate, looked up and stopped, her broom forgotten against the fence and both hands now firmly on her hips. She waited. Ernie, examining his welts, willing them to swell higher and redder, was blinking hard, desperately trying to make tears form in time so his hard-done-by story would be magnificently heart-rending. He poured forth his account. And Bessie calmly faced the teacher.

'Is that true, Mr O'Connor?' she said. Ernie's eyes twinkled. But before he had time to gloat, she turned. To him.

'Well, if you didn't do it this time, you've probably done it before. Mr O'Connor, take this boy back to school.'

'Mu-um,' said one stunned and check-mated rebel. Bessie's manoeuvre was skilful and complete, with the adults retaining control. Ernie slouched back to class, letting the peer adulation come his way, too embarrassed to confess the betrayal to his mates.

But Ernie had been too young to know his mother's desires for her children, too young to know that she dared to entertain hope when nothing but despair seemed on offer. She had listened closely when a concerned Welfare officer said she believed education to be the way for the children to get ahead. It was an opportunity never offered her, one she would dearly have loved. Ernie and his sisters would be staying in class as long as she could manage to keep them there. She was proud they were all learning to read and write, and looked over their shoulders at their homework, trying to learn with them. She made them read their early readers out loud, and slowly copy the words out as well, always standing nearby. Sometimes they found copies she had done, Bessie at the table reading Dick and Dora, Nip and Fluff, when no-one else was home.

Once a fortnight Bessie joined the women playing cards. She was still a novice, having had little practice since Reg and his mates had lounged in their house back at Woolgorong, a long time ago. She would take the money she had allowed herself for the one day when the world was at her feet, when she had some control, cash in pocket, food in the cupboard, and the illusion of limitless opportunities, at least for a day or so. Ulie, not interested in cards, stayed home to mind the children. Bessie went for company, for friendship, and of course to catch the gossip. This time, stories had gone on far into the night at Marge Comeagain's house, Bessie not wanting it to end. And she was winning, her notes sneakily stashed down the front of her dress, coins in a neat pile in front. Ernie had come this time, playing with the other kids and listening to all the talk. But waiting too long, he fell asleep, still in his school greys.

'C'on son, we're going home,' Bessie said quietly, as she nudged him awake.

Ernie jumped up, looked at her, and decided against saying anything. She must have lost, he thought. They stepped out into the chilly midnight air, Bessie pulling her cardigan tightly across her chest, young Ernie struggling to keep her pace.

'Didja have a good time, Mum?' he called after her, wanting to offer solace.

'Well yes, son,' she said through the blackness. 'But I had to leave 'cos you was fartin' like a motor bike.' Ernie's red face lit the night.

The embarrassing scene replayed in his imagination for a short while after. But he got over it as best he could. He'd had a lifetime's training in accepting whatever happened, the good times, the bad, even the odd case of flatulence. And if his Mum would keep quiet, none of his mates would ever have to know. But he did wonder just who else had heard that motor running.

For Ernie and the kids, living on the town fringe had many benefits, among them the reduced walking time to go swimming in the Dog Hole opposite the tip, and also getting to know the town activities. Ernie and Bruce would hang on the wire fence, noses poking through, gazing at the tennis players all properly attired in their whites, and race each other to recover and chuck back any balls which came over. Sometimes they wondered if they were merely imagining it, or did those people deliberately hit a few their way, a long way out, and then turn away, signalling a donation? Arms pumping they would bolt, prize in hand, the run exhilarating, their action satisfyingly scary, Ernie not aware for many years they could simply have acknowledged it with a thank you.

Visitors were just as frequent here at Four Corners as they had been at Between the Lines, and the Uncles would all come to stay, in town for a while in between jobs, their beds just their swags at the side of the house in front of the woodheap. It was always a big deal for Bruce and Ernie when they arrived. They would watch, waiting, hanging in there, ready for when it just might happen—two bob time. Uncles Les, Owen, Friday or Jimmy, all had the same routine, it being a favourite with the men pleased to have something to give, pleased to have something which could make them feel a man before the children, in a home so dominated by women, in a wider world which didn't pay them very well and which so often told Yamatjis they didn't rate. The teasing would begin, a hand in the side pocket raising a jingle.

'You been paid?' one Uncle would say to the other, clinking away.

'Yeah, earnt my money. I been paid too.'

'I worked hard for my two bob, and I've got my own, right here.'

Ernie and Bruce waited, their longing intense, building with each delay, no matter how many times this had been played before. And into their own pocket that one silver coin each would go. It felt good, and they both constantly checked to see if it was still there, pressing it into their skin. The familiar internal struggle was then in motion. To spend or not to spend, reluctance and want doing battle, such wealth rarely coming their way. Mullewa was a dusty place, and for many months overbearingly hot, the heat influencing such a tough decision. Frozen oranges from the swimming pool kiosk generally won out. And strangely so did they. The sound of the left-over money, the change, was even more thrilling, several pennies in a pocket producing a jingle-jingle so loud, and suggesting such infinite funds, they could not resist making those coins sing to all adults who came within earshot, but never near their mates—there they were always trying to avoid being cadged for half.

For Bessie and Ulie, infinite was not a word which could be applied to their finances. Ulie had her pension, but Bessie's only money apart from the poorly paid housework in town was the child endowment which she received, one pound per child per month. They were barely getting by. Bessie went back up the bush for a while, to a station working as a musterers' cook, grateful to Don Peet for organising it for her. The children stayed put with Ulie, and waited for their mother's return in about nine months. She came home, sooner than expected, walking in with a friend.

'I brought a son-in-law back,' she announced. Ulie said not a word. And Nobby moved in.

Chapter Eighteen

Up in the Gascoyne, Les, a free man for four years now, and with no Yamatji consequences in sight, had gone dogging and dingo-trapping, earning enough to buy a long-wheelbase Landrover, his 1937 Ford truck in 1965 well past its prime. His new second-hand vehicle, like the old truck before, provided more than mere transport. With few Yamatjis able to afford cars and forced to wait on remote stations for the weekly mail truck or a taxi if they were cashed up, money in hand, at the end of a season's job, the owning of a car gave a feeling of control, the sensation, even if an illusion, of pulling the strings. Round the Gascoyne and Murchison, Les could choose to go where and when he liked. And his choice of truck this time was important too, the long wheelbase a declaration to anybody privy to the code that he was the same as they were, a man of the bush.

He moved around a lot these days, all his belongings, his home, carried within, the side emblazoned with his name, Leslie Dingo, painted proudly in his swirling self-taught lettering. He was never a loner, instead confident to go alone, Yamatjis and whitefella friends pleased to see him again wherever he pulled in. One time when visiting Norm and Val Armstrong, he came bearing a crayon drawing of the country he loved, the hills nearby, for Val, the white lady who always invited him in to have his cup of tea. Val had the sketch on her wall for years, until it fell in two, age drying the paper, the hills ripping apart. A visit from Les was always something special. For his nephews and their friends, having Uncle nearby was a wonderful time. He'd tease, have fun with them, always laughing, often playing the clown, acting out funny segments he heard on the radio. When he'd say 'Comin' for a ride, you boys?' they would all race, a truck full of smiling faces, Les with the biggest.

There had been times when it looked like his freewheeling days were at an end, a couple of short attempts at living with girlfriends, but settling down was something he had been unable to do, his desire to create his own life, live his way, never disappearing, himself as the rodeo rider moving to the next town carved in his heart. These days, so far out from any of the towns, he rarely saw those visiting shows, his own buckjumping days long gone as he was close to forty years old, but Les, arriving at the stations in style, in his own truck, would still join the first muster he could find. Sometimes it would be rounding up wild goats, the station owner benefiting with a reduction in the numbers of the feed-devouring nuisances, Les gaining as well, permitted to keep half any proceeds raised from a sale.

If his riding preference was not on offer though, any station work would do, fixing fences, yardwork, or windmill runs, dogging demanding not only immense skill and unending patience but also another means of subsistence. There might be many animals snared on one trip, but few or none the next. A dogger had to be prepared for the long haul. The station owners knew Les was dogging, and with dingoes killing large numbers of their calves and lambs on their properties, would send word. And Dingo would pit wits against dingo. It was no pushover—for either. So after locating his prey and setting traps, he would have to mark time, and station work, and the tucker provided, were appreciated.

A dingo is never easy to defeat, and few men possess the ability. Les often spent weeks alone in scrub country, eyes peeled, every sense attuned, while he waited. Spotting a dog was the easy part, a catch, however, unachievable unless the dogger was as clever as the dingo, the animal sharp, intuitive, and with an ability to humble most, by sizing a situation up and taking evasive action. The dogs would watch all who entered their terrain, knew who were the regulars, the station men, and deduced which of the newcomers spelt danger, knew which one was after them. Doggers had to find crafty ways of covering their smell, of leaving not a trace on the traps, the dogs well able to skirt around, some eluding them for up to ten years. And some were even capable of pulling off breathtaking rescues.

Les's father, Dingo Jim, had been dogging early in his marriage, with Ulie along to help. He located the lair, and confident the mother and father were away finding food, had taken the puppies, tying the seven together, tossing them up the embankment to Ulie—who hadn't heard the female dingo approach. The determined dog grabbed the rope in her mouth and tore away, her offspring in tow, saved, even if still tethered together. But a bit of twine was a minor impediment, and easily gnawed through by such a strong-willed, smart mother.

A Dingo trapping dingoes is a strange concept. However, as Les and his family had acquired the name as a result of Dingo Jim's own dogging days, the incongruity diminishes. And Les, like most doggers, had the utmost respect for the animals who could outsmart him and them. He sent one unique pair of pups, beautiful cream fluffy bundles who were just coming into the white coats they would have as adults, on the mail truck to Mullewa and from there on to the city zoo, Icecream and Lickit as he had named them featuring in the Perth daily paper a few days later with their new names, Rinso and Surf.

Les was doing both dogging and general work on Dairy Creek Station—the very one where Bessie had been born, near the river which had nearly claimed her—when Cyclone Mavis lashed the coast. Flood warnings were issued to the area and residents battened down, preparing for the hundred-mile-per-hour winds. The cyclone caused serious disruptions as far away as the United States of America, where it threatened the American Gemini space launch, to be monitored in part from the Carnarvon Space Tracking Station. And locally, due to the downpour and winds, residents and farmers had to give up the idea of lighting bonfires when the astronauts whirled over. Back on land, the deluge cut roads, leaving transport vehicles stranded for many costly days, with no relief in sight. However the banana planters and vegetable growers were jubilant, bumper crops promised when the river finally reached Carnarvon. 'The Gascoyne River was doing a banker,' the local newpaper announced, as the normally dry bed flowed bank to bank, and swiftly.

Ernie with fellow cast member Lynette Narkle waiting for the Theatre-in-Education truck to hit the road for the tour of his first ever acting gig in Jack Davis's *Kullark*.

Ernie, in a distinctive tea cosy, with his mentor and closest friend, Richard Walley.

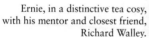

Director Bruce Beresford, Ernie and rodeo rider selected as Ernie's stand-in for a 'rough riding' rodeo scene in Ernie's first film *Fringe Dwellers* in 1984.

Bruce *(right)* with Kerry Ryder following family tradition by working on Woolgorong Station, for Ted Officer and his wife, Meg.

Bessie, Meg Officer and myself at Woolgorong Station on the site where Ulie's beloved house once stood. The Tamarisk trees she planted are still going strong, but the tree where Dingo Jim hid his parcel no longer stands.

The tin hut where Ernie was born on Bullardoo Station. The small room where Ulie acted as midwife for Bessie (which was attached to the left hand side) has been demolished.

Neatening the shells on Pearlie and Joe's baby's grave on Yallalong Station.

Wail homestead now.

Ronnie's grave located in 1996 during my research for the Dingo story.

Ulie had never been officially notified her son had died, nor did she ever know where he had been buried.

Bessie (on left) and Pearlie with Bessie's grandson, Baden Thorne, displaying old Yamatji ways and skills at the Mullewa show.

Ernie and myself with our much loved children, Wilara and Jurra.

Jurra, Wilara and myself presenting Ernie with his specially decorated birthday cake for his 41st birthday. I'm the one without chocolate icing as facial decoration.

Eddie Peet and Auntie Pearlie 'nursing' me. Bessie sitting close by finds it all pretty funny.

Inland, the lifeline to the stations, the mail truck, could not deliver in some parts. And Les was at Gascoyne Junction, having swum over from the Lyons River Station where he'd been paying a visit to his current girlfriend. A strong swimmer, he made the crossing easily, as he knew he would, and chatted to the mates he had come to see. When the truck arrived and the problem was voiced, Les, as helpful as usual, volunteered to swim the mailbag back.

Nobby, the son-in-law Bessie had brought home to Ulie, had found some work at Morawa, laying water pipes, and Bessie went too with toddler Ginny, Ulie, back at Mullewa looking after the others, making sure they all went to school.

At the end of the week, Nobby came home, left a chunk of his pay with her, and went to the local pub. Nobby, Yamatji but fair-skinned and with no identifiable Aboriginal features, was allowed to drink with the whitefellas. Bessie stayed home, and burst into tears. Something felt strange. Something could be wrong.

But she tried to ignore her weeping, knowing she was expecting again, knowing how her moods had swung with each pregnancy she'd had. Nobby returned, beerily happy, but Bessie, not wanting him in his state, breathing drunkenness over her while she and Ginny tried to sleep, refused him his place in the bed. She cried again when she was accused of cutting him out, of having another man. It was now a familiar refrain. Nobby was a jealous man. Bessie had chosen a man rendered insecure, the son of a whiteman and a Yamatji mother, both of whom had carted him many places, fought often, and separated when he was a boy. And there was another factor which Nobby tried in his own way to reconcile. Nobby was a Yamatji who looked like a whiteman, a whiteman who was not. There were fights when he was permitted to drink with the whitemen while other Yamatjis were refused, and there were fights when he answered whitemen back. He took refuge in the bottle, able to feel complete for a while. Down at the pub, for a couple of hours, when all was quiet, Nobby was the greatest of navigators through the uncertain territory he occupied. However, shouting whitefellas beers while he sought acceptance, yet also seeking to be who he knew himself to be—and staying too long and for too many rounds—he would change. Those fights would break out, and if they didn't happen there, they sure did at home. And Bessie, in contrast to Nobby, secure in the knowledge of the role she had to play, a mother, with the certainty of women's business always to attend to, copped the brunt. She also had to find food money from somewhere when he reclaimed the pay he had given her so he could return for another drink. Bessie hadn't known him well when she brought him home from the station where beer was only available on a Friday night, after a hard week's work, and then only one bottle each.

To a distant onlooker, Nobby's tendencies in town appeared the same as many of the white workers', who having endured lonely months on the stations where they worked hard, hit the pubs with feverish enthusiasm, all drinking as much as they had money for, all fighting when the drink got too much. All limping back to wait the next chance. Nobby, like them, was of the bush culture, but, unlike them, not accepted as a permanent player within. Nobby, a quiet, likeable fellow when he wasn't drinking, had a much harder road to tread. And it was all hard for Bessie to live with.

She woke, feeling empty, the strange sadness still with her, now compounded by Nobby's accusations. She put a roast in the oven and sat down, Nobby's Geraldton weekend paper lying before her.

'Gascoyne River,' she read in the Stop Press section on the back page, some of the few words she had learned to recognise, and she could read the two preceding.

'Man missing.'

Nobby's Auntie answered the door, but Bessie was there in a flash. Two policemen stood, one hesitated, then said what she already knew.

'Your brother Les ...'

Bessie fainted. The two men helped her to a chair.

Pearlie was working at Dairy Creek as well, the station Les was based at for the time. She was the order cook, serving workers' breakfast requests, in addition to helping with general meals and baking the daily loaves of bread. She was pleased she was getting paid there. The part of her life which had often consisted of following in a cart behind cattle, drovers' cook at the ready, had come to a close, finished with her marriage, Yamatji-way, of twenty-six years, white-way fifteen. Joe had worked away for long periods of time, always knowing he was part of the family, often taking his sons or nephews, teaching them patiently and well, often having to dodge a bullock or two when they made youthful, sometimes dangerous errors. But mostly he was elsewhere, working hard for long periods of time, blokes with blokes, and over the years the intimacy with his wife trickled away. Pearlie, though, remained ever-loyal to her Joe, and he in his way to her. She was glad her brother was at this station, family still near.

Les had been expected back, but hadn't arrived yet. Pearlie was in the kitchen, getting on with her chores, when shouting rang out from the yard, frantic desperate bellowing. The phone rang, Pearlie answered, and the internal station caller between buildings barked a question about another worker's whereabouts.

'Down at the yard, doing the horses,' said Pearlie, surprised at all the commotion and flurry. 'Can I take a message?'

'No,' was the hurried answer, and Pearlie, confused, watched people quickly coming over to the house.

Mrs Cornish, the missus, then appeared at the door, the workers behind. They were walking too slowly for Pearlie's liking. 'What now, what now,' she thought.

'He could be on a tree,' someone said, grasping any hope they could offer.

'No, he's not,' said Pearlie softly. Dingo Jim's daughter, like Bessie, and the entire family, always knew certain things.

Back in Mullewa, Ulie cried like she'd never cried before.

'I tried to tell my mate, I tried to tell him,' said a whitewoman at the Gascoyne Junction pub, reliving the warnings she said she gave, her words heavy with accusation and inference. But no-one would ever know.

Chapter Nineteen

At Mullewa, everybody was stunned. Strong, jolly, friendly Les, as Mrs Peet described him, had drowned. But not many were able to travel to the funeral up in Carnarvon, as little notice could be given before it was held, the burial having to take place as soon as it could be organised. Les's body had been submerged for two days, and there could be no delay. Don Peet though made sure Ulie got there, taking her and Bessie the 600 kilometres in his taxi. His position was an important one, he was driving the first family, the direct family, of the deceased. At the service and at the cemetery, all would part and make way for him leading Ulie. His brother Eddie, who almost twenty years earlier had been one of the young boys who idolised Les when he first rode the buckjumpers, one of the boys who had hung around listening to every word the laughing man uttered, was there too. Les had many many friends throughout the region. They were all saddened at his early death, and at the way he had died. Mrs Peet in Mullewa continued working her long hours in her shop, unable to get away. She stayed, and thought of him.

At Carnarvon, the night after his body had been located, the Yamatjis at the reserve prepared themselves, making sure everyone was ready to meet the Dingo family in the proper manner. Pearlie and her Uncle Bob Williams, who was Ulie's brother-in-law and therefore immediate family, and who had also been one of the trackers scouring the river, were both aware of the preparations there would be, and so spent the night camped away, giving the people time to get ready. And they also waited for members of their family, the Dingos, to arrive so they could then enter together, as one group, cry first with Hilda and Tommy, Jimmy and his wife, Joan Battle, as well as Friday and his wife, Joyce Dodd, before seating themselves on the ground in the middle of the specially cleared area spread with blankets, to cry then with everybody else. Circles of mourners formed around the main family who, heads down, leaned into one another, the men crying, women wailing. All those outside the first family were positioned in order of rank and traditional status within their respective families, each person fully aware when it would be their turn to come forward. The outermost circles were crowded with people watching for their time to move up, still on the ground, to cry with another family member, head down, touching each other somehow, a hand holding someone's arm, shoulder, even someone's foot. And eventually all mourners had reached every member of the immediate family. All had linked, all had poured out their sorrow, and all had honoured the dead man and family. It was an important time, grief to be fully expressed, the funeral later more subdued, all now accepting Les's returning to the earth, and his spirit moving on.

On the morning of the funeral, Ulie was given a pill to sedate her. Her grief had been hard to bear. But she watched, with everyone, the white handkerchief which floated down from the charter plane which flew overhead. Owen, flying in late from Onslow, had thrown it, reaching out to his brother, connecting by the only means he could see how from up there, before Les was entombed below. Ulie stood beside Pearlie as the coffin was lowered into the ground, then walked back to the car. Owen, finally arriving at the cemetery, came straight to his mother to 'meet' her and to cry, but was unable. Ulie had gone to sleep, and he didn't know what to do. It was not proper for him to receive condolences until he had grieved with her, for son, for brother, together. And yet all the mourners at the service, as soon as the grave was filled in and the mound neatened, were required to pay their respects, filing past to either hug him in quiet shared grieving, or pump his hand once, eyes averted, in an understood acknowledgement of his sorrow, an offering of their sympathy. The mourners all knew, and waited, leaving him to meet with his brothers and sisters as he should. He had no choice but to meet Ulie later.

Back in Mullewa, Bessie stayed on with Ulie, and with her children, knowing Nobby would head back when his job finished. Bessie didn't want Ulie to be alone, her mother so very sad all the time. Mrs Peet noticed the change too, the smiling Ulie she had known earlier gone, Ulie now older, sicker, and with her heart broken.

And Ulie was concerned with what she saw at home.

'Why go and get with this drunken man,' she would ask of Bessie, 'who can't help you look after the kids.'

And Bessie had not much to say. Her dream of a man to share her life, to ease the daily struggle, to love and help her, had not come about. And it would always be difficult to find what she wanted with Nobby, after all life was hard for him too. Lee Peters, a local Native Welfare officer, believed Nobby's drinking allowed him to obliterate what his life had to be, masked what he felt incapable of controlling, being, like most Yamatji men of the time, unable to move away from the circumstances in which he lived. And Bessie, of those circumstances herself, would not condemn him, would not give in. Bessie gave him chance after chance. Ulie, though, who in contrast to Nobby had known some purpose in her life on the stations, had felt some satisfaction in her daily work, and who knew with definiteness who she was, found his behaviour unacceptable. She thought a few simple home truths would do the trick.

'You got her,' she would say, reminding him Bessie, still in her early thirties, was quite a catch. 'Why don't you do the right thing?'

'Don't you reckon I'm doing the right thing?' would come the reply, Nobby sober once more, sure he was dependable because he came home every night, and even handed money over when he was paid. And after some drinking sessions, the guilt eating at him, he would take Ernie and the other kids and walk up to the tip, all searching for any copper, lead or brass to sell to the scrap metal merchant, Bessie getting the money. Until he asked for it back again.

'You *not*,' Ulie would emphasise, exasperated by his inability to see.

Bessie's and Nobby's baby Tania was born, and Nobby's brother Victor travelled to meet his new sister Bessie for the first time, and to greet his new niece. He was happy to hear the news of his brother's family. Victor was admiring the baby, making a fuss, when Nobby came back, drunk, after celebrating his own way.

'Oh, you here to see Bessie, eh?' Nobby accused, and began to push and punch, convinced his brother was another ready to cut him out.

Through his boozy haze, Nobby saw rivals wherever he looked. Many a fight was in response to an innocent query about where Bessie was. 'What are you asking for her for?' he would answer suspiciously. And another brawl would begin. Always when alcohol was his partner.

At other times, and there were many when he was sober, Bessie and Nobby struggled with the day-to-day realities of seven children, and three adults, in a small house with three tiny bedrooms. By now some of the glass louvres had broken, and at first they moved the top ones down the bottom, leaving the opening higher up, at least directing the airstream to some degree. When too many had smashed, Bessie used the flaps from a fruit box to make replacements, carefully cutting the cardboard to size. Ulie and Bessie didn't know it was possible to buy new ones, didn't have the money anyway, and the Native Welfare department didn't replace them, even though the agreed rent was being paid. Their house, as swept and scrubbed as Ulie and Bessie kept it, was looking a bit worse for wear.

The Native Welfare officers visited once a month, as they did all the Yamatjis, checking on living standards, those among them who were sympathetic attempting to help in some way, appalled at the poverty and the circumstances that the Yamatji people in the area had been placed in. And sometimes they would witness the generosity and dignity the Yamatjis allowed each other, in ways the outer world would not see. When Lee Peters came calling at Four Corners, sometimes for a yarn, but often to ask questions for the department, she watched the respect accorded Nobby, as Bessie became quiet, waiting, deferring to him, giving him an opportunity to speak. Bessie, in reality the powerful one in the relationship, would not usurp his family position, and would see that his status was maintained. And Lee watched also, when Ulie, seated inconspicuously and quietly in a corner, would speak up and, with just a word, utter the final pronouncement. The women ruled. And Nobby knew it. Like many Yamatji men struggling to grasp some control in their lives, he had little real influence at home, and even less in a world where real acceptance was denied. He did whatever he could to achieve a sense of self, and sadly, for both him and his family, drink had been the only solution he could see. The Welfare officers were not much help, those who wanted to, that is. They were mostly women, who dealt with the women, and they were white, never having experienced what it was like to live without the promise of a future. Male Welfare officers were rare, the men mostly working from the offices in Perth, pulling the strings, telling the Yamatjis what to do. The Yamatji men were on their own. And often blamed, from all sides.

For the kids, though, sheltered from such pressures, life, in their eyes, continued to deliver good times, interrupted only by the chores they had to do at home. Ernie always had a pile of wood to chop out the back near to Nobby's chook yard, and he displayed some skill inside as well. In the kitchen he was king of the cornflour custard, not minding doing his fair share, knowing the house rule that whoever cooked was excused from the worst part, washing and putting the dishes away. It was a useful rule for dodging those less palatable tasks, but there weren't many he could avoid. Ulie, who wouldn't tolerate idleness, was still the all-powerful matriarch even if slowing down, and he and his sisters had learned to accept what was, learned through experience it was the less painful approach to take, Ulie always handy with a springy branch from the tamarisk tree she had planted, the kids sent to select their own.

Over the years Ernie had learned to accept many things. He and his mates noticed but thought little of the way the local kids mostly divided themselves, a hierarchy seemingly in place. The town kids kept their distance from the black kids, so too most of the farm kids from the town kids, self-appointed it appeared as the elite, in town only to attend primary, before going off to boarding school in the city. Ernie and his mates also accepted as the norm the way people at the Mullewa swimming pool seemed to separate as well, in the water and under the shelters on the grass, the white children keeping to themselves, just like the Yamatjis. And at school black and white again mostly played separately. It seemed to be only the newcomers to the town, the children of railway employees, who mixed freely. Debbie Petit, daughter of the new station master, was even Ducko Papertalk's girlfriend for a while. But Ernie wasn't as lucky with his pre-pubescent romancing. He stared, pined, wouldn't talk, tried to befriend her brother, and even resorted to joining a recorder class just to be near the white girl who made his heart flutter. But Pauline Mowday didn't notice, and Ernie finally gave up, his non-love affair ending when he had to accept that the group, and Pauline too, was not for him. Ernie couldn't read music.

Pauline wasn't Ernie's only disappointment at this time. All the kids at school were excited when Australia's new currency came into effect in February 1966, Ernie just like all the others.

One of the white town boys had been to Mrs Peet's shop at lunch time, and returned tapping his pocket, coins clinking.

'Kevin Thomson, Kevin Thomson,' Ernie sang out eagerly, 'Show us the new money.'

'No,' came the reply, 'go and get your own.'

However, when competition basketball came to Mullewa, there were to be a few changes. Ernie and his mates were hooked, the new game their obsession, and so it was with some of the white kids. Basketball provided the first real opportunity for the children to fully interact, the newly formed local association placing Yamatji and white kids in the same team. Sometimes it looked as if the white kids pulled out so they could form their own team, but sometimes they stayed. Colin Jennings, a teacher at Mullewa Primary, introduced the boys to the game, teaching them the basics and taking them along to train where the adults played on the wire-enclosed asphalt court. The start he gave Ernie would later mean much, Ernie's involvement in sport and basketball in Mullewa leading to his eventual success in a much bigger world.

Ernie played every chance he could get, and so did his sisters, although they began with netball at first, with Ernie getting a taste. Before basketball had been introduced, he used to accompany them to their games, utilising any free court, throwing ball after ball at the netball ring. Now he had his own game, and there was a resurgence of serious intrafamily rivalry, especially in the home-based championships which regularly happened on the small front verandah. Marion, Ernie, Donelle and Audrey played two-on-two, whenever a tennis ball had been found. They pushed and shoved, feet scraping, hustling each other, shooting frantically, trying to score through the ten-centimetre gap between the rafter and the roof, smashing the ball down—until someone was inevitably smacked up against the wall, Ulie hearing the crying.

'Tennis ball a problem for you kids?' she would say. 'If you can't play together, give me that ball. *Give* me that ball.'

And with Ulie nearly always meaning what she said, their game would be over and they would have to wait until finding another, usually after the whitefellas had finished their social games. But basketball was a consuming passion now, and they wanted to play every day. They had to get their shots in. So they tied a backboard to the light pole out the front of the house, the wire also fixing the ring, a five-gallon drum rim, in place, and they were set. Together with any neighbouring kids who wanted to join in, they hammered any old ball through, all day and well into the night in the summertime, in the dust, in the heat, no stopping to notice the sweat dripping, and no need to worry about cars either, few ever coming up their red dirt street. When the Whitehursts, Comeagains, Greens and Lexie Maher turned up, the games, complete with rules of their own making, were played in deadly earnest. No-one owned a proper basketball, real ones only sighted at school or at the competition they now played in on Thursday nights, and those flash balls were never necessary. Instead, the variety of sizes and textures of the balls they used, scrounged from anywhere, sometimes even a new one, a cheap plastic one someone had been given for their birthday, all served to hone their handling abilities, taught them to be ready for anything, and established a skill base on which to add that Yamatji flair. None of them wanted to be seen to be playing like a whitefella, even though they all wanted to play the whitefella game. They wanted to do it their way, with their style.

Even when basketball appeared to be forgotten for a while, with the boys still venturing away from the town, shanghais strung around their necks, the day would invariably end again with a friendly game. Out they would head, five kilometres out of town to the waterfall where the artesian water had carved a rocky gully downwards from the flat dry Mullewa country. They would swim, or look for birds, lob a few stones with their basketball technique, then walk home, past the tip, and past Combo's Lane, with its name whispering Mullewa's and the Murchison's past. A combo was a derogatory whitefella term for a white man who had sex with or who lived with an Aboriginal woman, and this bush track was known as a place where many had taken women for that purpose. The lane's name was loaded with judgement and disapproval for the men, the condemnation however not for what would have been at the time illicit sex, some of which may even have involved coercion, but the fact that the men were with black women. The women themselves were of no concern, and in the lane's name there was no acknowledgement of their presence. At least Lovers' Lane, more acceptable and therefore closer to town, near the football oval, recognised two participants. For the boys, however, the track was just something they passed on the way home.

It was always a thirsty walk back, and such a day had often been long. However, it took only the sight of a light pole for a basketball scrimmage to begin again, usually when they had stopped for a few minutes to get a drink from somebody's house, sucking away at the outside tap. Someone would always find a ball and overhead shots went up outside many a Yamatji's tin dwelling, the ball bouncing off the imaginary backboard and ring in front of them. Not much else mattered if a game of basketball could be had.

But for Ernie, his new game meant more than merely a pastime to love. He began to glimpse what it could also give— recognition and approval. Ernie had always wanted to be just like the bigger boys, like Gavin, like Bruce, and used to hang around, listening, wanting to be included. Bruce was the cousin he idolised the most. With his quick wit and one-liners, and his position as main mischief-maker, he had been the leader of the Dingo kids, far and wide, for a few years now, and Ernie wanted to be him. Not only was Bruce amusing and fun, but he was liked by everybody as well, Yamatjis that is, most of the white people not yet knowing his humanness. One white town girl, with little direct contact with the local Aboriginal people, had been shocked to find herself sitting next to him on one occasion in school, she reported to me, embarrassed now at her reaction then. She had been frightened. With so many Yamatjis in town, but all on the fringe, such close contact was still out of the ordinary. In this social setting, basketball became one of the few means to become a person of note, though Ernie was unaware it would be his ticket to travel through the wider community. It was his own mob he was concerned with now, discovering early that a showpony could be seen, could stand out, and he could become, almost, one of the big boys. On the court he turned himself into a version of his fun-loving cousin, a bonier one, Ernie so skinny and all arms and legs. Bruce called him 'Showpy' as soon as he saw him play.

Chapter Twenty

'Why am I putting on these gloves to hit Ducko Papertalk?' Ernie thought to himself, the same thought he had every year.

It was another Boxing Day boxing day on their front lawn, and a big mob of people were there. On the lawn square in front of Ulie's tin house at Four Corners, a big tournament had become standard every year, with a few days organised over the summer as well. The lawn, Nobby had discovered soon after joining the household, was a perfect boxing ring, the right shape, with a defined boundary, red dirt, all around. Not long after they moved into the house, Ulie had supervised the kids as they dug the straight rows to her directions, planting the couch grass cuttings she had collected, never dreaming she was creating a sporting arena. It had grown beautifully too and she made sure it was watered every day, Bessie and the kids taking turns, with the legacy that Ernie today is blissfully happy with a hose in his hand, watering any bare patch of lawn anywhere.

Sometimes there would be as many as fifteen men standing round the lawn perimeter, with a few on the verandah watching, some having a sociable beer. And while the thirty-odd kids ran around, laughing and playing, they all waited for the sheep to cook. Friendly support would be offered to the two in the ring.

'Give 'im it then. Watch the upper-cut. Ooh, copped an upper cut. Heh! Told you to duck!' would be heard, no angry abuse or urging a kill allowed. Men from the generation before Nobby, Jack Comeagain, Charlie Green, and Eric Papertalk, were in charge, with a strong belief in self-discipline and fair play.

These were happy times, Yamatjis together, with young boys at the side being shown how to hold their pose, how to shadow-box, and made to punch into hands. Ernie's Uncle Friday was a boxer recognised in the town, the time he knocked his opponent out in the town hall still remembered today by those who were there. But Ernie didn't inherit his uncle's interest and, even though he could see the enjoyment and camaraderie it all gave, did not find it as fun-filled. His heart was not in it. But it had played an important role over the years for many.

In Mullewa, sporting achievement gave a pride which was difficult for Yamatjis to gain from their daily lives, a pride both personal and communal, and it also brought greater acceptance in the town. Life was easier for good footballers or boxers, as it had been for Les years ago with his rodeo riding, the Yamatjis apparently excused their 'nativeness' when their prowess helped them to be recognisable as people and when their achievements brought the whole town glory. Boxing had been important in the town since George Stewart's Boxing Troupes had first come through.

'Got any young fighters?' he would say on any return visit.

'Yep, we got fighters waiting for you mob,' Jack Comeagain would proudly answer, having trained the young fellas himself.

Men like Jack had been through a lot to survive in the town over the decades, and they were aware they needed to hand on some skills to the next generation, something to keep them strong, in mind as well as body, something which would help them cope with what they themselves had faced over the years, the Native Welfare department and not so long ago the so-called Protectors, whitefellas who the white law said could walk in and out of Yamatji lives, force their way in, leave when they decided, flaunting whitefella power over the now-rendered powerless. Teaching proper skills, Jack and his friends intended, would heighten the senses, sharpen the reflexes, mental as well, and would give them some strength to cope, at the same time reclaiming some of the abilities from former days when their grandfathers hunted and survived in the bush. And it would make them proud of what they could do. Unfortunately Jack wasn't always around to teach the rules he played by, and down the track rules and regulations, proper reasons for a proper fight, were forgotten or disregarded by the younger fellas, and fights started too easily, latent aggression born from frustration with their lot, including boredom, soon coming to the surface, especially after a few drinks. And skills which were meant to help achieve a personal victory over circumstances instead led many straight to gaol.

Marion and Ernie would join the other kids and gather outside the pub, help form the ring around two fighters, who, always after drinking, would be raring to go, a fight picked for many a petty reason, but really for a chance at some status, a chance to boast of manhood and strength. A fight was one of the few means to find something they could boast about, something which, mistaken as they may have been, would give them some recognition and prestige. When you have nothing, ephemeral glory, even if only in a mate's eye, is richness indeed. After a night on the grog, families fought other families, townies fought station Yamatjis who'd dare come to town, or any visitors from other towns. Marion and Ernie would stand in the circle, the ring moving to one side when the boxers moved that way, then back the other. The police would come, shine a light on it all, let the fighters have it out, then stop the punch-up, throw the loser in the van and take him off to gaol. 'Get home now,' the kids and crowd would all be told.

Nobby saw himself as a bit of a boxer, which probably caused many of his fights at the pub, Nobby always wanting to prove how good he was. And he did genuinely love it. Once when he was standing with his ear to the wireless in the fuse-box cupboard, the hinged door held open with one hand, the other punching the air as Muhammad Ali's moves were broadcast from a big fight, Ernie came round the corner at the wrong time, copping a blow fair in the face.

'Bessie!' Nobby yelled, hand still propping the door open, no second of this fight to be missed. 'Bessie! Get these kids away from here.'

With boxing so important, it was no surprise he was unimpressed when Ernie, gracing the ring on the front lawn, spent his time ducking, gloved hands over his face.

'G'orn. Get inside,' Nobby growled, embarrassed at Ernie's poor showing yet again.

Ernie slumped onto his bed, lifted the edge of his mattress

and took out the Phantom comic he'd stashed there. Sometimes he even had as many as three if he could prevent anybody from finding them. He lay across the bed placing the comic open on the floor below, reading with the least effort. And there would have been little involved anyway. After all, Ernie had read it over and over probably fifty times before.

'Still not fighting, eh boy?' Bessie said at the door, with a little smile. She always knew how to give comfort in just a few words.

Phantom comics didn't figure among the books Ernie's sisters Marion and Donelle read. Their preferences were more varied, and included a few unlikely to appeal to a young lad. Romance books, with *True Confessions* as Marion's favourite, were all passed from house to house, all eagerly read by those women and girls who could. Marion dreamed of travelling to the places where the stories were set, her ambition to spend a Christmas in New York, even though she hadn't seen Perth yet. But she would never allow the romance novels to turn her head, Ulie had seen to that, after Marion, who possessed her grandmother's own character- istic, a determination which could sometimes tip towards stub- bornness, had bucked against Ulie's authority again.

'When you get to be fifteen,' Ulie had said to her granddaughter, pointing to all the young girls in town with babies, some pushing prams, 'you gunna be just like them.'

Marion resolved there and then, that would never be. She would prove it to her Granny.

More serious and studious than her younger brother Ernie, and always with a book in her hand it seemed, she often read late into the night—until Nobby, annoyed at the electricity bills, decided to pull the fuses. They took to the streets, Marion, Ernie and Donelle, sitting in the gutter, reading under the lamplight, the girls a book each, a comic for Ernie. Nobby's action hadn't

Tim Officer Junior and Friday.
Not only was 'the sea rough' for
Friday's hairstyle but it looks like
Moses seems to have parted it as well.

Teenager Bessie
among the
wildflowers.

facto stepfather who didn't want the
essie's kids who weren't his. Nobby,
Bessie, would leave Bessie's five eldest
called his own children into his room,
them lollies and treats. The children
and Ulie, made no such distinction,
r sister.

the railways, on the tracks, and his
had ever seen before. But a heavy
ell enough to live with great comfort
in the house, and an aching, grease-
to rest over a few beers at the end of
ed to provide for all, and then to have
ld have been hard. He resented it, and
e pay for them, he said. What about
nt the kids around. And Bessie was
land and nowhere to go, didn't know
e'd always watched Ulie do, kept on,
as best she could. But the kids all
easing coldness. However, Bessie's
ed family, with the relationships
ead wide these days, eased her worry,
blood-tied or not, taking the four
and as many weekends as could be
young to go with them, but Ernie,
y stayed at many places throughout the
ons, Ernie spending time with Pearlie
more often with Queenie and Reg
Simpson at Pindar.
er Jimmy worked at a farm only about
Mullewa, and Marion and Ernie often

247

spent weekends there, camping with their uncle in the small shed in which he lived, helping with fencing sometimes, stacking hay others, even going back a few weeks later to turn the bales and running from the snakes which wriggled away underneath. When his nieces and nephews weren't there, it was a lonely life for Jimmy working like this and for not much money, the wheat-farming family not wealthy themselves and now back in Mullewa, leaving him alone to look after the machinery and the property. He had married earlier and he and his wife had two children, but after problems they separated, Jimmy finding work where he could in his own country, somewhere close to his sick mother, his wife and children a long way away in Carnarvon. He missed the closeness, the family he had as a boy, the family he had not wanted to leave when the mission people came calling. He missed the security he'd had, the confidence in who he was. Now he knew how hard it was for Yamatji men, telling Ernie many stories. Jimmy, already a drinker, already sad, turned to the bottle even more.

her Jimmy and Tim Officer Junior and
;orong Station.

Jimmy told Ernie which farms Yamatji workers tried not to go near, knowing from experience the treatment they would receive. And he also told of those where they knew they would be treated with fairness and decency—the Keeffes, Ullrichs, Waldecks and Tunbridges, all farming families who treated the Yamatjis as people of worth, even paying the two youngsters a few dollars when they came to give their uncles some help. Later on for the Tunbridges, there was an unusual benefit to be had. Yamatji workers everywhere would always get hold of a football if they could, and in the breaks used to teach any youngsters how to play their style. A generation on, a Mullewa lad, Brad Tunbridge, his father Norm taught by blackfellas, made it to the big-time, playing on the other side of the country for the Sydney Swans.

randdaughter Joan (Ilyama) with the
problem bicycle.

In town, Ernie concentrated on his basketball, the game giving him a purpose and a sense of achievement. It also gave him a place in the male community, and the acknowledgement he would never get from Nobby at home. His antics became bigger, but he kept them at first for his Aboriginal brothers and sisters, satisfied with being a small town character who was good at basketball. And away from Nobby, he had the same joy of living many in his family had shown, Les, Friday, Bessie too. He achieved what he wanted and along with his mates became well known in the poorer streets, the Yamatji streets of Mullewa.

It was a big thrill when coach Tosia Peet, who'd taught him to do lay-ups and worked on his technique, asked his mother, and included him in a B-grade team to travel to remote Mount Magnet to play in a social match. Ernie, still at primary school, was an eleven-year-old boy among the adults, and the only Yamatji included. So he was pleased when some of the Mt Magnet Yamatjis turned up to watch. And when he was awarded best on the court he was filled with pride. He had found what he was good at, which he could make his own. He blossomed and started showing his talents to all, whitefellas now too—showing off many called it—finding a place was what it was really all about and feeling good about himself.

Ulie's and Bessie's days were still sad, even though it was over twelve months since Les had drowned and the official mourning period had come to an end. At least they had one event to look forward to. Buddy Williams and his band were touring all the region's towns, big and small, and were coming to Mullewa again. All the Dingos liked Buddy's music, attending his concerts whenever he came, and were all eager listeners to the 6WF Country Hour on Perth ABC radio. A solid stick to prop open the hinged fuse-box door was all they needed to ensure good listening, the sound on Ulie's faithful wireless immediately clearer. They would roar with pleasure when they heard messages to people they knew, relatives as well. To the kids this was all new, though Bessie relived her happy days at Woolgorong when Lizzie had helped with all the letter-writing. Now, after regular airplay, everyone knew Buddy's songs. But there was one the Dingos hadn't heard, and didn't know about.

They trooped into the Mullewa Town Hall, all excited, all here, all except Nobby. But Bessie wasn't worried, and didn't expect him to come. And anyway, this was her night, hers and the kids and her Mum's, and Owen's who was staying with them for a while too. It all brought back wonderful memories of Les, when she used to travel up to Carnarvon to meet him, the two of them together at Buddy's concert, then following the show down to Mullewa, seeing it all over again. Buddy was a warm, caring, charismatic man, who was adored in all the country areas, showing many times over where his heart lay, and it was with everyone who struggled. He himself had started life in an orphanage, running away in his early teens from foster parents who it appeared saw him only as free labour for their property. He then found work in the Depression cracking rocks in a quarry, before discovering busking in the streets, and then work singing in hotels. Now he toured the country, knew many of his fans personally, and attempted always to help any way he could. And Buddy knew what it was like to grieve. His twenty-one-month-old daughter had been killed when a truck backed over her, while the family had been on tour in Tasmania, the song 'Little Red Bonnet' now part of his repertoire, his moving tribute to her. Buddy had known Les well, firstly from the buckjumping days, then through his presence at the concerts in the Carnarvon region, and through him Buddy had met the whole family. He now let them in for free, Ulie, Bessie, Owen and the kids. They were honoured. The place was buzzing, with only a few vacant seats up the back.

Going to a concert or to the pictures was a big deal in Mullewa, and everybody crowded into Mrs Peet's shop at inter-mission, customers sometimes standing six-deep while she struggled to serve them all before the time was up. Mostly they wanted the chocolate-dipped ice-creams she made herself, melting the chocolate over the little spirit stove she had bought for that purpose, the ice-creams placed into kerosene tins in readiness. As tonight was special, Ulie and Bessie had set aside some money and each of the kids was allowed one, joining the rest of the audience who congregated on the lawn at the hall front. Tonight certainly was a big night. Everyone finished eating, drinking and yarning, and took up their seats again. The second half was about to begin. Buddy and his band began.

The Gascoyne River was in flood
It was running wild and wide
Carnarvon town was cut right off
And was short of food supply.

The mailman couldn't get to town
Cause the Gascoyne was too high
So he left the mail for Carnarvon folks
On the bank of the river side.

A coloured man with heart so brave
Volunteered to get the mail
He swam the raging rivers wild
Les Dingo was his name ...

Ulie, as if in a trance, got up from her seat, and slowly walked up the centre aisle, her arms raised high towards Buddy on the stage. The audience watched, in silence, astonished, but knew what this was about. She stopped and stood in front, arms still stretched heavenward, still expressing her gratitude, tears streaming down her face. Owen's impulse had been the same, and he too walked forward, climbing the steps at the side, and now stood centre-stage behind Buddy, immeasurable pride and emotion on his face, which too was wet with tears. Les's mother in front, Les's brother behind—and Buddy's voice faded. Everyone in the band was crying, Buddy, his wife, son, concert-goers too. 'Tears was rollin',' says Bessie. Nobody moved.

Buddy and the band burst into song again.

Les Dingo was his name
Les Dingo he died game
A coloured man with a great big smile
Les Dingo was his name.

And a white lady came and comforted Ulie, and took her back to her seat. Where she just sat and howled.

But Ulie had to keep going, had to push through. And there still were a few times when she felt pleasure. She was glad when Jimmy Ryan agreed to take Bruce and teach him station work. He had only recently returned from Mogumber Agricultural school, where he was among those to receive what many Yamatji families had been struggling to give their children. Bruce completed a couple of years' schooling past grade five, primary level. He was one of the first in the region to receive some training assistance, albeit rudimentary.

For a couple of months now, Bruce had been one of the post-boys in Mullewa, Native Welfare finding him the position in the kindred government department. And he was happy to have the job. Wearing his PMG shirt and hat, he pedalled his shiny red bicycle round the town, and no-one—that is no-one—was allowed to touch his much-valued 'truck'. But Bruce, a powerfully built young man, wanted work like his father Owen and uncles before him. And he wanted to be with his mob. On the stations, although there was always a white boss to give overall instructions, out on the job they were Yamatjis working together, making their own decisions, but most treasured of all, speaking, laughing and teasing each other their way. Couldn't do that with whitefellas around. And in town, Yamatjis were constantly told what to do, how they should be, by Welfare, by the police, by the white locals. The Yamatjis felt as if they were always being watched. Bruce wanted a place where he could be himself, and he was indeed fortunate to have Jimmy Ryan as his uncle. Jimmy, Simon Keogh's right-hand man for a long time, had an excellent reputation among the station bosses. Ernie was saddened when his big cousin-brother left again.

Ulie was now ill, and Bessie took over, her mother no longer able to do much for herself. But, as always, her determination would never really falter. Even now, if Bessie came home from shopping without an item Ulie thought necessary, Ulie would comb her hair, put on a good dress if she thought the one she was wearing wasn't presentable enough and out the door she would go, heading to Peet's shop.

'Sit down, Ulie,' Mrs Peet would say kindly, getting her a drink, as Ulie arrived puffing and in obvious discomfort. And she'd sponge Ulie's face down, take what was wanted from her shelves, then organise one of her sons to get the car out and take Ulie back home.

The doctor told Bessie to let Ulie do as she wanted, to let her go.

However, not everyone was as mindful of Ulie's wellbeing as Mrs Peet or the doctor. Nobby would bring his mates home, talking and singing, all drunk, all noisy, late into the night, and Ulie, needing her sleep, would be woken. It was only when they finally crashed out on the bare verandah floor at the front, too charged to notice, that quiet came again and all in the house could rest. Bessie, now with another baby, endured it all.

Ulie had another stroke, her seventh, and was in hospital again. When Bessie visited her in the morning session, Ulie asked her to bring the baby in so she could see him again, so she could cradle her new grandson Les, known by his second name Swaine, as his Uncle's name could not be spoken. Bessie went home, got the kids all ready, and took them in. But by the time she returned, Ulie's earthly persona had retreated, and her soul was preparing. Her eyes were open, but she was no longer available to the outside world. Bessie held her baby up, trying anything to make her mother see, but it was too late. Ulie died several days later. It was 1968. No-one went into the darkness to send her away.

'Bessie! Bessie!' Ulie called the night after her body had died. Floating and ghostly she woke Bessie from her slumber. 'Where's Audrey?' she asked.

'I don't know,' Bessie answered, knowing she must not tell that her daughter, Ulie's favourite grandchild, was sleeping next door. Audrey's life was saved, Bessie still believes, when Ulie was unable to find her, unable to take a companion.

Chapter Twenty-One

Bessie's world had changed, and she became quiet. Ernie watched, stared at her, when he came home from the Pallotine Training Centre at Tardun, the school he'd been sent to after completing primary at Mullewa. He knew his mother carried great pain at Ulie's passing. But he wasn't around for most of the year, and he didn't know what he could do to help anyway. And he wasn't very happy himself. He felt alone, his big sister Marion sent to the much larger school at Geraldton on the coast after gaining a bursary from Native Welfare. Not every Aboriginal student was offered the opportunity Marion had been given, and Bessie hadn't money to pay for boarding fees for her son. A bursary hadn't come through for Ernie, an oversight, but one which wasn't rectified until the following year. And so he was sent further inland from Mullewa, to where only an elementary education was on offer, but where his costs were covered. Bessie packed his bag, holding up the Y-fronts she had bought for him from Moorhead's shop, the first underpants he had ever owned or worn. The girls all laughed, but that didn't matter, he said, shamed, because he wouldn't be wearing them anyway! Bessie also packed new sheets for the dormitory bed, sheets also a first, blankets only adorning their beds in the past. At least there had been no need to buy shoes. He had owned some for several years now, receiving his first pair when he was about nine, black vinyl, which he'd carefully polished with cooking fat. The shine was dazzling and he had been pleased with the result, until the flies hung around and dust refused to budge. And he also had his canvas Dunlops for basketball, *gooninye* he thought, but more than a lot of the other Yamatji boys had. They'd had to play, even on the court, in their black vinyl school shoes. Going to Pallotine meant Ernie had to leave competition basketball behind, the kids at the school, mostly Yamatji kids from the stations, unfamiliar with the game, and not used to team sports at the level he wanted. He missed it sorely. But Ernie went, as required, leaving his Mum and his family. Apart from brief holidays, he was never to live with them again. He would soon turn twelve.

After Ulie's funeral, when Bessie's brothers and sisters had all gone back, all now spread about the Murchison, Bessie bore her sadness alone, Nobby too tangled in his own struggle to notice his wife's wretchedness, too estranged from softer feelings to even care. All Bessie had were her younger kids, and she now joined the other Yamatji women every opportunity she could. With money scarce, card games, the normal excuse to get together, were only once a fortnight, so Bessie was always grateful when the Seventh Day Adventist minister and his schoolteacher wife drove in from Geraldton twice a week to visit families and to open up the hall and conduct classes. Neroli Douglas taught sewing on Wednesday afternoons, and on Saturdays she assisted husband Robert with the church meetings. Bessie and the kids were always there, Four Corners just over the back. Neroli thought Bessie sweet, gentle, and dignified, as well as a good mother. She also thought Bessie was shy, a trait which emerged in the company of white people, until Bessie got to know them and was able to relax. And Neroli noticed Bessie was quiet. But Bessie was not one to trouble others with her sorrow.

With kids scattered through the hall and underfeet, Bessie and the women listened when Neroli showed how to make the simple style children's clothes, and they chuckled away when she gently chastised them for using the wrong colour cotton for the material. But as much as they enjoyed whatever practical teaching she offered, they appreciated the most what she did not know she gave. She and her husband offered a meeting place, somewhere where the Yamatji women were fully accepted, where they could chat, leave the daily hardship and sameness behind and all be friends together. They soon were giving her advice, telling her it was time she started having babies, and telling all their gossip.

As a result, the Douglases participated in much of their new friends' lives. During the year, a wedding was held in the hall, a joyful and festive event to which all the Mullewa Yamatjis came, and Neroli, in addition to organising the day, made and decorated the cake. But when sharing Yamatji lives, sad times inevitably come too. Neroli and her husband soon had to organise a funeral, when Irene and Ike Simpson's baby died, only a few weeks old.

They approached the town undertaker presuming

arrangements would be made with appropriate dignity and ease, no further grief involved for the dead baby's parents. But not being from this part of the country, and both youthfully innocent, in their mid-twenties, they were not expecting what they heard. They listened with disbelief as they were refused. He wouldn't be paid, he rudely insisted. And so his Geraldton colleague carried out the duties, after Neroli and Robert forwarded their own money to make sure the funeral could go ahead.

At the ceremony, she played the organ, and cried. The Yamatji family and relatives, including Bessie, did too, all bedecked in black, a sign of utmost respect in Yamatji communities now and insisted upon, their clothes all sorted from the boxes of church supplies sent up from down south. No-one sang the hymns, no-one could through their sadness. But the Geraldton undertaker was unmoved, and when the service finished, he unceremoniously picked up the coffin, a small white cardboard box, and blithely put it under his arm when they went on to the cemetery. Neroli and her husband were shocked at it all. And the Simpsons, contrary to the mean-spirited belief the Mullewa undertaker expressed, repaid the Douglases bit by bit, week by week, until the funeral expenses had all been covered.

When Neroli and her husband moved on, shifted from Geraldton by the church on to another town, the Yamatji women all gave a card, a gesture intended to thank, but one which instead hit her hard. The women had to ask the local Welfare officer to write their names for them, with Bessie specially requesting hers to be done in pencil, so she could trace over it in pen herself. In all the time she had been with them, Neroli, an English teacher when not at Mullewa, had not realised the women could neither read nor write. She was devastated by her late discovery, convinced she had failed them by concentrating on the unimportant. But Bessie and the women didn't see it that way. The respect they had been accorded mattered just as much, even though they would have loved to learn to read somewhere in their lives, but so too did the unconditional support they had been given, and the open friendship offered. Bessie and her friends wanted their share of happy times, just like everybody else.

Bessie felt her mother's absence the most when she was alone. And alone she was and alone she felt when soon afterwards blood oozed from her nipple and she had to take her first trip to Perth, returning with one breast removed. She didn't expect Nobby to be any real help. And this was women's business anyway, but of a type not struck before, not for public knowledge she felt, even among the friends she saw regularly. With Ulie gone, she told no-one, her sisters too far away. She took the rice-filled bag, put it in her bra, and went home, the Mullewa Yamatji women not discovering her secret for many years. After a time the radiotherapy did its job, and she no longer had to sit staring at her children wondering what would become of them. Her cancer had gone. Through it all, Nobby drank, and the arguments and fights continued. And Bessie was still there, coping, but with Native Welfare talking to her because her house wasn't as presentable as it used to be. She was having trouble getting money for food, let alone buying cleaning products, now that Ulie's pension was gone. With Nobby drinking more than ever, she relied on child endowment money to feed her family.

In 1970, Ernie was moved from Pallotine over to Geraldton High School. He was relieved. And a new world opened up to him, starting with the train he and Marion caught together, Marion having been home for the holidays. Coming through from Meekatharra, it was already full of excited school kids by the time it got to Mullewa, and the two eldest Dingo children hopped on, swelling the numbers and grinning at all the noise and activity. They were met at Geraldton by people from Della Hale Hostel for Marion, John Frewer Hostel for Ernie. 'So you're Marion Dingo's brother' was the comment. Marion laughed when it changed within a year to 'Ernie Dingo's sister', now her tag instead, even though she'd been a prefect. In the one year she was enrolled when he was, she watched it all happen, saw Ernie become known by many in the large high school, 1400 students and eighty-five teachers its complement, his sporting achievements and the confident ease developed on the basketball court bringing him to their attention. But there were a few he had trouble winning over at first, the boys too well indoctrinated with their parents' attitudes.

The farm boys pinned him up against the wall. It had come to this after days of muttering under their breath. 'What would you know, you're just an Abo,' Ernie heard many times, although he pretended he hadn't. For variety, they substituted coon for abo occasionally.

'My Dad has to pay for my school uniform,' they snarled, determined to get some satisfaction. 'My Dad has to pay for my school bag.' The list continued. 'But you! The Government pays for your travel. The Government pays for your hostel—AND they give you pocket money on top of that. Aborigines have it easy.'

Ernie was bewildered, and wondered if this was what made people call his mob niggers. As soon as he was home, back to Mullewa on his first holiday break, he asked his mother that which had bothered him since hearing the boys' accusations.

'Why does the government have to pay us?' he said. 'Do they want us to learn to be like whitefellas?'

'Well,' Bessie said gently. 'We don't have enough money to teach whitefellas to be like Yamatjis.'

At the school of 1400 pupils, there were about eighty

students assisted by the selective bursary and scholarship schemes which had given Ernie and Marion the opportunity they now had. Hundreds had not and were not given the chance, not recommended by the Welfare officer or school. A year later, a universal secondary grant scheme came into existence, with Aboriginal children across the board at last given access to secondary education on a par with white children.

Ernie settled into hostel life quickly, well used to restrictions after Ulie's domination at home, and also his year at Pallotine. But more helpful was the hostel warden himself. Dick Johnson cared about the seventy-five students he was responsible for, black and white, nurturing Ernie and all the boys, helped by the two Yamatji house parents. Ernie responded well, appreciative of a male who believed in him. Mr Johnson, a talented cricketer and sportsman himself, would take the boys to the oval after school, organising sporting activities, encouraging them all to participate and to improve. Ernie was in his element. There was sport—and there was a telephone, Ernie having unlimited access to one for the first time in his life. He now had the means to fill any empty patches of the day. Every spare moment, it seemed to Dick Johnson, Ernie was on the phone, calling the girls at Della Hale, using some of his twenty dollars per term pocket money. Life was pretty good, thought Ernie. He smiled a lot.

'Ernest is a pleasant student,' said his end of year report after his first year, when he had received average grades in most subjects, with the only A's in Physical Education and Art. 'Great effort and concentration are required if he is to gain full value from his years at school.'

The Aboriginal boys at the hostel bonded together, even though from different areas, the Aboriginal experience in Australia shared by them all. Ernie had been fortunate. His family had for the most part known decent treatment even if they had never possessed much in their lives. But nevertheless, he knew what his Aboriginal brothers and sisters had been through, how they all lived, the problems they all had in common in white society. And he'd look after whoever came, as he'd been taught in his family. Like Les before, he had a healthy sense of his own worth, handed on from Ulie, from Bessie and gained from his own achievements, and he took on what Dick Johnson today describes as a fatherly role. Ernie became the person the new boys went to, yarning with them, showing them what to do, helping them fit in to the environment he was now familiar with, Ernie with his mother's trait of warming to just about everybody he met. Ernie was a people person. It showed in the popularity he was achieving. A few white boys tagged along as well, Gordon Gosper, Steve Cowen and Jimmy Cornell. The Aboriginal boys soon formed their own basketball team, the Royal Demons in the Dingo-inspired hostel competition.

Geraldton offered much to both Marion and Ernie, coming as they did from a small town with not a great variety of activities or new experiences, especially when Yamatjis were still not generally included, confined instead to the town fringes and with the town problems getting bigger. Yamatjis had come in off the stations after 1968, when equal wages for Aboriginal workers in line with white wages had been passed in the Conciliation and Arbitration Commission, with many station owners Australia-wide refusing to pay, others not able to afford to. Many stations in the Murchison tried to keep on workers, labourers being hard to come by out there, but the workers' families had to leave, the men soon following them to town, not wanting the loneliness or the separation. A lot of confused people had appeared in Mullewa, facing emptiness after a life of dignity and pride in what they had been doing. And the station people did not fit in with the town folk. There was tension throughout. The reserve, the only place they had to go, was overcrowded, even though there were only four permanent houses there, but plenty of corrugated tin structures, shelters in reality, had been erected in between by the newly dispossessed. Many tried not to go to the reserve, traditional taboos, Yamatji law, not permitting proximity to certain people or families. They camped as far away as they could, not far at all though in the end, the police always moving them back to the reserve, keeping them out of town, the object to make sure they were out of sight. It was a painful time for those still adhering to Yamatji law ways, and problems arose, more explosive tension, because their law could not be obeyed. Marion, Ernie, and all the kids were told to keep their ears closed, their eyes to the ground, and warned against loose talk. And in the nothingness many a Yamatji stockman who'd had to come in became a drunken ex-stockman, glory days in the saddle relived when they could, with the help of a few beers. It was a time when the world spat them out and forgot them, expected them to behave themselves and fade away quietly. Instead, they despaired. Mullewa did not offer a great future to anybody. And the street lights were still turned off at ten o'clock.

Marion and Ernie had escaped the position their family had been thrust into by historical forces—by the whiteman—only through the good fortune they had to be born when they were. If their births had been a few years earlier, neither would have been given such a chance to complete high school, let alone sent to a school like Geraldton High, the bursaries and scholarships only introduced in the mid-1960s, a time of transition in the political treatment of Aboriginal people. Marion and Ernie had been given what Les always wanted—a chance to participate fully.

And at Geraldton High, Ernie was making the most of it, but not entirely as intended, adding, in the same way he did on the basketball court, his own Yamatji flair. While Marion did her work, Ernie skimmed his. There were so many people to get to know, to laugh with. His infectious enthusiasm drew people to him, according to Dick Johnson. He had succeeded in becoming just like Bruce—except that Bruce, born a few years too early and not getting the same chances, would never be known by as many people. Marion was quieter. All she wanted was to be liked for herself, her Aboriginality acknowledged but making no difference.

As well as impressing with his own style of basketball and the level of competition he played at his age, Ernie emerged as a good long-distance runner, Mr Johnson introducing him to athletics, his long skinny legs and the stamina he'd built up through his time on the court all working for him. He ran easily, but again added his own touch. In his years at the school, he often competed wearing a cadet hat band round his head holding his hair in place for the distance. At the interschool sports events, the school population watched the end of the race from the level above the oval down below. 'Ernie, Ernie,' they chanted as one, as he came close. No matter how close, how tight, the finish, Ernie would look up, sweep his head band off and wave it in a big gesture to the crowd. He enjoyed them enjoying him.

Ernie had become known by nearly everybody at the school by the time he left and had developed a close relationship with the headmaster. Jim Trevaskis was a kind man who looked for the good in all his students and made young Ernie feel special, something he badly needed after Nobby's rejection. It was only years later that Ernie realised Jim Trevaskis made everyone feel that way, which only increased his admiration for him. But Ernie could never resist a bit of mischief. On the last day of the year he and some of his mates watched as Jim Trevaskis started his Volkswagen. The car spluttered and coughed. Mr Trevaskis turned the key again and accompanied by an almighty explosion, a potato shot out of the exhaust, the perpetrators with ringleader Ernie hidden in the shrubbery.

'Mr Trevaskis ...' said Ernie, at the office to own up.

'Not now, Ernie,' said the headmaster.

'But Mr Trevaskis ...'

'I'm sorry, Ernie, but there are some boys waiting I need to see—about an incident with my car.'

'But Mr Trevaskis ... I ...'

'Off you go, Ernie.'

'One student who has excelled in the sporting fields and been a great asset to our school is Ernie Dingo,' the journal profile in his final school year read. 'He is a well known personality of the school and town, and is a fine representative of both.' Ernie, it appeared, had conquered school—but in fact not quite entirely. He finished the four years with no-one suspecting he had never been taught general living skills within the white world, his apparent everyday ease giving the understandable impression he was well equipped. And Mullewa certainly did not—and his mother could not—give him the knowledge he would require. Marion learnt from the Whitehursts, Lizzy, Leslie and Garry, who now lived in Geraldton, and all the books she read, along with the secretarial subjects she had studied at school—bookkeeping, typing, even etiquette—taught her something of the workings of the wider society. But Ernie had not been exposed to that as he cruised through life. And with sport his overwhelming interest, he still preferred a comic over a book. For all his surface confidence, when he left the secure cosy school environment, there were many times he was in need of someone to guide him. In the city, Ernie, like Crocodile Dundee in New York, was an innocent.

Chapter Twenty-Two

'G'orn you mob,' said Richard, in between breaths on the didgeridoo. 'Get up and dance.'

'Dance what?' asked Ernie. The other boys looking similarly puzzled. They were a basketball team after all, a good one.

'Blackfellas playing A grade?' Ernie first thought when he'd played against them at the weekend carnival in Perth, his eyes lighting up. After the game, he'd asked if there was a place for him. And next carnival, two weeks later, Ernie was well and truly back to his old form, his Yamatji flair out of hiding, his flamboyant court antics dusted off, all fitting perfectly in this team. They all played the same way. Ernie had found a home, was on solid ground again. Now, to Richard Walley's urging, the Wildcats basketball team transformed themselves into a dance group, basketball shorts discarded, exchanged—on performance days only, though, basketball still their main passion—for *tjulips*, lap-laps.

It had taken a couple of years for Ernie to find what he wanted in Perth, and he'd always been confused about why he'd been sent, the guidance officer at Geraldton Senior High School organising a signwriting apprenticeship for him, and contacting a baseball team for him to join. Ernie thought there were a few letters missing from the sport they sent him to play, basketball having two extra, but it appears the guidance officer had indeed tried to give Ernie the chance at a life which would suit him, a full life, taking into account his sporting ability rather than just setting up a job alone, as he could have done for him in Geraldton. And Ernie had shown promise in the baseball he had played for John Frewer Hostel. Signwriting—while not a job Ernie had heard or thought of, a country fireman the extent of his ambition at primary school (at high school he'd had no idea)—did suit. He was artistic, his handwriting beautiful. But there would always be problems settling in. Ernie had never thought of a regular job before, having seen only Nobby and Bruce with one, and then only for a short time each. And so, while proud of his signwriting, as well as his lunchtime table-tennis triumphs at technical school, he didn't make the distance. After three-and-a-half years he left, six months before he would have qualified for his ticket. Young Ernie wanted to be with his own mob, much as Bruce had wanted in choosing station work over the PMG. He was working with whitefellas by day, having to rein himself in, then coming home at night to Katakuda Hostel, the boarding facility for Aboriginal boys working in the city. It was not enough. He wanted family, but not necessarily blood ties as decreed in the white world. Even though he was able to banter easily with white people and enjoyed entertaining them, Ernie was Yamatji, and he wanted the familiarity and sense of belonging a shared understood background gave. And he wanted the Yamatji sense of humour. Richard was Yamatji also, the two of them in among the Noongars, the Perth and south-west Aboriginal people. Ernie had found a brother, a very capable one. Richard led him through.

Ernie did have a family with him for a while when he was first in Perth. Marion had come down some time previously and was working in a secretarial job, but as soon as she was old enough she joined the navy, lured by the advertisement featuring the girl in uniform behind the desk in the *Woman's Weekly* each issue. 'That's me,' Marion always said. Bessie wasn't as enthusiastic, her daughter going to where they shoot each other, she was convinced. In Perth Marion had introduced him to Veronica. When Ernie was eighteen, an older age than many other Yamatji boys he knew who did the same, he became a father, his daughter Carlleen born in 1974. Veronica was studying in the city, down from Mount Magnet, but left alone in this strange place, no wider family here for her either, while Ernie worked all day and played sport most nights and weekends too, she returned to her mother, Carlleen being raised, as is the accepted Yamatji way, with the maternal family. Ernie saw her when he was permitted. It was when he met Richard he met his future.

'Do it properly, brother,' Richard now encouraged, and each of the basketballers suddenly turned into dancer as requested, sitting up like kangaroos, twitching and scratching, walking like emus, beaks pecking, and also nyumbying, doing shake-a-leg, to the didge reverberations—all very strange to the lads, Ernie included, who'd only nyumbied back when they were kids, or on the basketball court when they were playing the fool. But Richard had always understood their tomfoolery was beyond showing off, even if they had not recognised it themselves. They were declaring who they were to the whitefellas they played, and now Richard, an extremely capable man with plans, not just for himself but for whichever blackfella he could assist, wanted them to do it seriously. They couldn't refuse, all aware Richard's vision was wider than theirs.

'I've got some young blokes who can dance,' he began to say to anyone who asked him to bring his didgeridoo and perform. Richard knew how to negotiate both cultures, knew what was appropriate, and had sought and been granted permission to play the age-old instrument from the people way up north, didgeridoo not being from his country, his area. And he had requested permission to use the dances too. In the white world he also knew how to get things done, and had introduced himself long ago to the tourist authorities in Perth. The Middar Dance Group came into being, performing at first at basketball carnival entertainment nights, then at weekends at the Swan River Winery, sometimes even going so far as to rehearse for a few minutes before they performed, almost an overkill in their eyes, when they already knew what to do. They'd be right they knew, all of them so laid back, unaffected, anxiety unknown, after all, being on stage was just like performing on the court. At the Winery they gave a twenty-minute performance early afternoon while people ate and drank, but the performers were not generally as well fed as the patrons. Paid only when the Winery did their bookwork, Ernie and his fellow dancers mostly lunched on chip sandwiches, no sauce, whatever money they had pooled to buy a loaf of bread and a dollar's worth of chips. Belonging to this dance troupe was never going to bring in a fortune, a hundred dollars a performance split beween the number of dancers who showed not stretching far. But it did mean none of them had to go on the dole. And it also gave them something they'd never expected—a couple of trips overseas, the boys being invited to Germany and Switzerland, their fares paid but not much else. But they had travelled, shown who they were to the other side of the world. They'd all been excited at such opportunities, but were determined to present the same nonchalance they showed before a basketball game, such casualness the only way to avoid a thorough teasing from Franklyn or Theo. But their clothing was anything but casual for these trips, Louis Beers, who ran the men's clothing store Ernie now worked in part-time, giving them matching hire outfits, insisting they all dress the same.

The basketball team became Ernie's Perth family, a close one. They stood and leant on each other, arms slung around each other's shoulders, while being coached, hugged and held tightly those they hadn't seen for a while. And each team member's family became family too, all part of one big mob, all parents becoming Mum and Dad, any children nieces and nephew. They hung out together, Richard and Ernie, Franklyn Nannup, Theo Kearing, Trevor Walley, lounged in each other's homes, helped each other when it was needed. Ernie was cruising again, he had found family for himself. And he also had a live-in relationship with his girl-friend Christine and her young son. When he wasn't dancing, coaching or playing basketball or footy, or fooling around, teasing any young kids in the neighbourhood, he and Morton Hanson, a fellow dancer, would do the rounds, mowing lawns and visiting the old folk, the Noongars all glad when they came. The basket-ball team also served a useful role in helping some win a few battles against alcohol. Many young boys were brought into the team when it became clear to Richard, Ernie and the regular players that family members were falling for drink and blotting out their lives. The team tried to give each newcomer a purpose, even if only for a few carnivals, a chance to stay away from the grog, a chance for the 'youngfellas' to enjoy using their skills again. Many could not get a game in the white teams around country Western Australia.

'Got a job for you,' Richard announced over the phone to Ernie.

'That's good, brother. What is it?' said Ernie, expecting another dance job, maybe working with kids, maybe another footy season inland, where after a long car trip each Sunday he could sometimes make a hundred dollars for the week if they won, what with match payments, best on the ground, goal of the day, mark of the day and local farmers pressing a few dollars into their palms, pleased to see a win, all the money he and his mates made spread on the bed and then divvied up.

'Acting!' said Richard.

'That's good, brother,' said Ernie. 'Doin' what?'

'You know, like they do on television.'

'Oh yeah?' said Ernie.

The play would open in a month, explained Richard, instructing Ernie to go and see them. Jack Davis's play *Kullark* was being workshopped and rehearsed with performances scheduled at the four weeks' end. The role had originally been offered to Richard, but realising the division of skills in his dance group and basketball team and being a writer, and a mover and shaker while Ernie was chief performer both on the court and off, he sent Ernie instead. Or so he thought. Ernie, hearing that it would be what he thought was such a lengthy time before the show opened, went home to Mullewa to visit his Mum as he always had every chance he got ever since his school days.

But it was to a different house, a better one, fibro, bigger, and more presentable. Nobby had gone, Bessie enlisting Native Welfare to help change the house over into her name, finally telling him he had to leave. It hadn't been easy, he wanted to take his kids and let his sister raise them, and there had been a few fights. But life was more peaceful now, even if she'd had to live on emergency ration payments from Welfare for a while. Nobby died a few years later, hit by a car in Geraldton. He'd had a sad life, died a sad way. Poor Nobby had never known it easy.

Richard tracked Ernie down, phoned him via the Native Welfare office in Mullewa.

'What are you doing up there?' he asked.

'Seeing my Mum,' Ernie answered, wondering why his brother was checking up. 'I got another coupla weeks before the show starts.'

'You gotta go to rehearsals,' announced Richard.

'Oh!' said Ernie, amazed. But he wasn't concerned. He could wing this like he did everything else.

Ernie returned to Perth, turning up two weeks before opening night. Winging it, he soon found, would not be allowed. Richard gave him a few tips, explained what acting was about, and added a humorous Shakespearean-style rendition. Ernie took it on board.

The others had been busy at the rehearsal cum workshop, and all the rewrites were complete. Ernie began, reading very slowly, doing what he thought Richard meant, art-ic-u-lat-ing beautifully, pro-ject-ing as actors did, so he'd been led to believe, reading his lines, he now says, like a slow Queenslander, the blackfella he was playing strangled somewhere in the portrayal. Andrew Ross, the director, let him continue—there was no time to find someone else, and Ernie, known as a joker, was probably fooling anyway.

'Are you all right?' he finally said, taking Ernie aside, gently hinting something was not quite working, without actually saying so. 'Just relax a bit.'

And Ernie did so. But there was another problem still. Jack Davis, the playwright, approached. He'd watched for several days.

'Ernie, that word there, what is it?'

'Epi-tome,' said Ernie confidently.

'Do you know what it means?' asked Jack.

'Na,' said Ernie.

'Do you know how you're supposed to say it?'

'Na,' said Ernie.

'Epi-to-me.'

'I've heard of that!' said Ernie.

Ernie now jokingly takes the credit for Andrew working so successfully over the years with Aboriginal actors. 'I was his worst case,' he says.

Ernie learnt his role in time, his memory sharp, probably as a result of the oral tradition he was from. For Yamatji people, that tradition today takes the form of yarns recalled, and also the constant speaking of kinship and family lines which are still explained in detail, all recognised relationships contained within, expected to be memorised and acknowledged. Ernie had listened well and, on seeing someone of Aboriginal descent in the street, still asks their parents' names, working out which line they are from, listing others who are also related. And he is able to tell which area someone is from, having learnt which facial features indicate which particular country. Ernie is not unusual in possessing these skills. Most Aboriginal people have been taught the same way.

On opening night, in February 1979, now that he had worked out what was going on, realised scenes ran into one another, understood where he was to come out from and what lines were to be said where, Ernie was, he says, right into it. This acting game was pretty good. He loved it. *Kullark*, part of a Theatre in Education program, then toured south-west of Perth for three months, playing at schools and civic centres, Lynette Narkle, Mick Fuller, Richard Tullock, and Dawn Blay his fellow cast-members.

Kullark is the story of an Aboriginal leader who led a fight to try to rid his traditional country of the invaders, after his people were shot when they either tried to take potatoes growing on their land or speared sheep grazing there, shot as well when they attempted to camp near their normal watering places. Their lands were now gone, the whiteman said, and Yagan led the resistance. After a courageous fight, in a battle he and his people had little hope of winning, pitted as they were against men armed with bullets, he was beheaded, his head smoked on a stump and sent to England. Only in September 1997, it would happen, was it finally returned to his homeland. Jack Davis had written the play incensed by a 1979 official government publication which stated man had first come to Western Australia in 1829, the statement refusing an existence to all Aboriginal people who'd ever been. Ernie had heard stories like Yagan's before—most Aboriginal people knew them—and Richard, in his dignified manner devoid of hate or the need to exact revenge, told him more, and told him to show another way. Ernie listened, and learnt. And Jack's words he had to speak burnt deep. He began to understand who he was on a different level.

Ernie enjoyed the tour, didn't mind the endless setting up and dismantling, the moving from place to place. But there were people they performed to who weren't aware what a play was, small children convinced that what they saw was real.

'Oo-oo! They killed Uncle Ernie!' Richard's five-year-old niece screamed over and over, as Yagan's head, a mask of Ernie's face topped with a wig, was pulled out of the box. While the play continued, she was hurriedly taken backstage, to hug Uncle and see how well they'd put his head back on.

When the tour finished Ernie went back to basketball and driving a courtesy vehicle for the Aboriginal Medical Service, a taxi service for Noongars needing to get to a hospital or doctor. Acting had been an interesting interlude, taught him a lot, but was over, much like a basketball carnival. Another role had been offered him straightaway, but he had only lasted a week, the role, playing a man from India in a children's production, not for him. He still hadn't learnt that an actor acts, not is. And there were few Aboriginal plays yet written. But he didn't leave the production without amusing a few people with his ingenuousness again.

There she stood, an actress brought over from the eastern states. Ernie was excited, and walked straight up.

'I know you!' he said.

'He he,' she chuckled. 'Do you?'

'Yeah, I know you!' He paused. 'What were you in now?'

'Oh,' she sighed. 'Number 96.'

'Yeah, that's it! That's right!' Another pause. 'Who did you play now?'

'Um. Rose Gudolphis.'

'Yeah, that's right!' continued Ernie, still as thrilled as when he'd first started the interrogation. 'Wha's your name?'

She was probably glad he didn't stay for the season.

Ernie took the information a friendly Welfare officer had dropped at his house around to his mentor, asking him what to do.

'Richard,' he said, 'how do you write letters for jobs?'

And Ernie signed the application applying to work in Camp

Jungai in Victoria, doing it to keep everybody happy, to get them off his back, never for a moment thinking he had a chance.

'Hey, look-out! What's this?' he said incredulously when they wrote asking him to come for an interview, fares paid, hotel booked, and someone organised to drive him up from Melbourne, deliver him to the race relations camp in the Rubicon Valley near Lake Eildon. In the interview he was asked about his cultural background and knowledge, and back he went to Perth.

'Good, brother,' said Richard when Ernie blurted he'd been successful, a letter arriving in the mail. 'You'll be teaching them mob all about Yamatjis. They're called Kooris.'

'Yeah,' said Ernie, not knowing what a Koori was, '... b ... but I gotta go and live over there.'

'You'll be right,' Richard assured him.

Ernie went ahead, Christine and her young son joining him two months later. By the time she arrived, Ernie had joined the nearest basketball and football team, and fitted in well. For a time back in Perth, as a result of getting to know kids on the streets, he had worked with young people in Longmore Juvenile Detention Centre, and a course he had undertaken then came to his assistance now.

'What do you kids know about Aboriginal culture?' he would ask any new group who arrived, knowing how to get the classes involved.

And Ernie was learning a lot too. Now, he often sat asking himself just what did he know about Yamatjis. And he would sit and listen to other groups who came in, impressed by the knowledge the cultural speakers had, Albert Mullet, Wayne Atkinson and Gail Sculthorpe. Ernie's teaching became stronger and stronger. And so did he.

Jack Davis's play *Dreamers* had a run in Perth, and a national tour was organised. Ernie was contacted. He went home to Perth, rehearsed this time, and began the tour, Andrew Ross again directing, to Melbourne, Brisbane, the Sydney Opera House, even Tasmania. As they travelled Aboriginal communities came out to greet them, the people so proud to see an Aboriginal play touring the nation. Families would come and take them for meals, show them the sights, always looking after them.

Back in Perth, it was harder for Ernie to settle. He'd taken on a few challenges in the past few years, and felt good about himself. He was ready for more, but didn't know what. It was a difficult time for Christine. The man she'd lived with for several years had changed. And she was hurt. But there was no turning back.

'Brother, I gotta go,' said Ernie.

'Yeah, right, *koodah*. No worries,' Richard replied, giving his blessing.

Ernie caught a bus east to Melbourne, but travelled even further after running into someone he knew.

'Them mob looking for you back home,' the messenger reported.

No-one would think to look down in Tasmania. But someone did. Two months later, his job driving the bus at the Aboriginal Centre was cut short when someone managed to track him down. His appearance at the Sydney Opera House the year before had been noticed, he was told, and he was now invited to the 1983 National Playwrights' Conference in Canberra, to workshop Tony Strachan's play, *State of Shock*.

He arrived, a confident and beautiful young man, according to Bob Ellis. And after a fortnight working with his group, in the one performance they delivered to the conference at large, Ernie's performance, it was reported, was astonishing.

'I thought he was a star then,' says Bob, 'and later on when I saw *Bran Nue Dae*, I thought he was a particular type of star, like Henry Fonda. He seemed to walk in out of legend, partly to do with thinness and tallness. He came like a ghost out of the mist.' Along with several Aboriginal actors at the conference never seen before, Ernie was 'an epic figure'.

Jane Cameron, Ernie's first agent in Sydney whom he found the week following the Playwrights' Conference after being urged to come to the big city by those who assured him he could make a living this way, thought he needed considerable protection. She educated him about the film industry as much as she could, but left the rest—life—to him, not wanting to intervene, wanting him to stay his own person. Ernie ploughed in, had triumphs, made mistakes, sought company. And survived. We met five years later.

I collected a brightly dressed Ernie from his inner city flat and drove him as arranged by his agent to appear on the Ray Martin *Midday* show. He was annoyed. I had been later than he would have liked, never having met him before and unaware how earnest he was about his work. And he was nervous. But as soon as we were taken to the Green Room, where guests wait before an appearance, and he realised we were well within time, he relaxed—so much so that I was amazed. He was a man not confined by the behavioural norms I was familiar with, those of white middle-class Australia. He sank into the couch, leaned in close, and sang me a song, a response to author Frank Hardy's face on the screen.

> *Poor bugger me Gurindji*
> *Me bin sit down this country*
> *Long time before the Lord Vestey*
> *Allabout land belongin' to we*
> *Oh poor bugger me Gurindji*

Bessie in brother Les's hat, sitting on the shearers' truck at Woolgorong Station.

Bessie in *the* coat with *those* ankles.

Passengers about to catch the mail truck loaded with kangaroo skins aplenty on top of the wool bales.

Harry Moorhead (kneeling in front) hawking clothing and wares to the men on Byro Station. Owen, on left, holds a toy gun awkwardly, his skill with a real rifle in no need of play-acting. Next to him, from left to right, are fellow workers Jimmy Ryan, Clarrie Cashin and Joe Egan, Pearlie's husband. Obbie Peet, right, also holds a toy gun.

He sang it in its entirety, Ted Egan's song about the Gurindji people's struggle for their land, when Frank Hardy alerted and took the media along to meet these gentle people of the Northern Territory, helping eventually to achieve what they sought. Gough Whitlam poured soil into Vincent Lingiari's hand in 1973, granting him and his people a lease on which they now run their own cattle station. I was mesmerised, but not really sure of how I should be responding. It was a powerful song, deserving more than polite, nice approval. I opted for silence. I knew the Gurindji fight, having been at university during the Whitlam era, immersing myself in the dreams he permitted my generation. Here, while we waited, in my ignorance about big-city life, too naive to realise there were many circles, many people with differing life-styles, values and interests, I was relieved to finally find someone in eighties' Sydney who was aware of something beyond night-clubbing, making money, and going out to dinner.

The circles I had entered due to my work as a sales represent-ative for a television station, then radio, were all I had met in my couple of years' harbour city residency. And I had worked hard to find some acceptance, seeing only what was before me, getting myself into debt to buy the required clothes, leasing the right car, and going to the acceptable places, feeling empty, a fraud, denying who I really was, a small town girl with a different background from those I was meeting. Ernie allowed me to see what I had pushed aside. Australia was bigger than the people I knew, with history, with events of importance outside my own life. He took me away from who I had fooled myself I had to be in the big smoke. I looked at him, and saw our similarities, his gaudy shirt, leather trousers, the too many chains around his neck now understood, worn in an attempt to fit some social scene. He was an outsider, floundering, just like me.

Chapter Twenty-Three

'Look at me! I'm bigger already!' she said proudly, hands held above her head to measure. Wilara, our adopted daughter, had just turned four. But proud Daddy wouldn't be home until the following morning, and he wasn't happy not being there for the big day, missing her as he always did when he had to go away to work, his precious '*widjarnu*', the little stranger who had travelled to us, who had made such a difference in our lives. Wilara gave us family. And was family.

'We had a visitor last night,' said Virginia, Ernie's sister, soon after Wilara had joined our mob. Ginni, as she was known, had come to stay for a few days, along with Donelle and Marion, all racing to be the first to see their new niece. With a shortage of space in our small rented house, Ginni was on a mattress on the floor next to where Wilara slept, when she heard footsteps on the polished boards and recognised the sound from her childhood, one foot slightly dragging, on the way to the cot. Ulie was there, bending over her new great-granddaughter, making sure everything was all right, Ginni told us all, in matter-of-fact tones. I wanted Granny Ulie to come more often, and hung a painting of a red-tailed black cockatoo, her totem, to entice her.

'Sally!' Ernie's Mum chuckled sympathetically but incredulously at my mistake, shaking her head at what I had done. 'She can't come when that's there.'

It was forbidden to gaze upon your own totem, the animal or bird which was yourself, whether flesh, or image. I'd done it again, shown my naivety in Ernie's culture. There was still so much to learn.

In our early years together, before Wilara came to us, Ernie and I both had much to decipher, to understand, both had a long road to walk. It was not always easy, and it was not well defined. In the white world, Ernie's innate intelligence, his personality, and his intuitive acting skills, covered much of the unworldliness he still had, and covered much of who he really was. I learnt over time, after consistently being astonished. And it began when I witnessed his complete lack of artifice.

He led me from actor to actor at the cast and crew party on the American series *Dolphin Cove* being filmed in Queensland, holding out my left hand, beaming with pleasure at the engagement ring he had chosen and bought for me, failing to notice the startled looks on their faces. The American actors, no big names among them, were earning amounts unheard of by their Australian colleagues, one sixteen-year-old on the series, unknown to the screen as yet, out to score a few points by boasting he was earning four times per episode what Ernie was being paid. They peered, and blinked, the seven-hundred-dollar ring with three tiny diamonds not quite what they would have purchased. Ernie, though, thought it was exquisitely beautiful, and indeed it was pretty. I smiled, uncomfortably at first until I talked myself through, pretended I didn't notice and watched their faces.

And I also began to see beyond the convincing performance he carried off each day, the city bloke he could do so well, looking and acting the part faultlessly, so much so that it was easy to presume he had mostly left his origins behind. Instead, though, he carried them with him. Ernie was of the Dingo family, connected always, and a Yamatji to the centre of his heart. He missed his home and family badly, and Richard too. It was not surprising then when he paid for his mother to join us in Alice Springs immediately after our wedding.

Bessie's children were all grown now, and she no longer lived in one place, no longer had a house of her own, moving instead from daughter to daughter, helping with the grannies, the grand-children, as her cultural role prescribed. And she'd come at Ernie's invitation to get to know her newest, and it so happened, eldest daughter. She piled the toast high, the camp pie on each piece spread liberally with tomato sauce, both considered treats out in the bush when she'd been a cattle camp cook, and she lovingly placed the mountain of food before me, her offering sublime in its simplicity and beauty. We sat and talked while Ernie, out the back, on a chair, mug of tea on the ground beside him, leaned into the wall and hosed the patchy lawn. Ernie watered the small lawn square every day, morning and night, and glowed with serenity and contentment. This was a good honeymoon.

I was unprepared then, for what I took to be a betrayal, for what I interpreted as a lack of concern for me. Bessie stood and watched as a whitefella friend of Sister Betty's assured me the paddy melons growing in profusion on the side of the road were bush tucker, tasty, pleading to be eaten. I took the piece offered— and spat, the taste horrible, one which oozed into my flesh and stayed there, endless in its torment. Why? I asked myself through the tears I fought back, from hurt and bewilderment more than any real injury. Why had she been so loving one minute, so unfeeling the next? And when we pulled up at the waterhole, and Bessie instructed me to take a handful of sand and throw it, to introduce myself to Bimurda, the water snake within, saying 'I am your countryman,' I hesitated, wondering what trick was going to come now. I had believed, Ernie had told me, she would look after me. And she had presumed Ernie would step in. But neither had felt they could challenge the man. Both had stood, shy, unwilling to confront, powerless they believed. They let the man do what he would. I was angry with them both, and confused. And now it took some time to convince me it was essential to introduce myself to the spirit who lived in the stagnant water, that it was the first action one should take, one which showed respect, and one which would safeguard my family, the snake exacting revenge by an illness befalling a family member unless he was made aware I came in friendship. And it took some time to realise Ernie was often speechless before the whitefellas, unable to challenge, to contradict, unable to tell the man no. This time, Ernie couldn't walk away and pretend it wasn't happening, his most frequent response when people didn't play by the Yamatjis' rules he knew. I was in the middle. He watched. And tried to support, to comfort me later.

Back in Sydney, Ernie resumed his larger-than-life personality, all confidence, smiles, and the funny lines he was so good at, spreading the illusion the world was at his feet. He was Les brought back to life. On our own, though, he and I both knew the truth. I'd seen the shopkeepers keep him waiting till last, pretending he wasn't there, serving anyone but him. I'd seen the look on his face. I'd seen his helplessness as he stood on the footpath outside real estate offices, sending me in to ask the questions, to get the keys, to do all the talking. We found places to rent this way, but once, even with the lease signed, when we returned to look over the house, the owner who lived next door came running—and suddenly the house needed immediate repairs, was no longer available, not to us anyway.

And on a well-earned holiday at a resort in Broome, a package trip we had saved for, Ernie was ordered from the pool, shouted at to get out, the manager refusing to believe he was a paying guest. Ernie, still in the water, looked up at the towering figure above, nervously stumbled over his words and forgot our room number, the manager gleeful that he had indeed been right. This Aboriginal person in their swimming pool was lying! It was only when Ernie managed to hoist himself out of the pool, search in all his pockets, the manager standing smugly in his certainty, that on producing the key he received an explanation, but not an apology. There'd been someone in the pool who shouldn't have been, so he'd been told. And he'd come straight to Ernie, presumed guilty because of his race. I watched from a distance, horrified, wondering what to do, having made a recent decision that I shouldn't do it all for Ernie in my world, that he must learn to stand on his own. Many guests, some high profile, watched with their mouths wide open.

And once I was shamed by my own actions, after a disagreement, our first few years of marriage littered with such arguments while we both learnt how to be married. I refused on that one occasion to enact the technique most couples of our racial mix use to hail a cab. I refused to take my place on the street and attract their attention, sending Ernie instead. He vainly tried taxi after taxi, looking back at me pleading, pain on his face. With tears brimming in his eyes, he asked me again, and I stepped forward, the very next cab pulling to the curb. He ran and got in. I felt sick at how I had baldly, callously, laid before him the position he was allotted in our society. He knew it already. It was one of the reasons he tried so hard every day.

Ernie and I were firm friends within our marriage, both of us in Sydney with no family, no network of old friends, no-one to fall back on. We relied on each other, and enjoyed spending time together, regardless of our teething problems. I was always amazed at how artlessly open and affectionate he was, my own family one where feelings were presumed but never spoken. I was constantly told I was loved, still learning to speak such a strange language. But there were times when, no matter how we tried to bridge the gap between our worlds, it seemed unpassable, pushing us to the limit, forcing a decision between marriage or not. Our desire for children brought it all to the surface, confronted as I was with a man whose responses were not like mine, with a man still not easy with many situations white society presented. His job made it blow sky high.

As Ulie had done all those years ago, I waited for a pregnancy to occur. But unlike Ulie, after several years, and several false alarms with all the heartache they brought, we had no success. Each month delivered sadness, a sense of failure, each month I retreated further within. We became tense, disappointed. I felt guilty, a failure in a family with so many children. We sought help, and Ernie was sent for a test, one which was highly embarrassing for him, one which meant revealing too much, and one which, according to the way he'd been taught, was only for men to know. He was sent for a sperm test.

I gave him the results, not realising the need for extreme sensitivity in my delivery, too caught up in my own need not to be guilty, to announce I was not responsible. His count was low, very low. Ernie glowered, furious with me, the doctor, the world. He was hurt, and humiliated. But we still hadn't reached rock-bottom, even though it seemed as if we were so far down already. There was in-vitro fertilisation treatment to go through yet.

I submitted to the daily drugs, and the large dose of hope the highly publicised technology presented, even though the limited success rate had been explained. And my ovaries did as they should, producing multiple ova, eggs to be fertilised externally, then placed high in the fallopian tubes in the hope of simulating a natural fertilisation, in a few days embedding themselves in the womb wall. Drugged, partly sitting up with my legs high and spread wide to allow the surgeon to remove the ova, the nurse brought Ernie in from the waiting room, leading him past where the doctor sat, bringing him to be with me, the same as she did with other husbands, most of them wanting to be with their wives. On seeing Ernie appear, his eyes pleading and darting, his shoulders slumped, his look unbalanced, I tried to speak up, but my words were slurred and slow.

'Take him out,' I struggled to say.

I fought my tears when he was seated, shaking, next to me, when I could clearly see his face, horrified, fearful, helpless. I knew instantly he'd been unable to tell the nurse no.

'This is women's business,' I kept on, when my mouth would obey.

The nurse and surgeon were confused at first, stopped, then understood, the nurse leading him back to where he'd been. They were embarrassed and upset. I was too. Ernie was traumatised. And my burden felt heavy. There was no-one there for me. If I'd been close to family, my family or his, someone would have been there, a woman to see me through. And alone, I had somehow to support my husband. I found it hard, and wept a lot.

And I found it hard when Ernie couldn't understand the procedure we were undergoing. Three fertilised ova, divided cells, were implanted.

'Our little babies are in there,' he so gently and lovingly said, hugging me from behind, his head on my shoulder, his hands over my stomach.

I knew what he couldn't or wouldn't grasp. I knew our chances. I was scared as I broke the news. I didn't want him to cry. But he did. To him we had lost our children. I tried to comfort, but it could never be enough. We grieved separately, coping as we could. I resented his inability to be as white men, and closed up. And he turned outwards, as he had done all his life, desperately filling his moments with people, anywhere, on the road, in his work.

A sixteen-year-old niece of his arrived with her six-month-old baby, an indefinite stay planned. I watched as she filled the baby's bottle with full-strength powdered milk and two dessert spoonfuls of Milo, several times each day. And I watched as the baby threw it all up. His niece was raising her baby away from her own mother, and refusing to seek advice. Conscious of how delicately any suggestions needed to be put, we presented alternatives, but to no avail. And it was my turn not to understand, my turn to miss a few essential points. I did not consider her specific needs, failed to recognise just how different those needs were from someone like myself who was comfortable in all aspects of white society. We'd negotiated, and she'd agreed to attend a clinic a suburb away, but only if I would push the pram.

The stitches in my navel pulled, two more fertilised eggs implanted, and I bent over in pain, the hills at times too steep, the pram heavy. The nursing sister tried to speak to Ernie's niece without condescension, but unsuccessfully, failing to connect on a personal level, failing, it appeared, to know how. And Ernie's niece was intimidated, felt in trouble. She nodded, head down, at what she was told to do, meekly accepted the two tins of baby formula offered and left. Outside, she turned both tins over. The use-by date had expired.

'I'm not going to no white doctor again,' she said, her suspicions confirmed. 'She's trying to make my baby sick.'

Ernie's niece, a girl too young to be a mother, with too many unhappy experiences with whitefellas relayed through her family, was unable to trust or believe any would wish to help, and she reached the only conclusion she could allow. I was stunned such a mistake had been made after the effort to get her there, realised I should have taken her to where she would feel more comfortable, to where Aboriginal staff were available. And I knew that had been the last chance. But I also had to be aware the baby was not mine, had to be aware it was not for me to take over, the white middle-class girl with the knowledge my background gave presuming a superiority over a young girl whose family had been displaced, sent to the edges of perceived humanity. Ernie and I watched, bought new formula which his niece decided to use, and snuck the baby, now eight months old, bottles of diluted fruit juice.

In our own lives, at the month's end, we relived our devastation when our IVF had again not worked, our pain intense once more. And Ernie sent his niece home when she did what teenagers do, try to hurt where it would hurt the most.

'What would you know,' she said, 'you can't even have babies.'

•

Ernie and I were shellshocked by it all, turned away from each other, had a lot to work through if we wanted to stay together. And Ernie had the additional problem of increasing fame with more televison appearances, of people wanting to know him, telling him he was invincible, telling him he was something other than himself. For a time the fringe-dweller boy who grew up in a humpy, the boy who'd been called nigger, became ensnared by the fantasies fame peddles, beguiled by how well he'd been accepted, his innocence preventing him seeing the dangers which could arise. We were at crisis point.

'Slow down,' Bessie ever wise told him.

'Decide,' I said.

And Ernie chose family, had always thought family, but presumed one would always be waiting.

We'd come a long way, were different people from the two who fronted at the Registry Office in 1989. We could now move on. And Ernie, the bloke, decent and lovable, the mate who genuinely enjoyed people wherever he went, had his feet firmly on the ground again. It was good to have him back.

Chapter Twenty-Four

'Gavin, have you been drinking?' I dared to ask, taking his call. It was three o'clock in the morning, and his voice was strange.

'No, my sister,' Ernie's cousin-brother, my brother-in-law, said softly.

And we were on our way to Geraldton. Ernie was so very sad. We were on our way to a funeral.

I was familiar with Geraldton now, and Auntie Pearlie's camp as well, had stayed several times, most recently a couple of week-long visits on my own. I'd seen and heard a lot. I'd had dreams like no other while staying there, a spirit teasing me, testing me, so I was told, with Auntie Pearlie telling it to leave me alone, that me writing the family story was all right. I'd been smoked, had walked through the fumes, rubbing it in, coating myself in the protection it gave. I'd helped select and collect kangaroo tails from the pet meat supplier, listened as he, Bessie and Tania, my sister-in-law, discussed the different qualities of the carcasses hanging upside down, some too rich, others too gamey, rock wallaby too tough, while I gazed at the severed heads with gaping bullet holes on the table. And I'd eaten the kangaroo tails when baked as well as the stew. I'd had a ceremonial headpiece made for me, Auntie Pearlie sitting and yarning while she cut the pliable branch as far down as necessary, curling the narrow strips, feathering the whiteness, the only thing missing the corroboree.

And I'd made mistakes.

'Do you know what your missus has done now?' Gavin phoned Ernie in Sydney to report immediately, on how, with all the women present, I'd said *boogoo*, backside, while a man was in the room.

'I nearly fell over when she said that,' he'd said, laughing, even though obviously shocked as well.

And I'd heard stories, plenty of stories, surreal, other-worldly stories, of powers being handed on, of hands being 'opened', of manifestations of those powers travelling through people's bodies. I'd been told of fantastic dreams, of ice and water, of big white dogs with shining eyes, of visiting places while remaining at home. And I'd heard more talk of Dingo Jim.

Now we were on our way back. Bruce had passed away, died in Crummy Whitehurst's arms of a heart attack, as Gavin drove in the early hours of the morning, trying to reach the hospital in time. And the cousin-brother Ernie had idolised as a boy, the bigger boy he had wanted to be, was gone, only forty-four years old. The entire family was grieving.

We pulled in again to Auntie Pearlie's driveway, and again, no-one came to meet us, seated as they were in order inside, waiting to 'meet' us properly. And there were many more to come, many more to meet. Family was travelling from afar, and would be arriving in small groups, sharing lifts if possible, doing whatever they could to get here. It had taken a while to decide the day for the funeral. Obtaining a specific date for one was often difficult, the date dependent on when certain members of the family could travel, whether cars had to be fixed, and also whether anybody had money. Sometimes it could be delayed for a fortnight. On an earlier occasion I had called from Sydney, requested information about another.

'Lettin' you know the funeral is next pension week,' was the message left on our answering machine.

And it was up to me to then find out the specifics. Anyone with close community links would know the time framework had been identified, and could make approximate plans accordingly until the exact day was pinpointed. But such a loose and accommodating system meant problems for any family member who worked in the mainstream white world, that world possessing, it seems, little understanding of the organisational methods and family commitments of Yamatji Australians. I have even heard of Yamatjis who've had to resign from their jobs, just so they could meet the obligations, could honour the families within the extended kinship networks as required, and as they wished to.

Ernie, as cousin-brother, had come a few days early to help with the arrangements. He was the only one available to do so, others not yet arrived, most having to scrape the money together to come from Carnarvon, 600 kilometres away, Owen, Bruce's father, not in a position to help either, coming from Carnarvon himself, and now with one arm and leg amputated, the result of diabetes. And Gavin, who ran his own Aboriginal shearing team, knew he should keep his men working, most of them family, Crummy too, keep them shearing until the day before the funeral itself, keeping their minds focused, concentrating on the job. We travelled to the station where the team was working, and outside the shed, flock of sheep penned and bleating nearby, Ernie and Gavin moved to one side to meet.

Ernie and I rented a holiday unit in Geraldton, only an hour's drive away from Mullewa where the funeral and burial were planned, Bruce having made it known to everybody, he'd come back from Carnarvon to be in his country, his home, near to where his Granny was buried, near to Ulie who had raised him. The unit gave us the extra room we needed so a couple of the travellers could stay with us, Marion and her daughter Scottie having journeyed, like many others, from Darwin. It was night-time when Sister Betty came through the door, announcing quietly 'Your *koodah* [brother] here.'

Ernie moved quickly, and said not a word, pushing chairs back, out of the way, spreading a hastily grabbed blanket on the floor, over the carpet. Marion raced to go out to the car, eager to see the young nephew she knew would be there—and as quickly raced back, having suddenly been jolted with the realisation of why they'd come visiting, why the formal declaration they were here, and why the wait. Betty's job had been as emissary. Cousin-brother Larry, Hilda's son, had come to meet them, so too Betty's daughter Loretta, both having arrived from Perth, and Betty had been sent in first to give Ernie and Marion time to prepare. And they were ready, the blanket on the floor, when Larry and Loretta came through the door. I stood out of the way, never having met

Larry before. Larry, an initiated lawman, swiftly entered, dived straight to Ernie on the blanket, placed his left hand open over Ernie's heart, his right shaking Ernie's hand. And then they hugged, tightly, weeping, brother to brother, for their brother. Marion cried with Loretta. They moved on to the other, and cried again, although with less intensity, the ties between brothers much stronger. I was then introduced to Larry, who shook my hand warmly, calling me Sister. Larry was head to toe in new clothes, nothing too flash, but dressed up out of respect, to say goodbye to his brother Bruce. I was a little in awe. Larry's face was the most gentle I'd ever seen, his gaze tender and placid. And unwavering.

On the morning of the funeral, after the car trip where Ernie had talked about any and everything, all at an exaggerated speed, all to cover his nervousness, all to try to give the appearance of detachment, we joined the whole family, Bruce's immediate family, and went on to the Catholic church together. People milled about outside the beautiful handbuilt stone building, all dressed in as much black as they could manage to find, black regarded by Yamatjis as essential for any funeral. Many cried softly while they waited for the first family, the Dingos, to move in, and I watched as two small girls, only seven years old, solemnly reached for each other across the stone wall, to hug and cry together too. Sister Betty grabbed my hand tightly and cradled my arm as we moved on in.

'Su-nita, you take Nana Sally's other hand,' she said to her granddaughter, now my granddaughter too.

Su-nita obeyed without hesitation, and with two protectors, I was escorted through the crowd, gently led, and guided fully. No-one would allow me to make a mistake, my extended family watching, nudging and correcting. No-one would leave me to stumble.

At the cemetery Bessie, with more directness than I'd known her capable of, ordered me to stand behind her chair at the open grave, the coffin next to it. Uncle Owen was beside her in his wheelchair. And on the other side of me Larry's sister Netta stood, her position set by her status as the eldest sister in the full Dingo family. Auntie Pearlie, not as agile as Bessie, stayed in a van parked near with the door open to allow a good view. Ernie and the boys, men now, Bruce's brothers, Gavin, Michael, Trumby and Larry stayed together, only Brother Ronald missing, unable to get through a flooded area in time. The rest of the many mourners, all Aboriginal except for a handful of white people, all family friends, Obbie Peet, Les Clayton, John Macpherson, and Bruce's old school mate, Tony Ventura, stood in the hot sun, standing anywhere so they could see. Clarrie was there with his wife Thelma, as he always would be, Dingos his family too, and more so now that Cecil had passed away a few years before.

In the centre place, I felt conspicuous for a while, exposed, in full view of everybody, as I stood behind my seated mother-in-law as she had ordered. And I wondered whether I had committed a *faux pas* by placing both my hands on her shoulders when she sobbed as the casket was lowered into the ground. She then stood and held me, leaning in for support, and stayed for a while, as people started to come forward, one by one, shaking my hand once, as was the custom, with dignified gravity and lowered eyes, then moving on. By placement alone, without a single word spoken, my position in Bruce's family had been telegraphed to all the mourners. Introductions were then unnecessary, and I was offered condolences by people whom I had never met or seen before. No-one had been left to wonder who that widpella *nyarlu*, that white woman was. Personal introductions, for those who didn't know me, would come later, at a more appropriate setting.

Bruce's nephews, young men dressed in black trousers, crisp white shirts, black ties and runners, took the shovels and, in the hot sun, filled in the grave completely. It was important to neaten the mound properly, important to make a good shape, the mound to remain as is, with no headstone, no fancy granite or marble to mark who lay below, only flowers, shells and painted rocks for decoration. This mound, though, had a marker placed upon it, an enamel mug, with his name, Bruce Dingo, painted across it, carefully positioned at his head. When the flowers had been transferred to his grave, it was time for the family to say a final goodbye to their son and their brother. Sisters and sister-cousins knelt, and with their faces close to the soil, close to where his head lay, they cried one last time. It was finished now. It was time to go.

At the Mullewa hall where food and a cup of tea was provided for the mourners, speeches were made on behalf of the family, with everybody thanked for coming. Travellers fed, they could now start heading back, or visiting their own families around the town, while the immediate Dingo family went on for a wake, a barbeque, to talk openly for the last time, about their son and brother Bruce.

We drove through the masses of wildflowers which had sprung up after the rains, to Gavin's rented farmhouse, the brothers, cousins, nephews and nieces and me sitting outside on the back verandah steps, or on the base of the tank stand, anywhere we could find, some hanging one arm around the rotary clothes line, several items of washing still pegged, forgotten in all the sorrow. Many of the men were those who years ago stood to guard me, surrounding me at the basketball carnival social evening. It was a good feeling to be with the whole family again. Bessie sat on the cement ledge, nieces leaning on her, Uncle Owen, with his long flowing white hair, was in his wheelchair, joining in, and Auntie

Pearlie stayed seated in the van, door open, but with her nieces crowding around talking and, funeral now over, joking as well. Bessie, Owen and Pearlie were all who were left of Ulie's and Dingo Jim's children, Friday, Jimmy and Hilda all passed away now too. The family was pleased to have the three 'oldies' all together again.

As we sat, beers were available, not too many, just enough while everyone talked. My Yamatji family had changed out of their funeral clothes into more casual gear suitable for a backyard barbeque, the clothes carried in readiness in their cars. But I'd been unaware of this routine, and with no other clothes on hand, tottered around in my high heels still dressed in black, still in skirt and jacket. When I walked in front of my mob through the long grass on the way to Auntie Pearlie in the van, overdressed as I was for this setting, and a stubby in my hand, the only one they'd ever seen me with, they rolled around with laughter.

'Look at Auntie Sally!!' they pointed and squealed, delighted with what they saw as an incongruity.

'Excuse me, Jijja,' Sister Netta said, moving past me at the door of the van. 'You know what *Jijja* means?' she added, as a minor test.

'Yes I do,' I said proudly, pleased as well to constantly have my place reinforced. 'Sister!'

Netta nodded approvingly. And I told of my attempts to learn Wadjarri, of my few successes, and of the errors I had made on the way.

'I couldn't sleep last night because of my pubic hair,' I had said to Bessie over the phone, the Wadjarri word for mosquito too subtly similar for me to remember.

'That's no good,' Bessie had kindly and simply replied, after a short startled pause.

Netta couldn't believe it. She and her sisters hooted and tittered, staggered about so amused. They told and retold the story among themselves.

'Hey! Look out now!' Netta suddenly hissed, conscious such a story was not for all to hear. 'Man there!'

And the guffawing group went quiet. They watched until the coast was clear, and then started up again, examining just how funny my gaffe had been.

It was time for us to leave, Ernie and I having to get back to the children, Wilara and toddler Jurra, a family member we were now raising as well, both left with a baby-sitter for the day. Bruce had been remembered. Stories had been told again, of Buttercup, Bruce's friendly yellow car, of his beloved dog Ashtray who, jumping out the window with leash still attached, had hung himself, of Bruce's sorrow, and Ashtray's grave, where Bruce had always left flowers. And what could have been was also said. In another time, many agreed, Bruce could have been a successful performer. The wake was coming to a close. Ties had been strengthened, and people could go on, concentrate on those living.

'I'll go and say goodbye to my sister now,' said Larry, and I was deeply moved. I was in love with every member of my family.

Back in Sydney, far away from them all, I thought of the many phone calls we'd always had. I thought of the loneliness Ernie sometimes experienced when he travelled, making him seek out people so he wouldn't have to be by himself. I thought of how much happier he was, calmer, stronger, and more focused now he had a family base in Sydney as well. And I at last knew. I understood, after all these years. So much now made sense, who Ernie was, and so too his family, with the many requests, expectations, and obligations, even though we were so far away.

And the struggle for Dingo Jim's parcel was no longer so bizarre. Nothing would be allowed to tamper with what helped to hold the family together. It had been a dangerous undertaking, the forces the family had to oppose strong among those who manipulated the law. But it had been done, after much preparation, and was safely hidden away again. Oondamooroo, Dingo Jim, would go on, overseeing his mob. And Ernie who had been given his grandfather's tribal name as a child, Bessie instructed to hand it to her eldest son, could go on as well, moving out into the wider world, always knowing where he belonged and who he was.

And I was learning who I was as well. I had travelled to the dusty sheep and cattle stations, driving past kangaroos, emus, wild goats and magnificent wild horses. I had seen and felt the land. And I'd seen where Dingo Jim and Ulie had camped all those years ago, had seen the horse stable lodgings they'd been given which made them finally seek their freedom. I'd seen where Les rode his imaginary horse, where Ulie fell in the water tank as she looked for the planes during the war. And I had stayed at Ulie's beloved Woolgorong, meeting Tim Officer's eldest son Ted who with his wife Meg still owns the leasehold, still runs the family sheep station. I'd seen it all, even though times are not so good for the station owners in the Murchison and Gascoyne areas now. And it had crept into my blood. I loved this land. And I now knew the journey Ernie had taken, knew he carried Dingo Jim, Ulie and Bessie with him, knew they and all his family were part of who he was. I knew so much more than I'd ever dreamed for myself.

Epilogue

Epilogue

With confidence I can now assert that there are many people in Australia who want to take their place in an inclusive and compassionate Australia. This confidence is based on the wonderful feedback and support from people's responses to the hardcover version of *Dingo*. People turned up in large numbers to listen to Ernie and me during our tour of the national capital cities (six hundred people turning up on one night alone in Brisbane), all eager to know the 'other' story, all wishing to declare where their hearts lay, all asking question after question. Sales were spread throughout the country, not confined to the major cities, with boxes of books ordered by regional and remote parts of Australia, and bookstores in Darwin unable to keep the supplies coming fast enough. It was a heartwarming time for me, one which causes me to believe we can eventually create an Australia which embraces all.

I was gratified to know of the large numbers of Aboriginal people who read the book—some struggling, slowly reading a couple of pages a sitting; others having it read to them and others, with more whitefella education, with no trouble at all. As a white woman writing an Aboriginal story, even though my Yamatji family had given permission, I was grateful when they contacted Ernie and myself to give their approval and their blessings. One Aboriginal woman I met while waiting for my children to finish playing at a Sydney Mcdonalds told me how important it was to her to read about what other Aboriginal communities went through. It gave her a connection with people not her own, yet her own. One Aboriginal lawyer with the Department of Aboriginal Affairs told me he was planning to use some of my experiences to role-play with his white staff, to help them understand the complex subtexts which were often at play in any conversation with Aboriginal people, and of which most whitefellas, even those working on a daily basis with Aboriginal people, are frequently unaware.

Many non-Aboriginal readers wrote generous, often moving letters, a significant number saying in effect, 'I didn't know,' all expressing gratitude at the opportunity to know an Aboriginal family. It was an astonishing time for me. I did not know what response there would be. In my inexperience in the world of publishing, I did not realise my book would 'give' to people. And I did not realise the full impact it would have on many of the families featured in *Dingo*.

Ernie and I insisted on having a book signing for the family in Geraldton, Western Australia. We sat for six hours straight as people lined up and moved on, book in hand, many bearing photos to show us, anecdotes to tell, and family friendships to alert us to. Clarrie came for a while, so did Auntie Pearlie fiercely determined to last the entire time. She sat regally behind us, not wanting to miss it, beaming wih pleasure at seeing old friends and aquaintances again, enjoying her new found fame. Many people moved on over to her. During this signing, four beautiful young women, each in their twenties, fronted us. One of them had something of extreme importance to say and she knelt down so she could speak across the table to me without being heard by all.

'Thank you ...' she started, then choked, tears filling her eyes.

She was Tim and Jean Officer's granddaughter, as were the other three. Liz Robson, formerly Lizzie Officer, mother to two of the girls and aunt to the others, her brother Tim Officer Junior's daughters, waited and watched.

'... I didn't ever know,' the young girl finally continued, 'that my grandmother cried.'

The line of people stopped and it was as if only she and I were there. I felt as if I had become Ulie and she, her grandmother Jean and we were in the kitchen at Woolgorong once again, meeting Yamatji way. I had no idea such beautiful moments were to be given to me. And I had no idea that my gathering together the many strands of the story would give the Officer grandchildren their grandparents back again, even though I certainly felt I had come to know Jean and Tim as flesh and blood.

Just as the book was going to press we heard the very sad news that Ted Officer, Tim Officer's eldest had just passed away at a young age, tragically just like his father. Jane Officer, Lizzie and their families had come together for a family reunion just before he died. The whole Dingo family was shocked and grieved with the Officer family when they heard the news.

Many people provided more layers to the story I had told. Ted and Meg Officer's daughter Jennie wrote and told me of her cherished friendship with Bruce, or Brucie, as she called him, 'one of the most special people in my life on Woolgorong,' she wrote. Bruce may not have achieved the heady heights his cousin-brother Ernie has, in the white man's definition of success, but Bruce was indeed successful—he is remembered with great affection by many.

Jennie wrote about how excited she had been when Bruce had rung and arranged to return to Woolgorong to live, not long before he died, and how she had been looking forward to seeing him again and waiting for the resumption of his frequent snake reports.

Brucie used to fastidiously rake acres and acres around where he camped so that he could ascertain their movements. King Browns were his particular obsession

And Bruce had taught her to have a similar healthy respect, and fear.

I still ride flat out, feet up high as I can lift them, through a couple of wandarries where Brucie knew they lurked, and where he had told me gruesome stories about what they'd do to me. (Not as bad, mind you, as the fear Michael Ryan put into me about black bungarras—[black goannas] who could easily run my 80cc motorbike down!)

Brucie would also never eat snake. He often had bungarra on the coals, but snake was way too evil to eat.

Jennie remembered how he had arrived back at Woolgorong from town late one night and couldn't go to bed until he had given out all the presents he had bought 'a knife for Dad and this amazing huge frilly doll for me.'

> *There are so many memories of Brucie*, she wrote. *Most of all, I'll remember him for his bubbling laugh and huge smile, his witty comments, giving me tit-bits of kangaroo from inside his jacket where Ashtray would also sit so he didn't get cold on the motorbike, having a nibble now and then too and always knowing just the right thing to say at the right time to keep me giggling.*

She thanked me for describing his funeral. 'It made me cry and cry,' she confessed, 'although I know Brucie would have found something in all the grief to laugh about.'

Neroli Douglas, who had conducted the sewing classes at Mullewa and had assisted her husband Robert with his weekly church services, wrote about the memories the Dingo story brought back.

> *I remember so well*, she wrote, *those houses on the fringes of Mullewa. And how totally shaken I was after we visited the reserve out of town one day to give out clothing—my sheltered upbringing had never exposed me to such poverty ... I recall*, she continued, *how at one of the weddings that year, the [Yamatji] folk put on a terrific feast, lots of attractive food and so many friends and relatives came. We all had a wonderful time—then when we went back to Mullewa the following Wednesday, we couldn't help but notice how many snuck into the rubbish bins and hungrily ate the stale sandwiches and*

leftovers from the previous weekend's festivities.

Reverend Chris Ridings, who in 1966 was sent to the Methodist Church at Mullewa, 'for experience rather than with experience,' wrote of how the sight of the Mullewa reserve still remains with him today.

Each house was of unlined corrugated iron, freezing in winter, but even more stifling in the hot Mullewa weather for over half the year ... There were no rooms, just an opening in the roof in the centre for the smoke from the fire to escape.

What always amazed me, was that Yamatji children housed in those appalling conditions could find anything at all to laugh about.

Reverend Ridings also had a few words to say on the local hoteliers.

There were two hotels in Mullewa, like bookends straddling the town. The south one had a stringent colour bar, while Shanahan's on the north end, facing the reserve and station country was happy to serve anyone. However, they were prone to short-changing Yamatji customers after they'd had a few drinks, and then call the police in when there was a disturbance.

As the Manse was opposite the Police Station, I had Constable Harry Reid boarding with me, Law and Grace together. We pored through the Dog Act and other Acts to see how we could catch Mrs S[hanahan] in the act. She had a fine car and two overseas trips on her 'savings'.

Since the release of *Dingo*, my friend and a great friend to the Dingos, Mrs Peet passed away, aged ninety-two. I still remember going to meet her for the first time just before she turned ninety embarrassed about her appearance, conscious of the effect the small stroke she had suffered had on her looks. However she was still remarkable, lovely and with an impressively sharp memory recalled in vivid detail the times she had lived through and the people she had known, including the exact prices, wages and monies saved. It was easy to feel close to her and after meeting her, she was often in my thoughts, especially after her admission that even with the passage of time, more than seventy years on, she still went to bed each night dreaming and longing for her first love, a boy she had known back in Scotland in her teens. They would meet and walk together back then, but never so much as held hands. And once she had been convinced she had seen him, after she had married. I had a foolish romantic notion, desperately wanting her to experience delirious happiness again, even for a short while. However it was not to be. A further stroke meant she had to leave her home and enter a nursing home and her powers of speech were almost gone. But she struggled and struggled to say what she could. To see her cry when her body and mouth would not obey was heartrending.

Mrs Peet was thrilled when I took a copy of the book to her, and immediately wanted copies sent to her family in Scotland. Her devoted granddaughter, (Eddie Peet's daughter) Erica Eccleston read the book aloud to her over many long visits. Erica wrote:

Nana and I enjoyed reading the book together, and it was a very emotional time for both of us, as she relived both happy and sad times. There were many laughs shared, Nana sometimes expanding your narrative on a more personal level. At other times, we would both be crying so hard, I was unable to read on.

I was able to finish reading your book to Nana before she died. It gave us both a great deal of pleasure and was a special time for us together.

I was pleased that Mrs Peet had been able to see the book completed and pleased that I had been able to honour her life. Many people, throughout Australia, now know her.

Those who also felt honoured by the book's publication were the Dingos and Clarrie Whitehurst. After all those years of toil and struggle, they were being celebrated, just like the more publicly recognisable member of the family, their son and nephew Ernie. And they were enjoying it.

We brought Clarrie, Pearlie and Bessie to Sydney for the book launch, Owen was not well enough for the journey. Bessie had been to Sydney several times before and was an old hand, Clarrie and Pearlie never.

'Too big,' said Pearlie when she was driven through the streets.

'Don't leave me, don't let me get lost,' implored Clarrie, as Ernie took him down town to the R.M. Williams store. Clarrie, however, was delighted to find many items which suited an old bushie like himself, and bought a corkpot (billy). Which made him feel as if he were somehow at home again.

'You're not gettin' me through that tunnel—under the water!' they both insisted.

To Clarrie and Pearlie, the tunnel under the Sydney Harbour

was not normal not natural, and not to be tried. Ernie resisted for several days, always turning off in time. 'Blow these buggers from the bush', Ernie claims now that he thought then, (although I suspect poetic licence here.) 'This is city culture.' And he ran the gauntlet, driving on in. There was a shocked silence in the car. Then, click, click, flash, flash from the back seat. Pearlie and Clarrie grabbed their cameras as soon as they realised what was happening. We have not been shown the tunnel 'wall' photos yet as fascinating as I am sure they must be.

Ray Martin was coming to meet them, to do a story on the Dingo women. Bessie had come to Sydney early to make sure she had some teeth in time. Her plate had snapped in two and she wasn't letting Ray see her *gummy nyulunge* (with no teeth). Ray arrived, knowing their stories intimately, his copy of the book marked, underlined, circled and visibly well read. He yarned easily with them for many hours, but was not told what Bessie had endured in the dentist chair especially for him. Pearlie couldn't help herself and made him bend forward so she could feel his hair—with both hands. Clarrie was bitterly disappointed he wasn't filmed, not understanding how a story has to hang together, and in this case the thread was the women in Ernie's life. However Ray knew Clarrie's life story too, and off camera chatted in detail about Clarrie and his brother Cecil's exploits on the stations. Meeting Ray had been a major highlight for them. Bessie now calls Ray her boyfriend.

Back home in Geraldton after the Sydney launch, many things have changed. Many people now knew the family in different ways. People came visiting. Old acquaintances re-acquainted. Old times discussed. Young people got to see the oldies as people who had had lives as well. White people got to know black people, black people white. A greater sense of community developed.

Telling a story from all sides seems to be able to do that.

But the moment which says it all for me was one which Pearlie told. One of Les's old close friends came visiting, a white man now in his late sixties. Pearlie gave him a photo, a spare one she had from those I had copied for her from the book. It was Les, taken a year or so before he died, leaning on a cart, the quintessential Aussie bloke, hat pushed back on his head, chewing on a bit of wheat. His old friend looked at it—and burst into tears.

'Well, I was finished then too,' said Pearlie and the two of them cried together for a man they both loved. Black and white. No matter. One mob.

Glossary of Aboriginal Words

Yamatji
bardi (grub)
barndi (good)
bimba (tree sap)
birndu (quiet)
boogoo (backside)
gogola (bush banana)
gooninye (sad and sorry)
gudja (child)
gulyu (yam)
gumbadi (grandchild)
gurlgu (sling)
gurndi (men's fighting stick)
guwiyarl (goanna)
jhullo (bone marrow)
Jijja (sister)
koodah (brother)
maja (master)
marbarrn (magic)
mardong (boyfriend or
    girlfriend, wife or husband)

marnda (rump, backside)
mayu (child)
meeunga (sound a frog makes)
mili (light)
munninge (silly)
ngingari (zebra-finch)
Nyaji (sand)
nyarlu (girl or woman)
nyumbi loo binya (dancing)
Wabiji (son-in-law)
wandarrie (country)
widjarnu (little stranger)
Wilgarda (Jimmy)
Winja (old person)
yukkia (shout of shock)

Noongah
tjulip (lap-lap)

Billabalong Station
Vica Mullewa Part office
Sep 11 1949

Dear Sir
I am Just Writting you this few
Lines Just to Ask you hav Do I got
to See so I Can get hundon the
White mans hape so hav I got to See you
or hav So Please Will you Noder fiear
me About it Please or Do I got to
go Down and See you about it my
Sealff that Will Be the Best go
Down to my sealff and see you About
it. So Noatier fiear me Please
hopping to hear from you soon
from yours faithfully
Leslie Dingo